Verdi at the Golden Gate

BOOKS BY GEORGE MARTIN

The Opera Companion
(1961; 4th ed., 6th ptg. 1992)

The Battle of the Frogs and the Mice:
An Homeric Fable
(1962; 2d ed. 1987)

Verdi, His Music, Life and Times
(1963; 4th ed. 1992)

The Red Shirt and the Cross of Savoy:
The Story of Italy's Risorgimento, 1748–1871
(1969)

Causes and Conflicts: The Centennial History
of the Association of the Bar of the
City of New York, 1870–1970
(1970)

Madam Secretary: Frances Perkins
(1976)

The Companion to
Twentieth-Century Opera
(1979; 3d ed. 1989)

The Damrosch Dynasty:
America's First Family of Music
(1983)

Aspects of Verdi
(1988; 2d ed. 1993)

Verdi at the Golden Gate:
Opera and San Francisco in the Gold Rush Years
(1993)

Verdi in 1853.

VERDI
at the Golden Gate

*Opera and San Francisco
in the Gold Rush Years*

George Martin

with a Foreword by
Lotfi Mansouri

UNIVERSITY OF CALIFORNIA PRESS
Berkeley · Los Angeles · Oxford

University of California Press
Berkeley and Los Angeles, California

University of California Press, Ltd.
Oxford, England

© 1993 by
George Martin

Library of Congress Cataloging-in-Publication Data

Martin, George Whitney.
   Verdi at the Golden Gate : opera and San Francisco in the Gold
Rush years / George Martin.
     p. cm.
   Includes bibliographical references (p.) and index.
   ISBN 0-520-08123-4 (alk. paper)
   1. Opera—California—San Francisco—19th century. 2. Verdi,
Giuseppe, 1813–1901—Performances—California—San Francisco.
I. Title.
ML1711.8.S2M37 1993
792.5′0974′6109034—dc20
                                                          92-18674
                                                            CIP
                                                            MN

Printed in the United States of America
9 8 7 6 5 4 3 2 1

For my niece
Julie Cheever
who has made her life
in San Francisco

Contents

Illustrations

Foreword

If you look in the *New Grove Dictionary of Music and Musicians* under the heading "San Francisco," you will read that "Opera was the city's first musical love." One of the marvelous things George Martin has accomplished in *Verdi at the Golden Gate* is to demonstrate how the remarkable love affair between opera and San Francisco—a relationship that we take for granted today but that, viewed objectively, is a highly improbable development—came to be.

Of course, most people today are aware that San Francisco Opera is a major force in the world of international opera, and has certainly been the preeminent operatic institution in the Western United States since its founding in 1923. In fact, my first actual participation in an opera production was with San Francisco Opera when it toured to Los Angeles some 40 years ago, when I appeared as a supernumerary spear-carrier in an opera by Verdi, no less—*Otello*.

What many people may not be aware of, however, is the degree to which the Bay Area embraced the muse of lyric theater long before San Francisco Opera was even a glint in the eye of founder Gaetano Merola, or even before Gaetano Merola was a glint in his own father's eye. It's a highly entertaining and highly improbable story—but then, San Francisco has always had a rather improbable history.

Martin analyzes, among other things, how the city's unique qualities influenced its taste for opera. Bay Area residents today are perhaps a bit too quick to say, "Only in San Francisco," but as Martin so convincingly demonstrates in this remarkable book, it's a phrase that is, in this case, perfectly apt.

In his epilogue, Martin writes, "Most likely, depending on each reader's previous knowledge of San Francisco or Verdi, he or she will find in this history a different set of surprises." For a book as filled with surprises as this one, that is an understatement. Martin deals generously with all aspects of the city's cultural history, and part of the surprise comes from his vivid reconstruction of the tone and style of life in what was, at the start of the second half of the nineteenth century, probably the most rugged, coarse and primitive community in America. That opera would take root and flourish in a society whose populace was less than 10 percent female should go a long way in laying to rest the tired canard that opera is an experience to which women drag their reluctant husbands.

On the other hand, women receive credit from Martin for their sometimes disproportionately large share of performance duties, when mezzo-sopranos had to make up for the dearth of capable tenors or baritones. Indeed, the means to which early opera impresarios resorted in the 1850s will be very familiar to ambitious opera presenters in the smaller American communities even today.

Perhaps one of the most remarkable revelations for me was the fact that much of San Francisco's earliest exposure to operatic music came by way of artists who were engaged at the opera houses of Mexico City, Lima, Valparaiso, and Santiago. These were established citadels of culture at a time when San Francisco was a barbaric settlement of roughshod miners. Today, in our outreach and exchange programs, particularly through the activities of our San Francisco Opera Center, we have been establishing anew our musical ties with other countries on the Pacific Rim; how gratifying it is to learn that our own operatic impulses first came to us from some of those very regions to which we now extend our own cultural resources. In a wonderful way, it seems that we are merely beginning to pay off an old artistic debt.

The more one reads of Mr. Martin's engaging chronicle, the more the mind boggles. How it can change our perspective of American musical life when we learn that San Franciscans were hearing music by Verdi—an occasional aria, at least—at a time when he had not yet composed *Rigoletto, Il trovatore,* or *La traviata!* Martin, through his exhaustive research, shows us that the evolution of musical taste in San Francisco during the mid-nineteenth century was not, despite the area's extreme physical isolation, very far out of step with the rest of the world. As the author so poetically puts it, "Rossini's sun was setting, its laughter and brightness giving way to the dark, romantic dramas of Donizetti and Verdi."

Many people in our own time have been impressed with the ability of so relatively small a city as San Francisco to support an opera company on a par with those of urban centers five or ten times its size; how even more miraculous to see the far-flung frontier outpost of San Francisco in the 1850s become, to use Martin's term, "mad for opera." One of my favorite statistics the author has compiled is the fact that if New York in 1992 were to play to an audience proportionate to that of San Francisco in 1860, it would need to build twenty additional opera houses and run them every night of the year.

Each reader, however, has his or her own thrilling discoveries to make in this intriguing text. It's a narrative unlike any other, combining the most colorful, passionate, and theatrical of all art forms with the history of the most colorful, passionate, and theatrical of all American cities. The pairing now seems so obvious, so right, that local Bay Area sociologists and art historians might well feel some embarrassment that it was left to a writer in Pennsylvania to record this incredible story. Let us just be thankful that the task was left in such capable hands. San Francisco, opera, George Martin—truly a menage made in heaven!

I'd like to conclude with an addendum that illustrates a type of continuity, however tenuous, between the San Francisco that Martin writes about and the opera company over which I preside today. In 1914, Verdi was honored again in San Francisco with a statue erected in Golden Gate Park. As part of the dedication ceremony, Luisa Tetrazzini sang an aria from *Aida* to the assembled crowd. A little more

than a half century later, the Friends of Recreation and Parks decided
to revive this wonderful notion of combining opera with the beautiful
surroundings of that unique park, by presenting an al fresco concert
featuring the stars and orchestra of San Francisco Opera.

That concert proved to be such a success that it was repeated in 1973
and again in 1975, after which it became an annual event. Today it
attracts scores of thousands of opera devotees from every walk of life
every year to Golden Gate Park in an annual celebration of the
significant place that opera holds in the hearts of the citizens of this
beautiful city. The love affair between the residents of the San Francisco Bay region and that miraculous combination of music and theater
called opera—an affair that Martin so affectionately documents in this
fascinating chronicle—continues.

Lotfi Mansouri
General Director
San Francisco Opera

Preface

My aim in this book is twofold: first, to write a history of opera in a particular place and time, San Francisco during the Gold Rush years, concentrating the events around the works of a particular composer, Verdi; and second, by exploring Verdi's rise to popularity in this city, in these years, to make a contribution to the more general history of San Francisco and, even, to the westward movement in the United States.

Both aims, specific and general, seem worthy because, with regard to the first, we lack detailed accounts in American musical history of how music started in our frontier towns: who began it, who supported it, what was played; and with regard to the second, most general histories, to their detriment, largely ignore cultural matters. For instance, one such history of California that has enjoyed many printings has no section, however small, on music, and not a single entry for it in the index. Yet from the start San Francisco, with its Bay area, has been an exceptional community for music, a leader in the United States.

This attempt to combine operatic and non-musical history may strike some readers as odd or ill-conceived; and certainly it is unusual. Therefore, to avoid any misconception of what follows, let me offer a word of explanation.

I have nothing to say about Verdi's life or the musical, political, and social influences that molded him or his music, and next to nothing about his musical techniques. I do have some comments on his musical style, which contributed to his popularity, and I have much to report on how his music was performed in San Francisco and how it was received by audiences who, for the most part, were hearing it for the first time.

No one in San Francisco in the Gold Rush years knew the facts of Verdi's life, or cared about them, and none, truth to tell, wrote about his music with much perception or learning. Yet artists and music-lovers in the city during these years took his music to heart and enthroned him as the most popular of opera composers and even perhaps—because there then was no great difference between "popular" and "serious" music—the most popular composer of the day. How and why this happened are themes of the book.

In this sort of history, for instance, the circumstances of what seems to be the first public performance in San Francisco of any of Verdi's music is worth noting. The performance was not of an opera, staged by a resident or visiting company in a theatre, with sets and costumes; it was of an aria, "Ernani, involami," sung by a soprano with only piano and violin accompaniment, and presented as an intermission feature between a play and a farce. And the second sample of Verdi heard in the city, performed in a concert of more than forty artists (most, probably, amateurs), was a trombone fantasy on an aria from his opera *Attila*. Apparently no such fantasy at the time had been published, and so the trombonist, in all likelihood, had made his own arrangement from sheet music for the aria. And the same probably was true of the soprano and her colleagues.

These two performances most likely fit the pattern of how music first entered a recital hall in any town on the frontier—of which San Francisco, in some aspects of its founding, was one. It was settled, for instance, by immigrants moving into what they called "the Wilderness" and attempting to create a civilized society. In other respects, however, San Francisco was unique. Though isolated by thousands of miles from the nearest large cities of the American Midwest, it could be reached by water, by ships carrying hundreds of passengers and much cargo, so that in many ways it was more like a maritime colony of the East Coast than an inland town on the advancing frontier. Nevertheless, the steps by which music in San Francisco moved from the back room of a saloon into a recital hall and finally into an opera house were probably not very different from their sequence in the more typical inland towns of the frontier—except for their acceleration by the event of 24 January 1848 that set San Francisco apart: the discovery in the mountains behind it of gold.

In short, I have attempted to combine in a single account musical, social, and theatrical histories that more often are treated separately. If my experiment succeeds, it should tell us much about opera's growth across the country and also, I like to think, something about Verdi. In some circles such a book would be called a study of "the transmission and reception of musical culture"; in others, more simply but less descriptively, "cultural history." But whatever its label, my account will include as important events a frontier audience's first hearing and response to *Rigoletto, Il trovatore,* and *La traviata*—unimpressed, ecstatic, puzzled—and will tell of related persons and episodes such as the impresario who spat in the face of a creditor, a whorehouse Madam who sat in the wrong row of a theatre, her gambler-lover who later was hanged by vigilantes, and a fistfight in the audience that stopped a performance of *Daughter of the Regiment* and ended in a death by duel.

Verdi composed his melodramas in these years in a style that some persons found excessive, not only musically, but also in its pessimism. "People say," he once wrote of *Trovatore,* "this opera is too sad and there are too many deaths in it. But after all, in life there is only death. What else lasts?"

In San Francisco in these Gold Rush years, when good and bad occurred in frequent excess, the difference between life and art, often exaggerated by the prosaic, all but vanished. And the blurring of that usual division, I believe, in part explains Verdi's astonishing popularity in northern California—most of whose immigrants arrived by ship, sailing into San Francisco's great bay through a narrows called "the Golden Gate."

But of course, Verdi was not the only opera composer to achieve popularity in the West, or in the United States generally. There were also Rossini, Bellini, Donizetti, Balfe, Auber, and others, and taken all together, opera, Italian, English, and French, in these years had a great vogue.

There evidently is some confusion about this, for one distinguished music historian has concluded that "of all the kinds of art music of the American cultivated tradition between 1820 and the Civil War, the least significant, and the least widely heard, was opera." Another, writing more specifically about the arts in California, has lamented that by 1859 "we must accept a sad ending for the first chapter in the history of music on the Gold Coast."

Yet as I hope this book's accumulation of facts from contemporary journals will show, at least on the frontier of northern California and in the final decade before the Civil War, a great deal of opera was heard. And on the Gold Coast in 1859 opera was about to have a stupendous year, stupendous by anyone's measure. The truth is both more interesting and colorful than generally reported.

George Martin
Kennett Square
Pennsylvania

A word about the treatment of opera titles. In all quotations I have left the title—in language, in italic or roman type, with or without quotation marks—as it appeared in the original. In my own writing I refer to the opera in the language in which it was composed except when I am discussing a production that I have reason to believe was sung in some other language. Thus, in general I refer to Rossini's *Il barbiere di Siviglia,* but when writing of a production sung in English I call it *The Barber of Seville,* and in French, *Le Barbier de Seville.* All rules, of course, have exceptions; to state one: when referring to the overture to Rossini's *Guillaume Tell,* I call the opera *William Tell.*

Acknowledgments

In the research for this book I have been helped greatly by the learning, skill, and patience of librarians, chiefly those in San Francisco, Sacramento, New York, Boston, and Washington. I will not identify every individual in each institution who answered a question, produced a book or document, or made a fruitful suggestion—the number of names and titles soon would deprive the list of any meaning—but those libraries in which most of my facts were discovered or verified are as named below, and for the courtesy, learning, and willingness of their staffs, at all levels of authority, I am grateful.

San Francisco Performing Arts Library & Museum
San Francisco Public Library
California Historical Society Library, San Francisco
Bancroft Library, University of California, Berkeley
California State Library, Sacramento
Boston Public Library
New York Public Library
New-York Historical Society Library
Library of Congress, Washington, D.C.

I also wish to thank Jackson Research Projects of Davis, California, a business offering "historical consulting services," for its part in assuring the accuracy of many parts of this book. Although I did research myself in California libraries, living in the East I inevitably was forced often to rely on others to verify old facts or to uncover new ones, and on my application the Jackson company assigned to work with me Rand F. Herbert and, later, also David A. Riggs.

The people at Jackson Research Projects are experts in water rights, a subject of prime importance in California if the state's citizenry is to live at peace, and as I sent queries westward I soon was rejoicing in the exactitude of the replies I began to receive. Water rights, it would seem, make an ideal preparation for research in opera. Yet when I look back on our three years of work, I am surprised that the company was willing to take me on—and, I believe, there is some surprise on its part, too. In any case, though I still know nothing about water rights, Messrs. Herbert and Riggs have learned something about opera in San Francisco in the Gold Rush years, and the accuracy of this book owes much to their precision and sympathetic interest. And I delight in acknowledging their help.

Other individuals who have aided me in some way beyond the usual call of friendship or duty are Mary Ashe, Oliver Daniel, Barbara R. Geisler, J. D. McClatchy, Barbara McClure, Peyton Moss, Frank Pitelka, John P. Sweeney, and Thomas G. Kaufman.

For permission to use pictures and documents from their collections, I am grateful to the following libraries: for the photographs of Rosina Mauri-Pellegrini, Innocenzo Pellegrini, Mathilde Korsinsky–Von Gulpen, Giovanna Bianchi, and Eugenio Bianchi, the San Francisco Performing Arts Library & Museum; for the Alessandro Biscaccianti letter, the libretto of *Ernani*, the photographs of Tom Maguire and of his Opera House, the Bancroft Library, University of California, Berkeley; for the drawings of Catherine Hayes in Musical Hall and the interior of the Metropolitan Theatre, the California State Library, Sacramento; and for the title page of sheet music and the libretto to *I due Foscari*, the Pierpont Morgan Library, New York City. The remaining photographs are from my own, small collection.

Prologue

Verdi himself never set foot in the United States, but from 1847 onward, after a production of *I Lombardi* in New York introduced his operas to the country, most of them came over within three or four years of their European premieres, and many settled promptly and permanently into our musical life. How his music spread throughout the larger cities of the Atlantic coast follows a predictable pattern of opera productions fully staged, with glamorous, European stars; how it spread in the emerging cities of the West, many of which at the time lacked an opera house or even a theatre, is less well known.

In the United States at the start of the decade 1851–60, Bellini, with *Norma* and *La sonnambula*, probably was the most frequently performed opera composer, and in countless arrangements and translations the aria that ends *Sonnambula*, "Ah, non giunge," was a popular song. At the end of the decade, however, Verdi had displaced Bellini—a reason to concentrate this history on Verdi's operas.

How did his music penetrate the towns of the West, or his operas make their way in cities only just building their first theatres? Of his operas, which were the first to be produced, and the first to succeed? How did the first theatres emerge, and what were they like? And what of the early opera productions: the orchestra, chorus, scenery, and

1

lighting? Who made up the audience, how did it behave, and how did the people react to Verdi's music? Not to the singer's voice and personality, please note, but, to the extent these can be subtracted, to the music itself, to Verdi.

Given the breadth of the country west of the Mississippi River and the variety of persons moving into it, the questions are large, and I will focus here on a single city, San Francisco, which in the 1850s joined Boston, New York, Philadelphia, and New Orleans as a center for opera. It achieved the distinction partly because it was a port, accessible to ships and steamers plying the western coast of Central and South America and consequently able to attract a few adventurous singers from an existing Pacific opera circuit. At this time, the opera houses of Santiago, Valparaíso, Lima, and Mexico City employed chiefly Italian artists, and some of these, though never a whole company, were willing to risk themselves and their artistry in the raw, new city to the north.[1]

For exploring the arrival of opera in a city, San Francisco offers several advantages, and one singular disadvantage that directly affected opera production: the city lacked women. In California in 1850, because of the rush of men into the state after the discovery of gold two years earlier, only 8 percent of the population was female, and, initially at least, many of those were women of ill repute. Among the French and German immigrants, the most active music-makers, the percentage was even smaller. Reportedly, among the French in San Francisco in March 1851, though the figures seem remarkably low, there still were only ten or twelve French women to upward of several thousand men; and even eighteen months later, the coming of a hundred French women caused an excited news-story headlined "Large Arrival of Women."[2] Not until about 1900 did the statewide proportion of men and women become equal. For this reason, therefore, as much as because of any belief that the theatre was inherently sinful, in the 1850s in San Francisco many operas requiring a women's chorus were produced without one. Either the men's chorus sang the women's melodies, or the music was cut.[3]

Nevertheless, despite this oddity, the city makes a fine sample for study. The swiftness of its growth insures that it did not start the decade with an established preference for any particular style of opera; indeed, probably none of any sort had been staged there. In 1848 San Francisco was a village of 500, and in 1851, the year of its first reported opera, a city of 30,000. Thus, throughout the 1850s the first production there of any opera was a regional premiere. In 1854, for example, a partial list of works heard for the first time in the city, and most likely for the first time anywhere west of the Rocky Mountains north of Mexico City, includes: Auber's *La Muette de Portici* and *Fra Diavolo;* Balfe's *The Bohemian Girl* and *The Enchantress;* Donizetti's *Lucia di Lammermoor, Lucrezia Borgia,* and *Don Pasquale;* Flotow's *Martha;* Rossini's *Cinderella;* Verdi's *Nabucco;* and Weber's *Der Freischütz.*

The variety of musical styles in this list reflects the diversity of the city's population—omitting always in this book the Chinese, whose operas fall outside the Western tradition. Among the immigrants of American and European background, however, the latter being chiefly Spanish-Mexican, French, Italian, German, English, Irish, and Scots, no one group by wealth or numbers was able to determine the city's musical life, as did those who spoke French in New Orleans, English in Boston, and, increasingly in this period, Italian and German in New York and Philadelphia. And because in San Francisco no group by itself could support a resident company, the operas of all nationalities were forced to compete in the same few theatres for an audience. By the end of 1859, the last year before Verdi began to dominate the repertory, by a rough count the most popular operas in the city's first nine years of opera were Donizetti's *La Fille du régiment* (17 performances), Balfe's *The Bohemian Girl* (17), Bellini's *La sonnambula* (15) and his *Norma* (15), Auber's *The Crown Diamonds* (14), Donizetti's *Lucrezia Borgia* (13), Verdi's *Il trovatore* (11, all in 1859), Weber's *Der Freischütz* (10), Donizetti's *La Favorite* (10), Balfe's *The Enchantress* (9), Verdi's *Ernani* (9), and Rossini's *Il barbiere di Siviglia* (9).[4] Though no Spanish composer is represented, Spanish or Mexican songs were much sung in the city's many saloons and frequently appeared as finales or encores to recitals of opera excerpts.

In addition to this mixture of cultures, another aspect of San Francisco in the 1850s that aids a study of Verdi's rise to popularity is the city's isolation. Transcontinental telegraph became available only in 1861, and regular overland mail, by pony express, only in 1860, and by railroad, in 1869. Until the mid-1860s the city could be reached from the east with any ease only by transshipping across the isthmus of Panama or by rounding Cape Horn, both routes long and expensive. As a result, unlike eastern cities San Francisco was left free to sort its preference in opera undisturbed by the arrival from elsewhere of fully staffed companies whose excellence created an immediate demand for a particular operatic style. In New York in 1843 and 1845, for example, visits by a French company from New Orleans, with operas mostly by Auber, Meyerbeer, and those by Donizetti to French texts, such as *La Favorite* and *La Fille du régiment*, had excited an enthusiasm for French opera. Then in 1847 a company from Havana, with good conductors, a fine orchestra, brilliant singers, and a repertory mainly of Rossini, Bellini, and Verdi, had established as the dominant style Italian opera.

Yet despite the isolation, in the years 1851–60, as Verdi ultimately became the city's favorite composer, San Francisco's taste for opera swelled into such a passion that if today's citizens of New York took to opera with equal exuberance—number of tickets sold relative to the population—the Metropolitan Opera Company would have to build twenty additional houses (cap. 3,800) and play them every night.[5]

A focus on San Francisco, therefore, is helpful to the book's more general purpose of examining how opera came to the West, for the very speed and severity of the city's intoxication with opera, by magnifying the steps of growth, makes them easy to follow. First, a city must have a theatre so that music unsuited to church or cabaret may have a home and be heard. Then comes the celebrity, typically a soprano accompanied by her husband as manager, and she includes an aria or two in a program of songs and ballads. Later, though still in recital, the soprano, modeling a variety of costumes and often with assisting singers, begins to present operatic scenes; and these in turn are followed by staged productions of the entire work, frequently in an English version, usually severely cut, with vocal lines mangled by transpositions and favorite arias of other composers inserted. Finally, there are full productions, increasingly in the composer's language, moderately cut, properly cast, and with few or no interpolations.

There is nothing extraordinary about this progression; in its outline it exemplifies the history of opera in much of the United States throughout the nineteenth century. Though seldom so clearly or fully developed, it was repeated in many towns on the frontier as they more slowly than San Francisco grew into cities.

But if an account of how Verdi's music triumphed in San Francisco can serve as a general model for how opera took root elsewhere in the West, in its details this account, because of the city, is highly individual: for in the 1850s, San Francisco was not like other cities. In the neighboring foothills of the Sierra Nevada, gold had been discovered, and from all over the world came fortune hunters. The city, nurtured by greed, was crude, savage, corrupt. Yet, perched on the rim of the world, it was also wholly new, unfettered by traditions, class distinctions, or received opinions, and it had a unique spirit. Immigrants, few of them older than thirty-five, found its atmosphere exhilarating. One, from New York, was Stephen J. Field, who later helped to create California's legal system and in 1863 was the first lawyer from the state appointed to the U.S. Supreme Court. He arrived in the city on the evening of 28 December 1849, sailing in through the Golden Gate. After disembarking, as he started up the street in search of cheap lodgings, he met acquaintances from New York, all of whom remarked in their greeting, "It's a glorious country," or "Isn't it a glorious country?" or "Did you ever see a more glorious country?" And soon, though he had but a dollar in his pocket and no employment, he found himself saying to everyone he met, "It's a glorious country."[6]

PART I

ONE

Toward a Theatre

There was music in California before the Gold Rush, chiefly on the large ranches in the countryside and in the settlements that clustered around the twenty-one Dominican (originally Franciscan) missions. It was music of Spain and Mexico, played usually on some combination of violin, trumpet, and harp, backed by guitars of several kinds and sizes and a variety of percussion. Aside from the individual songs and dances that livened family parties, picnics, and weddings, for the most part it accompanied religious festivals, leisurely, colorful events in which the whole community participated and which, because of the moderate climate and country life, often were held out-of-doors. Throughout the year there were many saints' days to be celebrated. At Christmas there were pageants, at New Year's, childrens' masquerades; and among the many events of Easter was a favorite of boys, the punishment of Judas Iscariot. His two-faced effigy of straw was strung on ropes between two buildings, and the ropes, jiggled and jerked in response to cries of abuse from the boys below, caused him to dance in pain. For a finale he was put to the torch, exploding in a stunning display of light and noise as firecrackers concealed in his limbs dis-membered his flaming body.[1]

Though there was drama in these fiestas, it did not lead to opera.

The religious and familial purpose of the events, together with their setting—out-of-doors, in the church, or in some ranchero's private house—was against it. Opera, lacking religion's universal appeal, required a sizable population from which to draw an audience, as well as public theatres. And Mexican California had neither.

In these years, for instance, the chief port for northern California, the seed of what later would become San Francisco, was Yerba Buena. Located on the tip of the peninsula, a mile or two from the Mission San Francisco de Asís (popularly known from a nearby stream as Mission Dolores), Yerba Buena was a cluster of twelve or fifteen buildings of which the largest was a barracks, the *presidio*. The others were rough houses or sheds for the storage of hides. On the empty hills behind were corrals for cattle. As for population, at this time the entire future state of California contained an estimated 15,000 persons, of which 10,000 were Indians and the balance white or mixed.[2]

One historian, summarizing the region and its people under Mexican rule, reported:

> [Visitors] confessed themselves astonished at the frailty of the Spanish and Mexican hold: a society without schools, without manufactures, without defenses, administered by a quasi-feudal mission system. . . . It was a society so backward that its plow and ox-cart were those of ancient times, so disorganized that in spite of the fact that countless cattle roamed its hills, it had to secure dairy products from the Russian colony at Fort Ross and have leather shoes shipped round the Horn from Boston.[3]

In 1847, as the result of the treaty closing the U.S.-Mexican war, the Mexican province of Upper California, the future state, passed to the United States, and in March of that year a contingent of the U.S. Army arrived in Yerba Buena to take possession, and the village was renamed San Francisco. With the surge of immigration from the United States that followed the flag, its population quickly increased, and following the discovery of gold in 1848 the numbers exploded. By December 1850 San Francisco had become a city of 30,000, almost all men.

Many came, no doubt, simply to get rich quick, by mining, gambling, or any way that opened. Others were tinged with idealism, eager to help in creating a new society in a backward, almost vacant land. The lawyer Field, for instance, was stirred by the thought of "going to a country comparatively unknown and taking a part in fashioning its institutions.... I had always thought that the most desirable fame a man could acquire was that of being the founder of a State, or of exerting a powerful influence for good upon its destinies."[4]

The excitement of that larger adventure, something more than the pursuit of gold, surfaces in many accounts of those who went out in "Forty-Nine" or the years soon after. Another, even more prominent theme in their journals, letters, and newspapers is their report of a startling return to a life of primary experience. On arrival, life suddenly became, as it often is in opera, a sequence of emotions and events that are overwhelming in their intensity and simplicity. In the words of the historian Kevin Starr:

> For a few brief years, in far-off California, the bottom fell out of the nineteenth century. Americans—and not just Americans of the frontier—returned en masse to primitive and brutal conditions, to a Homeric world of journeys, shipwreck, labor, treasure, killing, and chieftainship.... The Forty-Niners themselves were not unaware that they were being reduced to the elemental. Moments of stark experience, recorded without self-consciousness and yet shot through with mythic power, filled their narratives: there were murder, death, the falling-out of friends, food by a fire, gestures of voice and action appropriate to the mining camps of California.[5]

The same awful moments fill the accounts of those trying to create a decent city at the region's capital, by the Golden Gate. At times the task must have seemed beyond human capacity. Six times in eighteen months the city, or its major part, was destroyed by fire. And while the glut of gold no doubt provided wealth for quick rebuilding, it brought problems of its own, chiefly inflation and gambling—between which there was little difference in effect: both led to cheating, violence, drunkenness, and suicide. In hindsight, amid all the masculine brawling in this city that lacked women, the growth of a desire for art, chiefly good theatre and music, seems a miracle. Evidently, though, that desire is as elemental as the lust for gold: late or soon, it will appear.

In the pattern usual for frontier towns, public entertainment presented by paid performers from a stage first appeared in saloons. The rougher sort of these, known in San Francisco as "bit houses" because the price of admission was either one bit or two (twenty-five cents), had a small stage at the back of the building, with access, even for performers, only through the barroom. In the area before the stage were tables and chairs at which men drank, smoked or chewed tobacco, and gambled. Frequently they overturned the tables, and fought. The air stank of sweat, and the floor, soggy with tobacco juice, was often red with blood. Sometimes, facing the stage, a small gallery clung to a wall, and sometimes, instead of tables, there were rows of chairs—though in that case the back of each chair held a rack for bottles and glasses. To the side were rooms for gambling, their doors invitingly open; of the card games, monte, which in its simplicity is almost impervious to cheating, was the most popular. The entertainment, accompanied perhaps by a single piano or violin, a pair of guitars, or a wheezy accordion, consisted mostly of recitations, farces, songs, and dances performed by artists who were old, penniless, or simply untalented. The tone of the show, as well as of the audience's response to it, was rough, and no women, except for "hostesses," entered either the saloon or its "theatre." The show, good or bad, was quite incidental to the liquor and gambling.[6]

More expensive, refined saloons, sometimes called "melodeons" after the portable reed organ that occasionally substituted for an orchestra, offered a better grade of liquor and barmaids, spittoons for the tobacco-chewers, and private rooms for gambling, along with more complicated games of chance, like roulette. They also sometimes offered better entertainment. But again, the only entrance to the theatre usually was through the barroom, and though the audience was perhaps less coarse in language, dress, and behavior, it was still almost exclusively male, still only marginally interested in the show. Nevertheless, on occasion the music was well enough performed to draw in some men to listen.

In the spring of 1850, for example, one of the more famous of these saloons, the Bella Union, instead of a melodeon offered its patrons five

Mexicans playing two harps, one large and the other very small, two guitars, and one flute. According to one who heard them,

> The musicians were dressed in the Mexican costume (which, however, was nothing very noticeable at that time, as many of their auditors were in the same style of dress), and were quiet, modest looking men, with contented, amiable faces. They used to walk in among the throng of people, along to the upper end of the room, take their seats, and with scarcely any preamble or discussion, commence their instrumentation. They had played so much together, and were so similar, seemingly, in disposition—calm, confident and happy—that their ten hands moved as if guided by one mind; rising and falling in perfect unison—the harmony so sweet, and just strange enough in its tones, from the novelty in the selection of instruments, to give it a peculiar fascination for ears always accustomed to the orthodox and time-honored vehicles of music used in quintette instrumentation.
>
> Their *repertoire* contained the popular waltzes and dances of the time, and many weird, curious airs of old Spain, sad refrains and amorous *Lieder ohne worte;* the listener knew, intuitively, though he heard the music without the words, that the same sounds had, with words, centuries ago, floated on the moonlit night in old Seville, beneath the iron-latticed balconies where lovely senoritas listened with bated breath, and thrilled with sympathetic recognition.[7]

Soon those who cared more for theatre than for liquor or gambling began to separate the stage—just a little—from the saloon, and on 18 October 1849, in Sacramento, the first building in California erected expressly for drama, the Eagle Theatre, opened with a melodrama, *The Bandit Chief.* The two-story building had a wooden frame with walls of canvas and a roof of sheet iron and tin. Its stage, roughly twenty feet wide and sixteen deep, was built of packing boxes, but unlike saloon stages it had three all-purpose, painted-canvas backdrops, representing a street, a wood, and an interior. It also had a drop curtain that, when the bell rang to signal the start of the performance, rolled up. When down, the curtain displayed a California scene, described by the visiting journalist Bayard Taylor as "a glaring landscape, with dark-brown trees in the foreground, and lilac-colored mountains against a yellow sky."[8]

By Taylor's count the Eagle seated 400, of whom 100 were in a

gallery grandly titled "boxes." No seat, however, was numbered or
reserved, and for the first few performances there were no seats at all
on the parquet, merely bare ground. When rough benches were added,
the men used them during intermissions for gambling tables. Though
the only entrance to the parquet was, as usual, through a saloon, the
gallery could be reached by an outside stepladder, permitting respectable women to attend. And to forestall any violation of their modesty
by Peeping Toms, the management nailed canvas to the underside of
the ladder's rungs.

Unlike the saloons with their nightly variety shows, the Eagle put
on plays only three times a week, at a set hour, and to an audience that
regularly included women. But that was about the extent of its sophistication. The canvas kept the theatre hot; and the men in the audience,
in long heavy coats and flannel shirts, removed clothing, drank,
smoked, chewed, spat, gambled, whistled, yelled, and sometimes threw
vegetables at the actors. The opening-night play, *The Bandit Chief; or,
The Spectre of the Forest,* was a story of knights, ghosts, and a lone damsel.
According to Taylor, the company's single actress, a Mrs. Ray who
advertised herself as "of the Royal Theatre, New Zealand,"

> rushes in and throws herself into an attitude in the middle of the stage: why
> she does it, no one can tell. This movement, which she repeats several
> times in the course of the first three acts, has no connection with the
> tragedy; it is evidently introduced for the purpose of showing the audience
> that there is, actually, a female performer. The miners, to whom the sight
> of a woman is not a frequent occurrence, are delighted with these passages
> and applaud vehemently.[9]

Though the play, of course, filled the main portion of the evening,
music had a part. There was an orchestra of five, which Taylor reports
was led by an Italian and played well; it opened the program with an
overture and closed it as accompaniment to a postlude of songs and
duets. Thus music, on the coattails of drama, entered a space, a theatre,
that might be used as a recital hall or opera house.

San Francisco was only a fortnight behind Sacramento in erecting
what was probably its first public theatre, a temporary arena for a

circus. Then, on 16 January 1850, its first theatre proper opened with a drama, *The Wife*, by the well-known Irish playwright of the day Sheridan Knowles; and as was the custom then, the tragedy was followed by a farce. The theatre, Washington Hall, occupied the second story of a building that at street level housed Foley's Saloon. After only a week, however, the actors abruptly ended their season—reportedly because their treasurer had lost all the box-office receipts gambling—and the saloon took over the hall.[10]

During the next three months several more theatres opened, and one, the National, was for the time remarkably grand. It was partly of brick, stood on its own plot between Montgomery and Kearny streets, and seated 700, 400 on the parquet and 300 in "boxes," which, except for two stage boxes, may have been merely a gallery. The theatre opened in February with a French vaudeville company and in May, in one of San Francisco's many fires, burned to the ground. But before then it had housed an important event in the city's musical history.

On 2 April a pianist of international reputation gave San Franciscans what seems to have been their first purely musical event, certainly the first of note. Henri Herz, of Paris, who was nearing the end of a five-year tour of the United States, Mexico, the West Indies, Peru, and Chile, arrived from South America via Panama and, hiring as assisting artists a local bass-baritone and a flutist, gave a recital at what were surely the highest prices yet charged: $6 a seat for the boxes and $4 for the parquet. Though the flutist's two selections are not known, he probably performed arrangements of popular songs or operatic arias; the bass-baritone, a Frenchman, sang an aria from Donizetti's *La Favorite* and two French songs; and Herz, playing four times, offered variations on music from Hérold's opera *Le Pré aux clercs*, Bellini's *I Puritani*, Donizetti's *Lucia di Lammermoor*, and a medley of American, French, Italian, and German popular songs that ended with a triumphant inflation of Stephen Foster's "Oh! Susanna."[11]

Though the recital had not sold out, Herz scheduled another for 6 April, with the same flutist but a new singer, and this time, among other works not identified, he rhapsodized on "The Last Rose of Summer" and introduced his *Voyage musicale* for piano in which he mingled a

"Storm at Sea" and "The California Polka" with the national songs of
the world's principal countries, representing the United States by
"Yankee Doodle." The daily paper *Alta California* reported that portions of the *Voyage* were "perfectly electrifying."[12]

Herz's prices, however, left many seats empty, and for his third
concert, five days later, he lowered the scale to $5 and $3, announcing
a "Monstre Concert" in which, in addition to a cornetist and two
singers, he promised a finale in which four pianos would combine on
a *Marche nationale.* Though not described, it probably was another
Voyage musicale. The lower prices and more varied program pulled in
a full house, and he left for Sacramento on a storm of praise.[13]

Returning before the end of the month, Herz played his "farewell"
on 27 April, repeating his *Voyage musicale* and again selling out the
house at the reduced price scale. After the performance he was entertained by admirers at the Hotel du Commerce. According to the *Pacific
News,* "The occasion was one of the most pleasant re-unions in the
happiest French taste; the viands were delicious, and the wines most
choice and rare."[14]

The reception, with its touch of elegance, marked a change taking
place in the clothing as well as habits of some in San Francisco. With
the city's growing prosperity, men in the business community, particularly among the French, had begun to replace the miner's slouching
felt hat with a narrow-brimmed black beaver, the flannel shirt with
white linen, and the long, rumpled outer coat with a frock or dress coat.
Trousers, too, increasingly were tailored; but no man, so long as
spitting indoors or out was common and every street was a bog in
winter and a bin of dust in summer, was ready yet to give up the knee
boots into which trousers could be tucked.[15]

Herz, a witty, stylish man who enjoyed meeting people, assisted the
sartorial transition. As the first artist of front rank to visit the city, with
his recitals and receptions he not only encouraged those interested in
music to want more but also gave those who wished to dress up the
opportunity. In Sacramento, for example, only men with starched
shirts were admitted to his recital, and afterward he was entertained
with a ball, albeit in a cottage. While there was still smoking, spitting,

drinking, gambling, and much brawling in the theatres, he helped to advance the idea that they could be places of reasonable, orderly behavior.[16]

In his farewell recital, however, he put music's cause in retreat by engaging for the intermission a non-musician, a magician. Worse still, three nights later he played the piano as a turn in the man's show, once more relegating music to the subordinate position from which he had just rescued it.[17] On the other hand, before leaving the city he declined an offer of $2,000 a month to remain and play nightly in a saloon. Though the offer was perhaps too low to tempt him, his refusal, reported in the *Pacific News*, sharpened anew the distinction between music as an end in itself, however sugared to taste, and music merely as an accompaniment to other activities.[18] At very least, by his success he had demonstrated that the city, with its population now approaching 30,000, was almost ready to support serious musical endeavors—recitals, concerts, and opera.

TWO

The First Opera

The first sample of Verdi's music presented by a professional musician to an audience in San Francisco cannot be named with certainty, but the earliest yet discovered is the soprano's cavatina or entrance aria from *Ernani*, "Ernani, involami." It is an aria of leisurely, arched phrases, followed by an extended rush of intensity as the bride-to-be, unwillingly engaged to an elderly uncle, invokes her secret lover to snatch her from the old man's horrid embrace. The singer, making her local debut, was Mathilde Korsinsky, an artist of German background who before coming to San Francisco had sung professionally for five or six years in New York (Fig. 1). And the occasion was the intermission between a drama and a farce at the Jenny Lind Theatre on 4 November 1850.

The theatre, the city's newest, had opened only five nights earlier, on 30 October; and although on the previous day everyone had celebrated California's admission to the Union as the thirty-first state, the Jenny Lind's first night was also an event and, for the time, well reported. Its name reflected the "Lindomania" then sweeping the East as the "Swedish Nightingale" toured the bigger cities, St. Louis being her only stop west of the Mississippi. The theatre, built in traditional style and seating about 700, perched on the second floor of the Parker

House, a large building on the main square, or the Plaza. Directly beneath it was a saloon, with a piano and entertainment, and upstairs, with easy access to the theatre, were rooms for gambling.[1] The theatre had its own entrance, however, and though its seats were unnumbered, those in the front, or so it advertised, were "reserved for ladies."[2]

For the theatre's inaugural night the proprietor, the saloonkeeper, had put together a gala program consisting of Mme Korsinsky–Von Gulpen, as she sometimes was known, a man who sang ballads, and another who performed magical tricks and also was an expert on the slack wire.[3] This variety show—which on 1 November the volunteer firemen of the St. Francis Hook and Ladder Company attended in full uniform[4]—played four nights, and in Mme Korsinsky–Von Gulpen's bit of the evening, at least on the first night, she sang an unidentified Spanish song and "On the Banks of the Guadalquiver."[5] While there are several songs with that title, hers almost surely was the one by the Irish composer Michael Balfe, which then was very popular.

On Monday, 4 November, the Stark theatrical troupe took over, and between the drama *Damon and Pythias* and the closing farce *Dumb Belle,* Korsinsky–Von Gulpen sang her Verdi aria. The next day the *Evening Picayune* reported (with several names misspelled):

> The cavatina from *Ernani* was sung by Madame Korsinski with a power and brilliance of execution that drew down the house in the most enthusiastic demonstrations of delight. She was rapturously encored, and will afford one of the most popular attractions of this theatre. The orchestra consisting of a grand Piano played by Mons. Van Gulpen, and a violin by M. Pascal, was quite sufficient to fill the house, and they discoursed really delightful music. The hall is the neatest and most commodious affair of the kind in the city.[6]

Music in an intermission was then a common form of entertainment, and Korsinsky, who had been engaged for the week, apparently repeated the aria at least once.[7] Because of her marriage to the pianist, Carl Von Gulpen, which seems to have been recent, she soon would drop from her professional name the "Korsinsky," thus creating a sharp division between her career in New York and in San Francisco. She was never a singer of top rank, but in New York, appearing with the

Fig 1. Mathilde Korsinsky–Von Gulpen, who sang under her maiden name, Korsinsky, in New York City and under her married name, Von Gulpen, for the most part, in San Francisco. (San Francisco Performing Arts Library)

Philharmonic Society as Korsinsky, she had won a footnote in history as the mezzo-soprano in the U.S. premiere of Beethoven's Ninth Symphony. In San Francisco as Von Gulpen, she perhaps earned another for introducing the city to Verdi.[8]

In her next appearance, on 16 December 1850, she produced what seems to have been the city's first recital organized primarily around a singer. For the event, which she advertised as a "Grand Concert," she rented the Armory of the First California Guards and, as assisting artists, hired a cellist and two male vocalists. Although no one sang or played any Verdi, she did offer an aria from Rossini's *Il barbiere di Siviglia* and a duet from Donizetti's *Lucia di Lammermoor,* both before the intermission; after the break, she and the others sang only songs. Apparently, she gauged the audience's taste correctly, for the following day a newspaper's one-sentence comment was an invitation, albeit conditional, for more: "There can be no doubt that two such concerts monthly, if well managed, would succeed admirably."[9]

Before she was able to act on the suggestion, other artists had put together a musical miscellany that the *Alta California* described as the city's "first Grand Concert of Vocal and Instrumental Music." Assembling on the afternoon of 22 December in the large hall of the California Exchange, more than forty musicians, with perhaps twelve or fifteen of them forming an orchestra, offered a mishmash of operatic overtures, arias, and popular songs. The paper in its review, which omitted first names, partially identified only two soloists and their selections. A Señora (Francisca) Abalos sang the "soprano cavatina" (probably "Come per me sereno") from Bellini's *La sonnambula,* and a Signor (?) Lobero played a trombone arrangement of "the Grand Aria" (probably "Dagli immortali") from Verdi's *Attila.*[10]

At this time Verdi, born in 1813, had not yet composed *Rigoletto* (1851), *Il trovatore* (1853), or *La traviata* (1853), and the trombone "fantasy," as such instrumental arrangements of arias then often were called, was drawn from one of the more popular of his early operas. Of the fifteen of these works preceding *Rigoletto,* the best known probably were *Nabucodonosor* (generally called *Nabucco;* 1842), *I Lombardi alla prima crociata* (1843), *Ernani* (1844), and *Attila* (1846). Of these, *Ernani,* based on a play by Victor Hugo, had won the most fame, and its soprano cavatina, "Ernani, involami," more than any other of Verdi's arias, carried his name around the world. Sopranos could not ignore it. In San Francisco, as will be seen, it became a touchstone; by its rendition artists were judged.

Though Von Gulpen was a mezzo-soprano, or even contralto, and probably transposed the aria down, her success with it had been real, and for her next recital she returned to it, announcing another "Grand Concert," with herself as producer and star, for 29 January 1851 at the Adelphi Theatre. The Adelphi, which stood on the south side of Clay Street between Kearny and Montgomery, was a focus of the city's French community, a frequent home to French plays and farces. Its acoustics were doubtless better than those of the Armory, and it also had several advantages over the Jenny Lind: it was slightly larger and, most important, free of competition from the piano in the saloon.[11] As her assisting artists Von Gulpen hired a flutist, a cellist, and a bass-baritone, and offered a program that included a fantasy for flute on melodies from Bellini's *Sonnambula* and *I Puritani,* duets for herself and the bass-baritone from Donizetti's *Belisario* and *Elisir d'amore* (the latter to be sung in costume), and, as her most demanding solo aria, placed as the finale before the intermission, Verdi's "Ernani, involami."[12]

Before this event took place, however, two others leading toward the production of opera in San Francisco intervened. On Sunday evening 12 January, at Foley's Amphitheatre, a small group of resident French musicians, led by the violinist Louis Theophile Planel—usually referred to simply as "Mons. Planel"—gave a concert of vocal and instrumental selections, ending with the final act of Donizetti's French opera *La Favorite:* the first attempt in the city to present an entire act of opera, however much cut. But their effort, or at least its vocal part, for which Mme Hortense Planel served as prima donna, was judged a failure. The *Alta California* dismissed it in two sentences: "We confess ourselves disappointed. The instrumental portion was far the best of the entertainment." In his next concert, Planel shied away from opera.[13]

Meanwhile, an event of more lasting significance had occurred. On

8 January, at 1:00 P.M., the steamer *Tennessee* from Panama via Acapulco, San Diego, and Monterey, a voyage of twenty days, had docked with freight, mail, and 101 passengers, among whom was a troupe of three Italian opera singers and a pianist, arriving unexpected and unknown.[14] Promptly their leader placed an advertisement in the *Alta California*, which he ran for three days:

ITALIAN OPERA

MAD'ME ROSINA MAURI PELLEGRINI, SIGNOR INNOCENZO PELLEGRINI, SIGNOR ANGELO FRANCIA and SIGNOR JAMES WEITZ, forming a company of the first and most distinguished vocal performers of the lyric companies of Peru and Chile, under the direction of Signor Pellegrini, a celebrated tenor, and lyric artist of highest repute, who has sung in the first theatres of Europe, private singer to H.M. the King of Denmark, Fellow of the Academy of St. Cecilia at Rome and also of the Philharmonic Society of Rome, and Bologna, whose voice is among the sweetest Italy has produced, and of the most modern school [Fig. 2].

Mad'me MAURI, prima donna soprano, also a very distinguished Italian songstress [Fig. 3]. Signor ANGELO FRANCIA, an Italian baritone, and Signor JAMES WEITZ, an excellent pianist, and much prized by Americans, and whose talents have raised his reputation to place him on a par with the most distinguished of modern pianists.

The above mentioned artists intend giving a few entertainments, in which will be represented and sung whole acts of the best modern operas, and complete operas, with gorgeous dresses, which they have brought here, not omitting the best orchestra to be engaged in this city.[15]

Pellegrini scheduled the first concert for 24 January, at Foley's Amphitheatre, hiring to appear with his singers several dancers, the Llorentes, who made a specialty of character skits. And where the local French, in the vocal part of their entertainment, had failed, the newly arrived Italians succeeded. Unfortunately, neither Pellegrini in his announcements nor the newspapers in their reviews disclose what was sung.[16]

Capitalizing on his troupe's success, Pellegrini scheduled a second concert at the amphitheatre for 28 January, preceding by only a day Von Gulpen's "Grand Concert" at the Adelphi, with its program of arias by Verdi and Donizetti and a duet "in costume." Such a quick succession of operatic events was new in San Francisco and a sign of how swiftly the city's musical life was growing. Also in this week, and possibly in time for his second concert, Pellegrini expanded his troupe by hiring two additional soloists: Señora Abalos, who in the previous month had done well with the cavatina from *Sonnambula;* and a bass-baritone, Signor V. Acquasoni. Like the first concert, this second was a success, and though details are lacking, a news item hints: "The programme promises selections from the operas of Donizetti and Verdi."[17]

Meanwhile, Pellegrini had announced in the *Alta California,* though without dates, staged productions of complete operas; and finally, at the Adelphi Theatre on 12 February, as the opening of his season, he presented San Francisco with its first opera: Bellini's *La sonnambula.* The cast included himself as Elvino; his wife, Mauri, as the sleepwalk-ing Amina; Abalos as Lisa; Acquasoni as Count Rodolfo, and Francia in the small role of Alessio. Possibly Weitz, who no longer is men-tioned, served as a vocal coach and rehearsal pianist, and perhaps also as conductor, though the fact that neither the advertisement nor the review of the performance mentions a conductor suggests that the small orchestra was led by the first violinist from his chair, a frequent but unsatisfactory practice. (Except when he stopped playing to direct, the violinist usually led simply by playing loud, stomping time and making faces at the players and singers.)[18]

The next morning the *Alta California,* with an unsigned paragraph, published the city's first review of an opera:

ITALIAN OPERA — A crowded house greeted the opening of the Italian opera troupe, at the Adelphi, last evening. The opera was Bellini's cele-brated production, "La Sonnambula." We were not previously aware that San Francisco contained such finished musical artists as appeared last evening, and the torrents of applause that continually broke forth [it was not yet the custom to await the aria's close to applaud], exhibited the appreciation of the audience. We trust these talented artists will receive the support from the San Francisco public which they richly merit.[19]

Indeed, so pleased was the public with what it had seen and heard that Pellegrini was able to repeat the opera three times in the fortnight.[20]

Fig 2. Innocenzo Pellegrini. (SF Performing Arts Library)

Then, adding another local artist, Von Gulpen, to his troupe, on 27 February he presented Bellini's *Norma,* and it, too, had a triumph. According to the *Alta California* the next morning: "Signora Abalos [Norma] did not possess a large amount of talent, but her voice is strong and musical. Von Gulpen–Korsinsky [Adalgisa] is a great acquisition for this company." Four days later they sang *Norma* again.[21]

All these performances, if like those soon to follow, were severely cut, lacked a women's chorus, had a men's chorus of six or fewer, and were accompanied by an orchestra of not more than twelve or fifteen—at most four or five violins (with the first-desk man doubling as conductor), a viola, a cello, a doublebass, a flute, two clarinets, two horns, a cornet, and a trombone . . . but, it seems likely, without tympani, which apparently were slow to reach the city.[22] The players, again judging from later performances, were usually either French or German immigrants—with the latter predominating, for the Germans, numbering nearly 5,000, were the city's most active music-makers.[23] Germans also customarily manned the chorus, whether recruited individually or as a group from one of their four fraternal singing clubs, of which the most important, the Turn Gesangverein, was the usual source.[24]

The Adelphi, which housed San Francisco's first opera season, had about a thousand seats, all unnumbered, except perhaps for those in the stage boxes. When the theatre opened its doors, therefore (usually a half-hour before the performance), within any price range it was "first come, best seated"—a practice about which the press, always on the lookout for perquisites, soon complained.[25]

Because the city did not have gas until February 1854, the Adelphi's auditorium and stage were lit by either candles or whale oil, probably in some combination. Each had a disadvantage: the sperm-whale oil had an unpleasant odor, and the candles required attention. Candles in the footlights, for example, often wanted their wicks trimmed during the performance, a duty frequently assigned to a member of the orchestra. As for the auditorium, once a chandelier had been lit and raised to the ceiling, its candles could not be trimmed, and sometimes dripped—a reason the pit, or orchestra floor close to the stage and directly beneath the chandelier, was neither fashionable nor expensive. Respectable women shunned the area, and men sitting there were apt to keep on their hats.[26] Indeed, throughout the house generally it still was common to remain "covered" during the performance, on the rationale that a theatre was a public place. Even the actors, whether the scene was indoors or out, frequently wore hats, for the stage, too, usually was lit by a chandelier.[27]

Pellegrini's price scale at the Adelphi was, private boxes (probably only the stage boxes or those adjoining the proscenium), $4; other boxes (apparently unenclosed and merely the lowest of the three galleries), $3; second gallery and parquet (probably the entire orchestra floor), $2; and top gallery (to which, at the Jenny Lind at least, Negroes were directed), $1.[28] Von Gulpen at her recitals had charged $3 for all seats at the Armory (with a $1 discount for escorted ladies) and $2 at the Adelphi. A drama troupe playing the Jenny Lind had a top price of $3. Pellegrini's scale, therefore, was not high; indeed, compared to what Henri Herz had charged a year earlier it was low, and tickets sold well.

In the gold fields at this time a miner who was skillful, lucky, and hard working might average $100 a day; and two who struck it rich went off with $10,000 in two days. In the city, meanwhile, a dinner with wine cost $3.50, a stevedore or porter could charge $3 or $4 to carry a trunk, and a skilled workman could earn upwards of $20 a day. At the most elegant saloons a woman, invariably French, would sit at a man's table for the evening—nothing more—for $32, and a woman known to be fastidious and willing to entertain a man for the night might earn $400. Among musicians there was the usual spread: an orchestra member might earn $32 of an evening; popular soloists, five or six times that amount.[29]

Inevitably, the great majority of the audience were men, many in work clothes.[30] According to reports of later performances, the most elegant in dress and manners were the French, and the most raucous, the Irish.[31] During the intermissions those of European background would stand in the lobby or on the sidewalk outside, smoking their cigars and discussing the performance; the Americans would rush across the street to have a drink.[32] In the theatre, peanuts and fruit were sold in the aisles, and purchasers munched throughout the performance.[33] Many in the audience smoked. After Pellegrini's first concert, at Foley's Amphitheatre, the *Evening Picayune* had complained of "the disgusting habit of segar smoking . . . the theatre was filled with tobacco smoke, and several ladies were compelled to leave in consequence."[34] Ten days before the first *Sonnambula*, the *Alta California* gave theatregoers a tip: "We would respectfully advise gentlemen, if they must eject tobacco juice in church or in the theatre, that they be particular to eject it on their own boots and pantaloons, instead of the boots and pantaloons of others."[35]

After two performances of *Norma*, Pellegrini brought back *Sonnambula* for one, the city's first operatic revival, and then announced in the *Alta California* as his third production, to be presented on 28 March, the "First representation of the celebrated opera of Ernani." Though the notice listed the singers of the four leading roles, it nowhere named the opera's composer: Verdi.[36]

Pellegrini's casting for *Ernani* was strange, reflecting not only the small number of his company, but also a problem in mounting the opera that, in turn, suggests a way in which many of Verdi's early works may have sounded distinctive to audiences. Pellegrini's roster of voices for leading roles (and plainly, judging by the casting of the first two operas, he did not think Francia's baritone good for much) counted three female and two male: the sopranos of Mauri and Abalos, the mezzo-soprano of Von Gulpen, his own tenor, and Acquasoni's bass-baritone. This was adequate to cast most of the contemporary costume dramas, which typically required one or two sopranos, a tenor, and a bass-baritone; but it would not do for *Ernani*, which wanted a single female voice and three male: tenor, baritone, and bass. This imbalance in favor of men's voices was not unusual in comic opera, but with only a few exceptions, like Donizetti's *Marin Faliero* or Bellini's *I Puritani*, it was rare in the romantic melodramas then popular. For contemporary audiences, therefore, part of the special quality of *Ernani* was its strong masculine tone.

Finding a satisfactory baritone, however, must have proved difficult, for ultimately Pellegrini assigned the role of Don Carlo to Von Gulpen, who would have to sing it an octave higher than composed and, in all probability, to rewrite many of its phrases. In these years Verdi's baritone roles often were troublesome to cast, for he wanted a voice higher than the traditional bass-baritone, yet lower than the tenor. The true distinction between bass and baritone, according to Charles Santley, a contemporary English artist who sang many of Verdi's baritone roles, lay not at all in the ability to sing higher notes—for many excellent basses could manage an F or G above middle C—but entirely in the "quality of the voice" that a singer could bring to the upper end of his range. That quality often was slow to stabilize, a fact that led many men to concentrate on their lower notes, to become basses, when they might have done better to train as baritones.[37] Verdi was not so much "creating" a new type of voice, as was sometimes said, as calling into greater use a range of a voice already existing and often needing only some further training.

Pellegrini, in producing *Ernani*, was not the first impresario to find himself without enough male voices, or voices of the required range and quality, to cast the opera properly. In 1847 the Royal Italian Opera at Covent Garden, unable to find a baritone for Don Carlo, used a contralto for the part, Marietta Alboni. But however fine Alboni's low notes, she cannot have descended to Don Carlo's lowest, an A at an octave and a half below middle C; and like Von Gulpen, she, too, must have transposed the vocal line upward.

With his *Ernani*, though, Pellegrini's luck turned against him, and on the morning after the supposed performance on 28 March 1851 the *Alta California* carried a brief explanation of its sudden postponement:

> We are requested by Signor Pellegrini, director of the Italian Opera, to state that in consequence of the sudden departure of Madam Von Gulpen for Sacramento City, without having given him notice, he will be unable for the present to produce the opera of Ernani, upon which he has made great outlay.[38]

Von Gulpen never disclosed to the public who or what had called her to Sacramento, but she evidently was able to reconcile herself to

Fig. 3. Rosina Mauri-Pellegrini. (SF Performing Arts Library)

Pellegrini, for he soon announced for the evening of 8 April, as the final performance of his season and a benefit for himself as "manager," the production of "Verdi's magnificent opera of Ernani."[39] There is no review of it—a lack that for 1851 in San Francisco is not uncommon—but the journal of a local theatrical agent, John H. McCabe, records the performance as having taken place.[40]

Soon thereafter Pellegrini, Mauri, and Acquasoni (no mention of any others) gave four concerts in Sacramento, which could be reached by the Union Line's river steamer in nine hours, at a charge of $12 for a cabin, $9 for a deck chair. In their concerts the trio offered selections from operas by Bellini, Donizetti, and Verdi. At the same time, Pellegrini sought by newspaper advertisement "fifty gentlemen [who] will subscribe twenty-five dollars each" to underwrite a season of *Sonnambula*, *Norma*, and *Ernani*.[41] But the sponsors were not forthcoming, and even the concerts of operatic selections may not have been too successful, for the announcement of the last promises that Pellegrini "will sing in English the popular song, 'The Death of Warren at Bunker Hill' "— surely a concession for a fellow of the Philharmonic Society of Rome and of Bologna.[42]

Then, on 3 May 1851 in San Francisco, occurred one of the city's celebrated fires, the fifth of six within eighteen months. This one started in a paint shop on the west side of Portsmouth Square, as the Plaza now was called, and, burning all the next day, destroyed twenty-two blocks in the heart of the city. Among the buildings lost, estimated at 1,800, were all the newspaper offices, except that of the *Alta California*, and, without exception, all the theatres. Every one.

Perhaps discouraged by the fire and not conceiving how the city could recover, Pellegrini and his wife apparently concluded that San Francisco no longer was a town for opera—and they vanished, utterly.[43] Possibly they were lost at sea. Pellegrini, however, was the first, forever the first, to produce opera in San Francisco: five performances of *Sonnambula*, two of *Norma*, one of *Ernani*.

THREE

The Celebrity Sopranos

Though Pellegrini bequeathed to San Francisco a memory of *Ernani*, Verdi as yet cannot be said to have had much impact on the city, and in 1852, when no operas were staged, he had even less. This year two visiting celebrities, both sopranos, dominated the musical life, each with a series of recitals in which she surrounded arias and scenes from operas with English, Scottish, and Irish songs. A typical program began with an orchestral number, usually an opera overture, played by a band of ten seated on the stage; it continued with a song or aria sung by an assisting artist, and then presented the prima donna. She would be greeted with cheers and stamping feet, "thunders of applause," which she would acknowledge with demure smiles and imploring glances until allowed to sing. Thereafter, each of her selections, if all went well, would gather more applause as well as a harvest of bouquets, either thrown from the galleries or, the theatres being small, handed to her directly. Sometimes these offerings concealed gold coins or small pieces of jewelry. In response to appeals, several times of an evening she would repeat a song or aria or, instead, move to the piano and accompany herself in some unscheduled, highly popular number such as "Home, Sweet Home."

In those days, throughout the United States and not only in San

Francisco, an audience's approval was not expressed merely by clapping. Even at musical events, which by their nature were more quietly attended than plays or minstrel shows, there was a great deal of whistling, stamping, and yelling, particularly from the cheaper seats. The more reticent members of the audience, sitting for the most part in the boxes, might express their approval by clapping or knocking their canes against the wooden chairs or using them as poles to twirl their top hats. The more noisily inclined, however, held nothing back, and if in a mood of disapproval, hissed, groaned, yelled, and sometimes hurled vegetables at the artists, though this was more frequent at plays than at concerts.

Even when pleased, however, the audience did not reserve its applause for the end of the song or aria, but broke in after any admired passage, often obscuring the one that followed. Thus a repeat, even if sung exactly as before, might reveal beauties as yet unheard, and perhaps for this reason, as well as for fear of offending a capricious audience, repeats, when vigorously demanded, often were granted.[1]

The amount of whistling and yelling always startled European visitors. In 1851 a French immigrant to the city, Albert Bernard de Russailh, noted in his journal that enjoyment in the theatre was expressed by "shrill whistles and savage yells," and he went on to add: "Most of the Frenchmen here cannot live on friendly terms with the Americans, whom they consider a savage, ignorant people."

The French in San Francisco, in 1851, had cause to dislike their American neighbors, for the American-dominated state legislature, in a notable display of racial animosity and greed, had imposed a prohibitive "Foreign Miners Tax" on all but U.S. citizens, and efforts in the mine fields to collect the $20-per-month fee had led to furious protests and riots. So angry was the response to the tax that it soon was repealed, but among non-citizens distrust of American motives and actions lingered.

De Russailh, though he did not share the French aversion to Americans and thought French exclusiveness a foolish trait in California, nevertheless was appalled by the aggressive spirit of American nationalism and the violence that accompanied it. In commenting on the frequent barroom and gambling brawls, he remarked: Americans "have all the characteristics of savages and think only of death and slaughter. They always carry revolvers, and they draw them on the least provocation and threaten to blow your head off . . . As a race they laugh at honesty and decency whenever it is to their advantage to do so."[2]

Even the American sense of humor distressed him, for he saw in it the same tendency to violence that permeated their daily life. At a circus, he noted, they want "a good clown. When they see him kicked in the behind, they scream with laughter, and they love a fellow with plenty of jokes, who can roll around in the sawdust and make funny faces while his partner belabors him."[3]

Possibly De Russailh's views exaggerate American failings, but they also support three plain truths about theatrical life in San Francisco in the Gold Rush years: the behavior of the audiences for drama and music was as rough as legend tells; the French in the city had a strong civilizing influence on audience behavior and the development of the arts; and the artists, like Herz and those who followed him to the Golden Gate, had courage.

The first of the two celebrity sopranos to arrive, on 14 March 1852, was Eliza Biscaccianti (Fig. 4), with her husband Alessandro, a cellist, acting as manager. In anticipation, the *Alta California* asked music-lovers for their attention and good behavior. She was coming, the paper stated, despite the "remonstrances" of friends and "moneyed inducements" to remain in the East, and was relying on "the good taste of the Californians." San Franciscans should "show the world that the Muses have as many admirers and supporters here as elsewhere."[4]

Because she had been born in Boston of a New England mother, Biscaccianti was known popularly as "The American Thrush," but she had studied in Europe and sung in Paris, Milan, St. Petersburg, and London, founding a claim to be the first American to sing opera in Europe. In the ten months that she remained in California she sang at least seventy recitals, thirty-five in San Francisco, thirteen in Sacramento, seven in Stockton, and the balance in smaller towns.[5] In San Francisco she opened with a series of ten recitals, all sung at the American Theatre (cap. 2,000) during March and April 1852.[6] In the

Fig. 4. Eliza Biscaccianti in costume for the "Bridal Scene" of *Lucia di Lammermoor:* a title page for sheet music published by Atwill, New York.

third of these she sang Verdi's aria "Ernani, involami," and in the eighth, the soprano's prayer (including the initial recitative), "Sempre all'alba," from his opera *Giovanna d'Arco.* Both selections won applause, yet despite her skills the music evidently made little impression and, unlike the finale of *Sonnambula,* "Ah! non giunge," which at its first presentation had to be repeated twice, neither Verdi aria won a repeat or was rescheduled. Mozart did no better; "Porgi amor," from *Le nozze di Figaro,* similarly failed.[7]

What succeeded were the old songs, sometimes sung straight, sometimes embellished, though the latter were not to everyone's taste.[8] Among the most popular were "Comin' Thro' the Rye," "John Anderson, My Jo," "I Am Queen of a Fairy Band," "Believe Me, If All Those Endearing Young Charms," and a new one—her only American number—Foster's "Old Folks at Home" (1851), which in popularity was beginning to rival Bishop's "Home, Sweet Home" (1823). She also did well with some song of Schubert that she retitled "A German Romance" and offered with a cello obbligato played by her husband; it not only earned a repeat but was rescheduled twice.[9]

Of the operatic selections in this first series of recitals, besides "Ah! non giunge," with eight renditions, only the duet for two sopranos from *Norma*, "Deh! con te," with four, caught the public's ear and required an immediate repetition and rescheduling. And only "O luce di quest'anima" from *Linda di Chamounix* and "Spargi d'amor" from *Lucia di Lammermoor* won even a single reappearance. The other three arias, from *Sonnambula, Beatrice di Tenda,* and *Robert le diable,* like those of Verdi and Mozart, were heard once and dropped. The songs, therefore, greatly outnumbered the arias. Nevertheless, her art deeply stirred her audiences, and after her opening night the *Alta California* reported, "The next day the people went about in a daze and even the most sober minded and judicial subscribed to the decision of the press that the evening marked an era in the musical, social and fashionable progress of the city."[10]

In the city's small theatrical world, however, where an undifferentiated audience attended all entertainments of whatever kind, any artist's success or failure was likely to be translated promptly into a comic skit, and Biscaccianti's triumph was no exception. On 30 March, the night after her fourth recital, in the very same theatre a group of comedians presented an "original local quizzical, outrageous burlesque squib," *Mr. and Mrs. Biscuit Chanter.* The *Alta California,* without revealing details, reported that the players had won "a great deal of applause," and presumably the company's chief comic, James Evrard, had mocked by excess all the mannerisms of a prima donna: the entrance, the acknowledgment of applause, the discreet cough (to

discount in advance any failure), the careful positioning of herself
and her dress (ending in a nod to her accompanist when ready to
begin), and finally all the bodily and facial contortions of a soprano
in full bravura flight.[11]

Biscaccianti's success continued into the summer, and after a tour
that included Sacramento and the towns and mining camps to the
north, she returned to San Francisco in July to offer a second series of
ten recitals, appearing this time in the Jenny Lind Theatre, which
because of fires was now in its third incarnation, no longer on an upper
floor but standing on its own lot and enlarged to seat 2,000.[12] She also
sang a benefit to raise money for the Washington Monument Fund,
"realizing" $503,[13] another for the Firemen's Charitable Fund, and one
for Grace Church—for which occasion the parishoners set up a bar in
the church—where she presented, presumably backed by the church
choir, soloists, and organ, the local premiere of Rossini's *Stabat Mater*.[14]
But for the most part, her programs remained much as before.

Evidently she liked San Francisco, for early in December, in an
open letter to the *Herald*, her husband proposed that subscribers underwrite a season of Italian opera, with Biscaccianti as prima donna,
backed by an Italian company then in Lima, Peru. To persons he
thought might subscribe he sent the proposal direct, with full details
of the scheme (Fig. 5).[15] He envisaged importing not a troupe but a full
company: nine soloists, a mixed chorus of twelve, and an orchestra of
twenty-one, with the first violinist as conductor. In addition he wanted
to include a prompter, who might also serve as a copyist, and a chorus
master who would be in charge of costumes. The salaries and other
expenses, he estimated, would come to $16,000 a month, and he pro-
jected a season of six months and fifteen operas.

In every way the project was more than the city's musical community was ready to undertake, and for lack of support his effort to
found a resident company—which he referred to as "the first San
Francisco Opera"—failed. Instead, on 15 January 1853, he and Biscaccianti departed by the steamer *Golden Gate* for Lima, where at the
Teatro Principal opera was mounted on a grander scale; and soon
reports came back that Biscaccianti was enjoying a great success.[16]

Tehama House, Dec. 11 1852.

Mr Gregory Yale

Having received private intelligence that the Italian Opera troupe at present performing in Lima express a desire to visit this city professionally, and being personally acquainted with the principal *artistes* composing said troupe, I have thought of a plan by which an engagement could be effected with them, and thus contribute to the desire of the many lovers of music in this refined city of San Francisco.

To carry out this project, it would be not only necessary to engage the principals composing this troupe, but also the secondary parts, chorus, orchestra, and finally every individual connected with an Operatic establishment. Allow me, if you please to give you a list of them :

Prima Donna,	Second Tenor,	Comprimaria,
First Barytone,	Seconda Donna,	Barytone Comprimaria,
First Tenor,	First Basso,	Tenor Compramaria.

CHORUS.

Four Tenors,	Two Sopranos,	Four Bassos,
	Two Contraltos.	

ORCHESTRA.

First Violin and Director,	First Clarinetto,	Three First Violins,
Second Clarinetto,	Three Second Violins,	First Horn,
Two Tenors,	Second Horn.	First Violioncello,
First Trometto,	First Contra Basso,	First Trombone,
Second Contra Basso,	First Drummer.	First Hauto,
Prompter and Copyist.	Chorus Mast. and Costumer,	First Flaggioletto.

The joint salary of this company, consisting of forty-four individuals, according to my calculation, will amount to the sum of about $10,000 per month   Add to this the rent of the theatre, printing, advertising, illumination, attendance, scene painter and others employed in the establishment, a wardrobe for a series of fifteen Operas, with the purchase of the same Operas with orchestral parts, and expenses of traveling for the entire troupe, will augment the sum to near $16,000 per month

A certain number of subscribers would be necessary for a season of six months, sufficient to cover two-thirds of the expenses. The following are the conditions of the subscription :

Each subscriber will pledge himself to pay, for a season of six months, the sum of $60 per month, holding the right for the same of a reserved seat in the Opera House for twelve representations each month.

The Managers will pledge himself to give to the subscribers three representations each week, during the operatic season ; and to produce at least two new Operas each month, with appropriate costumes and scenery.

The sum of about $10,000 is also necessary to defray the traveling expenses of this entire troupe, together with the wardrobe. I would suggest that this sum should be raised by those subscribers who would be willing to assist this enterprise, by advancing one month's subscription, which would be refunded in the course of the operatic season, by the administration, in the following manner, viz :

Each subscriber who had advanced this sum, instead of paying $60 per month, will be required to pay $50.

Should this plan meet with your confidence and support, I will leave immediately for Lima to make the necessary arrangements for the transfer of the *artistes* composing that troupe to this city. In this connection, and in behalf of Madame Biscaccianti, I beg to state, that should this scheme succeed, the pleasure she derives in contemplating a protracted stay, and an engagement as the *Prima Donna* of the first San Francisco Opera, is as unfeigned as the pleasant recollections which are cherished of her warm reception here, and the friendships which have been formed during her visit to California.

In conclusion, I beg to add, that the above scheme is a *fac simile* of the one of the Astor Place Opera, in New York, and of all others where the Italian Opera has been introduced.   I have the honor to subscribe myself, very respectfully,

ALESSANDRO BISCACCIANTI

The soprano who matched Biscaccianti's success in San Francisco in 1852–53 was another international artist, Catherine or Kate Hayes, "The Swan of Erin" (Fig. 6). She arrived on 20 November 1852 accompanied by her mother and a German Swiss bass-baritone, Josef Mengis, whose first name, curiously, journalists seem never to have used, always referring to him as "Herr Mengis." Hayes had imported him from Europe, and he soon proved his worth, for although she had a pleasant, well-trained voice, she was not so impressive a singer as Biscaccianti. And to hold her audience during the half-year she remained in the city she relied far more than her predecessor on her assisting artist, changes of costume, beauty, charm, flair for comedy, and flamboyant publicity.[17]

She was "under the direction" of P. T. Barnum, whose agent, W. A. Bushnell, preceded her to the city,[18] and after she arrived, he staged frequent ticket auctions and torch-light parades, often making use of the city's volunteer fire companies, which the city did not replace with a professional, salaried department until 1866. Until then, particularly in these early years, much of the city's social life centered on the volunteer companies. The fire station, sometimes with a steeple for the bell, was often the most imposing building on the block, and between companies there was great rivalry over the polish and design of the engine, neatness of the station, and speed of response to an alarm. To raise money there were benefits, balls, parades, and picnics, and to aid in spending it, outings as far afield as Sacramento, with the festivities continuing for days. On all these occasions the men would wear their uniforms, red flannel shirts or smocks, blue trousers, boots, hats of leather, and their special insignia. At a "benefit night" in a theatre, whether for an individual company or the Firemen's Fund, they would drape the house with their company banners, attend in uniform, and loudly compete in their applause.[19]

Some of their events, however, may not have been entirely spon-

Fig. 5.   The proposal of Biscaccianti's husband to found "the first San Francisco Opera," which failed for lack of support. (The Bancroft Library, University of California, Berkeley)

Fig. 6. Catherine Hayes: a concert in Musical Hall, Bush Street; published in the *Golden Era*, July 1854. (California State Library, Sacramento)

taneous. When George Green, a butcher in the Pacific Market, on Central Wharf, and the foreman of Empire Engine Company No. 1, bid $1,125 for the best seat to Hayes's third recital, surely some persons then, as now, wondered whether Green, who asked that the ticket be put in the name of the Engine Company, might not receive a rebate in some form from Barnum's agent.[20]

Nevertheless, Hayes was a serious artist, opening her first recital, on 30 November, with "Ah, mon fils" from Meyerbeer's *Le Prophète* and continuing, after an assisting artist's piano fantasy, with a duet for herself and Mengis from *Norma* and a comic scene for the two of them from *Don Pasquale.* She also sang many songs, among them "The Last Rose of Summer," and these led to calls for a repetition. In the excitement some Irish immigrants in the audience threw their hats and money on the stage. The *Alta California* disapproved.[21]

Hayes presented her first eight recitals in the American Theatre, which had just been refurbished and its seats for the first time numbered. To make sure the audience grasped the new rules for seating, presumably the theatre, not Hayes, paid for the extra-large advertisement for her recital. Besides announcing the time, date, and place, it explained: "The ticket must be given up at the door, but the numbered check is to be retained and exhibited to the usher.... The first applicant [at the box office] will have the choice of seats except those reserved for the press.... A diagram of the theatre" would be on hand to show the seat's location.[22]

This change, which made it more difficult for the noisy, drinking members of the audience to bunch together, apparently was accepted so readily that, despite its significance, it drew surprisingly little comment. In its review of evening the *Alta California* merely observed, "The house has been rearranged.... The seats were numbered, and ushers were in attendance." Apparently, as soon as was practical the other larger theatres adopted the practice without raising opposition or feeling a need to state their reasons.[23]

The American, however, was one of the city's biggest theatres, and for her remaining recitals Hayes moved to a smaller hall, the San Francisco, which may have been more flattering to her voice. Reviews

of her performances stress her charm, her gift for comedy, her purity
of tone and ease of execution, but suggest that her voice, though sweet
and rich in its low and middle registers, lacked brilliance and power
at the top.[24]

Still, whether in the large theatre or the small, Hayes faced nightly
the disadvantages that plagued all theatrical events at this time in San
Francisco. The city as yet had no water, lighting, or sewage system; the
theatres continued to be lit with candles, oil, or some combination; and
the unpaved streets in an hour's rain could become knee-deep in mud.
At her first recital in the San Francisco Theatre the audience was small
because of rain; at the third, therefore, her manager advanced the
indoor event to take advantage of clear skies. As the *Alta California*
explained, the manager "stole a march on the weather last night. The
concert announced for this evening was given last night, on account of
the propitious state of the elements."[25] Plainly, with recitals often
scheduled at a rate of three a week, tickets for a performance usually
went on sale only the morning before.[26]

For her recitals at the San Francisco, which ran through late December and January 1853, Hayes offered a series of seventeen "concerts-
in-costume," the first of record in San Francisco.[27] The programs,
staged without scenery or properties but displaying a variety of costumes, which were much admired in the somewhat drably dressed city,
were made up chiefly of ballads and operatic scenes, and she included
among them a number of "operas-in-brief." These, to use the titles by
which they were advertised, were the *Barber of Seville, Daughter of the
Regiment, Elixir of Love, Don Pasquale, Lucia di Lammermoor, Norma,* and
Sonnambula. As the many translated titles suggest, probably most of the
operatic scenes and excerpts in this series were sung in English.[28]
Doubtless, too, many of them were cut, resewn, and transposed downward to display her soprano at its best, for although in Mengis she had
an exceptional supporting artist, particularly in buffo roles, it was
always her show.[29] Verdi's operas, if only because of the weight he gave
to men's voices, were ill-suited to her purpose.

In mid-February, chaperoned by her mother, she left for a vacation
in the mountains and then, after a tour that included Grass Valley and

other outlying towns and mining camps, returned to San Francisco for another series of recitals. Her farewell appearance, on 14 May 1853, was a benefit sponsored for her by the city's fire companies, and she drew the operatic portion of the program entirely from Rossini's *Il barbiere di Siviglia* and Donizetti's *L'elisir d'amore*, with the selections apparently now sung by herself and Mengis in Italian.[30] Two days later, having given some fifty recitals and, by newspaper report, gained a profit of $30,000, she departed by steamer for Lima and Valparaíso, accompanied as always by her mother and also by Mengis and her agent, Bushnell.[31]

Undoubtedly her recitals, in which Mengis played such a large part, had strengthened the position of music in the city, and her operas-in-brief must have excited many who heard them to want the operas fully staged. Her success, as well as that of Mengis, is proof of what an astute singer with a sure sense of limitations could achieve. Though in the period 1847–49 she had sung at Verona, Florence, and Genoa the premieres of Verdi's *I masnadieri,* by 1853 she evidently had decided that the role of Amalia, with a gorgeous aria composed specifically for Jenny Lind, was beyond her powers. In San Francisco she kept her programs conservative and modest, relying entirely on the light, simple, or familiar, and never including an aria or duet by Verdi.[32]

FOUR

More of *Ernani;* and the First Resident Company

Not long after Catherine Hayes sailed for South America, the four singers who in the remainder of 1853 would do the most to promote Verdi's music in San Francisco announced their first concert. They were two men and two women, all amateur or church soloists, who had been singing locally for some months, though without much reputation or publicity.[1] Now, banding together and calling themselves "The Pacific Musical Troupe," they hired a chorus from the Philharmonic Society along with its orchestra of sixteen players and offered the public seven concerts in four weeks, 26 July–23 August.[2]

To lead their forces they engaged the Englishman George Loder, the city's leading resident musician who, besides conducting, on occasion served as a composer, arranger, pianist, flutist, or doublebassist. A short man with a magnificent beard, he had arrived in February 1852, in time to conduct Eliza Biscaccianti's first series of recitals and also that of Hayes.[3] In addition, in the summer of 1852, at a time when the city had 350 licensed saloons, twenty-seven "dancing and fandango houses," eighteen gambling halls, and four theatres,[4] he organized on a cooperative basis San Francisco's first Philharmonic Society. From its ranks of some thirty women and fifty men he drew both a chorus and an orchestra; rehearsing regularly in the Baptist church on Pine Street, he soon had a well-drilled band and what apparently was the city's only trained mixed chorus.[5]

It seems likely that Loder had a large part in launching the Pacific Troupe and selecting its programs. He was the only professional among them, and he was a man of considerable reputation. Before coming to San Francisco he had been a regular conductor of the New York Philharmonic Society for seven years, and his retirement from that post marked the beginning of the rise to dominance in orchestral music along the East Coast of German and Austrian musicians. Many of these, after the failure of the European, liberal revolutions of 1848, had emigrated to the United States, and by their number and talent they soon caused a sharp turn in the country's musical taste and history. Loder, for instance, was the last non-Germanic conductor of the New York Philharmonic Society until 1902, a stretch of fifty years, and in the thirty following his departure the percentage of German-Austrian works in the orchestra's programs shot up from seventy to ninety, dropping back only gradually thereafter.[6]

His preference in music ran more to English, Italian, and Classical Viennese composers, particularly Haydn, than to the newer romantic Germans, though it was he who in 1846, with the New York Philharmonic, conducted the U.S. premiere of Beethoven's Ninth Symphony. And while in New York he evidently had discovered Verdi's operas and liked them enough to poke fun at them. Once, as the chief conductor of a theatre specializing in light music, he had composed a "concerted piece with kitchen utensil accompaniments" for use in a burlesque of *Ernani* entitled *Herr Nanny*.[7] No doubt he intended to caricature Verdi's orchestration, which in comparison to Bellini's or Donizetti's was considered noisy; clearly, he knew the opera well.

For the Pacific Troupe's first concert, opening the new Music Hall, on Bush Street, near Montgomery, Loder scheduled works by such now-forgotten composers as Stigelli, Glover, Mornington, Spofforth, and Kücken (a favorite with Germans), along with pieces by Balfe, Bishop, and Spohr. He also included two numbers from *Ernani*, in English: a chorus, "Oh hail us, ye free" (possibly the bandits' chorus for tenors and basses, Act I, "Eviva! Beviam!"), and the finale to Act III,

"Crowned with the Tempest" ("Oh sommo Carlo"). The latter starts with an aria for Don Carlo, the baritone, who then is joined by the other soloists and chorus in a majestic chorale with a strong melodic outline. The *Alta California*, in taking note of the piece, called it "oratorio-like," but for many of the audience, probably, its greatest appeal lay in its overwhelming rhythmic impulse, an aspect of music in which Verdi in his ensembles was proving himself a master.[8]

So great was the finale's success that the singers scheduled it for the second concert, and this time the music won critical comment in the *Herald:* "[It] elicited the most enthusiastic applause. It is a splendid piece of composition, and Mr. [J. Connor] Smith has exactly the voice to give it effect."[9] The sixth concert offered another selection from Verdi, apparently sung in Italian: the trio for soprano, tenor, and baritone from the final act of *Attila*, "Te sol quest'anima."[10] And for their final appearance the Troupe brought back "Crowned with the Tempest." Thus, in a four-week period this finale to the third act of *Ernani*, in which the baritone predominates, was featured in three of seven concerts, more often than any other selection, and among at least a core of music-lovers in San Francisco it presumably established Verdi as a composer with a strong individual style—a long step toward popularity.

The newspapers' notice of the music was unusual. After most concerts at this time the music, as opposed to the singer's talents, went unreviewed. Personalities, of course, generally are considered more newsworthy than discussions of abstractions like music, and most songs perhaps were too well known for comment; but with the less familiar music there may have been also another reason. Whereas the singer's personality was considered part of the next concert, and therefore news, the particular musical work, once performed, belonged to the past, was unlikely to be repeated, and therefore was not news. The *Pioneer*, having failed one time to review an opera promptly, excused itself with a revealing remark: "It would afford us great pleasure to comment upon the beauties of the production, and the singing of Anna Bishop, but it is useless now to speak of things so long past. The present is all that interests Californians."[11]

For San Franciscans, in these early Gold Rush years, a newspaper was as much a bulletin board to the future as a record of events past. As a consequence, a large part of any of the city's twenty or so newspapers, only one or two of which had a circulation of more than 1,500, was filled with short news items and paid announcements of what was available or about to happen.

Every day in the *Alta California*, for example, besides the many medical practitioners offering "Quick Cures at Low Prices," a hundred others in business would list their wares and services, and the paper's four large pages, made dense by the many short announcements— "We beg to inform the public . . ."—would be clarified and enlivened by appropriate colophons at the start of each advertisement. To signify a dentist there was a pair of dentures; for a hair restorer, a man's bald head; for an optician, spectacles; for a blacksmith, horseshoes; and for a music store, a spinet piano.

Frequently there was a column headed "Stages," though not for theatrical news. It announced the schedules of the local stagecoach lines, most of which by 1853 offered the Concord wagons that could squeeze in about nine or ten passengers, with as many more "on top." Boots at the front and back carried mail and baggage.[12]

Shipping news was of paramount interest, and for most of the decade any large ship's arrival at Long Wharf was announced from Telegraph Hill by the firing of a cannon. In a theatre at the sound, a large part of the audience would rise quickly and leave; until the completion of transcontinental telegraph in 1861, any foreseeable "steamer night" insured a poor house. Once, according to an eyewitness, an audience at an opening night of *The Merchant of Venice*, eager to learn the results of elections in the East, kept its ear cocked to the cannon's boom. "In the middle of the fifth act it came. Without a second's hesitation, men dived for their hats and rushed out of the theater. Women rose and gathered their wraps. On the stage the actors stared at us, and then the curtain was rung down."[13]

Typically, the next morning the newspapers would blossom with advertisements by stores proclaiming what they now could offer. "NEW BOOKS! NEW BOOKS!" trumpeted J. McGlashan & Co., of

127 Montgomery Street, after the arrival of the mail-steamer *Sonora*. The store, careful to list something for everyone, began its notice with "Vol. 2, Judge Edmonds on Spiritualism" and ended with "Leslie's Gazette of Fashion."[14] But this view of a newspaper as chiefly an advertising sheet for small businesses and daily services was modifying, and gradually, in the second half of the decade, the city's papers began to lengthen their reports on musical events that had taken place, sometimes even commenting on the music. Such reports, however, unlike those in the New York papers, were not signed.

In the autumn, after a visit to Sacramento, the Pacific Musical Troupe returned to San Francisco for three concerts, but without Loder. He was replaced by a young pianist, Rudolph Herold, who had come to California as an accompanist for Hayes and, remaining in the city on her departure, soon became one of its most active musical leaders. But apparently he was less familiar than Loder with *Ernani*, and despite the Troupe's great success with the finale to Act III, the piece was not repeated.[15]

Yet it had made its impression, and later in the year evidence of its impact appeared in a different sort of musical event. Miska Hauser, a violinist who had played often and to great acclaim, in November announced a "farewell" concert with a program of popular numbers. Besides including his own composition "Echo of San Francisco," he played as the finale before the intermission, the usual spot for the evening's major work, a "Grand Fantasie" on arias from *Ernani*.[16]

In that same period, though without Verdi, opera took another step forward. Mons. Planel, still the leading musician in the city's French community, organized with local artists a French Opera Company, with Mme Planel as prima donna, and intermittently, on Sunday and Wednesday evenings at the Adelphi Theatre, he presented a season of five French operas. Opening on 18 September 1853 with Donizetti's *La Fille du régiment*, he continued in a leisurely fashion, producing a new opera every two or three weeks. Besides *La Fille* (4 performances), he offered Donizetti's *La Favorite* (3), Boildieu's *La Dame blanche* (2), Albert Grisar's *Gilles Ravisseur* (2), and for closing night a performance of Rossini's *Le Barbier de Seville* (making its city debut sung in French).

The Grisar *opera buffa,* first performed at the Opéra-Comique in Paris in 1848, became in San Francisco on 30 October 1853 the city's first U.S., and most likely Western Hemisphere, premiere. Neither Planel nor anyone else, however, noted the fact. Possibly, because of the lack of communication between cities, he was unaware of it. In any case, in these years when new operas continually were appearing, premieres were of less importance than in later years.[17]

Planel's season was well supported by the city's French, for with the exception of Rossini's *Barber,* all the works had been composed to French texts, including the two by Donizetti, and even the *Barber,* though composed to Italian, was based on one of the most famous of French plays. His audience, as he no doubt expected, delighted in hearing French sung and spoken onstage.

Earlier in the year the Adelphi's interior had been converted into an arena for an equestrian show, or "hippodrama," and afterward restored with improvements, including new cushions and decorations throughout. Commonly called "the French Theatre" because of its constant programs of French vaudeville, farce, drama, and opera, it was declared by the critic for the *Golden Era* to be "the most cosy and comfortable house in the city,"[18] and its size (cap. 2,000) evidently did not overwhelm Planel's unpretentious productions. The *Barber* won from the *Alta California* a comic opera's highest compliment: "Between the wit of the plot and the notes of the musicians, the audience were amused and content." And *Gilles Ravisseur* was "an excellent union of laughable incident with fine music and good acting."[19]

This gathering of local musicians into a viable organization must be counted San Francisco's first resident opera company, doubly so because at the season's end it did not disperse but in the spring, with a visiting soprano, presented a second season of French opera. It also, for the record, was the first company in the city to produce that perennial favorite *The Barber of Seville,* albeit in French, and the first to present, in *Gilles Ravisseur,* a U.S. premiere. Of more immediate importance, however, it brought back staged opera to a city that had lacked any for eighteen months.

Anna Bishop and *Judith* (*Nabucco*)

For the next two years, 1854–55, the leading soprano in San Francisco, though not without competition, was Anna Bishop, unquestionably the most accomplished singer to perform there during this first decade (Fig. 7). She was a dramatic soprano, with a larger voice than either Biscaccianti or Hayes, greater agility, better trill, wider range, and more extensive repertory. Aided by a regal presence, an ability to act, and an extraordinary eagerness to sing, she became one of the most widely known artists of her day, touring incessantly until she was seventy-three and performing on every continent. With her inexhaustible energy she was a kind of elemental force let loose in the world of opera. Wherever she was, like a prevailing wind she promised to return and sing again, and nothing could stop her. In 1866, when she was fifty-five, she sailed from Honolulu for the Orient, was shipwrecked on a reef near Wake Island, endured with twenty other survivors more than four weeks and 1,400 miles in an open boat, and then, upon reaching Guam Island, resumed the tour.

In 1854, coming from New York via Panama, she arrived in San Francisco with her companion and manager, Nicholas Bochsa, a French composer and conductor who was also the world's premier harpist. For him, in 1839, she had deserted three children and a husband

Fig. 7. Anna Bishop: a title page for sheet music.

twenty-four years her senior, Henry Bishop, the composer of "Home, Sweet Home." Bochsa, who was said to weigh 300 pounds and was himself twenty-one years older than she, thereupon had transformed her, as if by hypnosis, from an unexceptional singer of English songs and sacred music into a stirring diva of opera. In this respect, at least, the extravagantly gaunt Svengali in George du Maurier's novel *Trilby* is said to have been based on Bochsa and his artistic relation to Bishop.

Besides the scandal of the elopement in 1839, there were other matters in Bochsa's life to be lived down. In 1818 a French court had convicted him, in absentia, of issuing forged documents and had sen-

tenced him to prison and to be branded—so his tours with Bishop did
not include France. In England, even before his liaison with Bishop, he
was accused of having two wives, one in France, the other in England;
and also in England, in 1824 he was declared bankrupt, much to the
injury of his creditors.

Nevertheless, his musical talents, combined with hers, won them
both at least a partial pardon, and when in 1846 they returned to
London, after a long period on the continent, the *Morning Post* greeted
her debut in Balfe's opera *The Maid of Artois* thus:

> This lady has rare qualifications for the stage, a soprano voice of excellent
> quality, unerring intonation, facile execution, artistic feeling, and, what is
> uncommon even among the best vocalists, perfect musical accent. Her
> register extends from E flat on the first line to D flat in alt. She is of middle
> size and symmetrically formed—her eyes are large, lustrous, and full of
> fire—her actions free, graceful and dramatic. We welcome Madame
> Bishop as a rich addition to the English lyrical drama.[1]

In 1847, however, when the couple first performed in New York,
some journalists had questioned the propriety of attending their concerts. Would not the purchase of a ticket, the lending of one's presence
to a performance, support immorality? Yet the public had accepted
them, apparently deciding that an eight-year-old English scandal was
irrelevant to high art in the United States. And in San Francisco, seven
years later, the issue was not raised.

They arrived on 2 February, hired the Musical Hall for a series of
six recitals, and published announcements promising operatic scenes
"in appropriate costumes" and "elegant books . . . on the programs."
The subsequent advertisement for the first recital carried an "Especial
Notice," which stated: "A diagram of the hall has been prepared and
all the seats numbered" and explained how and where the tickets
might be purchased. Thus another of the city's concert halls began to
number its seats.[2]

On 7 February 1854, only five days after their arrival, Bishop and
Bochsa presented themselves, she singing, and he interspersing among
her numbers his harp solos, which he called "bardic effusions." At their

third recital there was a moment's embarrassment. A member of the audience asked Bochsa to improvise on "The Arkansas Traveler," and he refused, saying the audience was trying to make a fool of him. A more adroit artist, such as Henri Herz, would have complied, or found a less contentious ground for refusal, or at least offered as an alternative a song of Stephen Foster. Four years earlier, in Herz's time, in fact, such a blunt refusal might have turned an audience against an artist. But now it was passed over, and the portly Bochsa soon became a popular figure in San Francisco.[3]

After six joint recitals Bishop performed alone for the state legislators in the Assembly Chamber at Benicia, then the capital of California. In none of these seven appearances does she seem to have sung any Verdi, though along with the standard English, Scottish, and Irish songs she offered scenes from the operas of Rossini, Bellini, and Donizetti. The "elegant books" that accompanied the recitals soon disappeared and after the fourth no longer were offered. One critic had found them "silly," quite beneath the artistic standard of the performance, which was "very fine." And even her costumes, which were sumptuous, seem to have been overshadowed by the impact of her voice, though they probably were no less colorful than those of Hayes and in one respect added something new: for the landing scene from Rossini's *Tancredi*, culminating in "Di tanti palpiti" and requiring her to impersonate a man, she promised a "gorgeous warrior costume." In New York, and no doubt in San Francisco, the costume included a moustache.[4]

Meanwhile, Catherine Hayes, having returned from her tour in South America, on 24 April at the Metropolitan Theatre presented a staged version of *Norma*, with her faithful Mengis as Pollione and a bass new to the city, Francesco Leonardi, as Oroveso. The production was a mistake. Until then Hayes had managed her programs most skillfully, never exceeding the limits of her talents or those of Mengis; but the length, weight, and drama of *Norma*, even when cut, proved beyond her, and it is hard to imagine Mengis, a buffo bass-baritone, making much of Pollione's tenor line without disfiguring cuts and transpositions. Though the performance marked the return to the city of two

popular artists, the *Alta California* was harsh in its review, ignoring
Mengis and bluntly stating that Hayes, while good in songs, lacked the
power and volume for grand opera.[5]

Still worse for Hayes, Bishop six days later in the same theatre
performed *Norma* to greater acclaim,[6] and then on 7 May, after squeez-
ing in several more recitals, opened her first opera "season": two
performances each of *Sonnambula* and *Norma,* and three of *Don Pasquale,*
with Leonardi as Pasquale and Mengis as Malatesta. In addition, she
sang a benefit concert with selections from Rossini, Bellini, and Donizetti—all within eight days.[7]

Music-lovers argued the merits of the two sopranos,[8] but Hayes,
after a repeat of *Norma,* avoided any further artistic confrontations. She
staged no more operas, or even "operas-in-brief," but instead sang a
number of concerts for which she hired an orchestra, with George
Loder conducting, and shared her programs chiefly with the new bass,
Leonardi. On 7 July, before sailing the next day for Australia, she sang
a farewell concert and then attended a reception at the Hotel Oriental,
where her admirers gave her a gold brooch valued at $1,100. For Hayes,
California was ever golden.[9]

This time Mengis remained behind, and so, too, did the bass Leonardi. Like Pellegrini, Leonardi had arrived in the city without advance notice, but for the previous four years he had been singing
leading roles in Santiago, Valparaíso, and Lima and evidently had been
persuaded by Hayes to accompany her to San Francisco. Though he
evidently had a sufficiently strong top to his voice occasionally to sing
baritone arias and roles, he performed mostly as a bass and quickly
established himself as "the best basso that has appeared in California."[10]

In Lima, Valparaíso, and Santiago he had sung frequently in Verdi's
operas, particularly *I Lombardi, Attila,* and *I masnadieri,* and in sharing
four recitals with Hayes he introduced several Verdi arias to San
Francisco. In their first recital, as one of his selections he sang a scene,
"Dagli immortali vertici," from Verdi's *Attila;* in the second and third,
arias from Rossini and Donizetti; and in the fourth, besides "La ca-
lunnia" from Rossini's *Il barbiere,* the "Profezia" from Verdi's *Nabucco.*

In all their programs his selections provided the greater musical substance, while she with her songs, such as "Home, Sweet Home," "Auld Robin Gray," and "The Irish Immigrant's Lament," doubtless drew the greater applause.[11]

The scene from *Attila* is for baritone, not bass, and possibly Leonardi transposed it down. It presents the Roman general Ezio, whose army stands between the city and the Huns, in two contrasting arias reflecting a sharp change of mood. In the first, and slower, he mourns Rome's vanished glory: Who, he asks rhetorically, in the present weak and timid city, can see the former capital of the world? Who can see? Who can see? The phrases describing Rome's former grandeur rise and fall in long, swelling arcs in which passion forcefully expressed alternates with the refrain "Who can see?" uttered in fading, smothered tones. The shift from full to hushed voice, without a stop and fresh start, is hard for a singer, but in it lies the aria's drama, and Leonardi, "the best basso," apparently managed it.

The scene's second, contrasting aria is fast, energetic, and enriched by historical connotation. After a few lines of recitative to establish news of a plot against Attila that promises a Roman victory, Ezio decides not to retreat as his emperor has ordered, but to attack. He sings *con forza*, "É gettata la mia sorte," or "my lot is cast," a reference to Julius Caesar's remark "Iacta alea est"—The die is cast—when he decided to ignore the order of the Roman Senate, to cross the river Rubicon, and to lead his army against Rome. Again, to sing the aria with the dignity of a Caesar and the excitement of a conspirator at a crux of history is not easy. For many years this scene with its double aria was much studied by young singers and, onstage or in a recital hall, was a touchstone of a baritone's ability.

Leonardi's other scene from Verdi, the "Profezia" in *Nabucco*, for bass, is a vision of Babylon destroyed, sung by the Hebrew prophet Zaccaria to his people held captive in Babylon by Nabucco (Nebuchadnezzar). Its text is a paraphrase of the prophecies of *Jeremiah* (chaps. 50 and 51): "Hyenas will come to squat upon the skulls, and snakes to slither among the bones; in the dust blown by a dry wind a deathly silence will pervade; and only the owl with its sad lament will mark the approach of evening." Among Verdi's captive Hebrews, the prophecy revives their hopes for freedom and a return to Jerusalem. The music, which properly should have a chorus to join the soloist, begins declamatory and descriptive, with an imitation in the accompaniment of the owl's mournful hooting, and ends with a rolling song of triumph. The scene always has been somewhat overwhelmed by the artistic success of the immediately preceding chorus of the Hebrews weeping in Babylon, "Va, pensiero," which is based chiefly on Psalm 137 and ranks in Italy as an unofficial national anthem. But the "Profezia," even when sung without chorus, is not without power, and doubtless in the mid–nineteenth century, when audiences were familiar with the Bible, the music's imagery and rhythm could stir interest.

Like J. Connor Smith with the baritone aria and finale from *Ernani*, Leonardi with his scenes from *Attila* and *Nabucco* seems to have made a strong impression on the city's audiences, though the newspapers at first all but ignored him. And to Smith and Leonardi must be added a third bass-baritone, a Mons. Emile Coulon, whom Hayes employed as an assisting artist for her farewell recital in July. On that occasion he, too, introduced a Verdi aria to the city, "Sciagurata! hai tu creduto" from Act I of *I Lombardi*. It is sung by the opera's villain, Pagano, but, being a declaration of love, momentarily arouses the audience's sympathy for him. In its dramatic function as well as its structure, and particularly in the way it blooms melodically in its last third, a mark of Verdi's style, it resembles "Il balen" in *Trovatore*.[12]

Coulon was a local French artist who had sung frequently in recitals and with Planel's French company; though consistently praised for his work, he had never achieved Leonardi's acclaim. It is noteworthy, however, that he, Smith, and Leonardi, the assisting or secondary artists, and not Hayes and Bishop, the celebrity sopranos, were the singers introducing Verdi's music to the city. Behind that fact lie some reasons reflecting a shift in musical style and the economics of music publishing.

Basses and baritones had a long, unbroken tradition of importance in Italian comic opera, but in serious opera their position, always less secure, in recent decades had slipped. In the years 1825–40 Bellini and

Donizetti, replacing Rossini's serious works with a new style of romantic opera, increasingly had focused their music on sopranos and tenors,
relegating the other voices to supporting roles. Verdi, though composing in the new romantic style, tended to treat the singers more evenly,
sometimes even preferring the lower voices to the higher. Thus in the
early 1850s, when his music, by then firmly established in New York,
began to spread westward to the Mississippi and, with a long jump by
sea, to San Francisco, basses and baritones looking for new arias to
show off their voices found them in Verdi. Sopranos, however, with all
of Bellini and Donizetti to choose from, and with an eye to what
already had proved itself at the box office, tended to be less adventurous. It is remarkable that Hayes in her two visits to San Francisco never
sang a note of Verdi and that Bishop in her first six months there still
had not done so.

Certainly, finding new arias to sing cannot have been difficult.
Leonardi in Peru and Chile had sung in at least five of Verdi's operas
and so had a strong acquaintance with the music, but the other two,
who had not, would have had to look no further than the city's music
stores. These, like those in the East, kept standing orders with publishers in Boston, New York, or Europe, and a shipment from New York,
crossing the isthmus at Panama, could arrive in five weeks. The chief
stores at this time were Atwill & Co., an offshoot of a New York store
and music publishing house; Woodworth & Co.; and "Salvator Rosa,"
named after the Neapolitan painter and poet. The last, on Clay Street
to start out and later at 157 Montgomery Street, was the most closely
tied to opera and in advertisements for productions often was stated to
have librettos for sale. All three, however, served as postal drops and
bulletin boards for artists: for example, anyone advertising for pupils
would ask those interested to leave their names and addresses with a
clerk at one of the stores. And undoubtedly, just as in music stores
today, there was a great deal of leafing through the stock. An enterprising singer like Smith or Coulon would have had no trouble finding new
music to suit his voice.[13]

Equally, anyone hearing a new aria could expect to be able to buy
an arrangement of it, and sometimes the advertisements for the recital

would state at which store the music was available. These arrangements might be for piano and voice (with the text in any of three or
four languages); piano solo; piano four-, six-, or eight-hands; or with
piano accompaniment for the two most popular home instruments,
flute and violin. Almost as common were "fantasies" for harp, guitar,
clarinet, cello, or even trombone. The variety and numbers of such
arrangements kept in print by publishers were huge, running for the
more popular operas, *Norma* or *Ernani,* into the hundreds. Everyone in
the industry of opera understood the importance of these arrangements
in making new music familiar, and publishers, stores, and artists pushed
them hard; newspapers in the more populous East sometimes reviewed
them. In San Francisco, at this time, it is likely that more of Verdi's
music was available in the stores, and sung or played in homes, than
yet was performed professionally.[14]

During this spring of 1854, in the months before Hayes's departure,
audiences in San Francisco had a choice of four operatic sopranos,
evidence of the city's growing enthusiasm for opera. The least well
known, and little threat to Bishop, was Clarisse Cailly, an artist of
French and Belgian background who arrived in the city from Lima
early in April and was greeted by the *Alta California* with a suggestion:
"There is a very good French operatic company here, who can afford
a most excellent support to Madam Cailly, and we hope soon to see
her produce some of the French operas."[15]

Taking the hint, she joined forces with Planel's company, which
included the reliable Coulon and a good tenor, Mons. [?] Laglaise, and
they promptly offered a single performance at the Metropolitan
Theatre of *Lucie de Lammermoor,* with Donizetti's quintessential Italian
opera, like Rossini's *Barber,* making its San Francisco debut in French.
With this venture a success, Cailly and her colleagues then scheduled
a short season at the Union Theatre, opening on 4 May with a single
performance of Paer's *Le Maître de chapelle,* an *opéra bouffe* popular in
Paris and new to San Francisco. There followed one performance of
Rossini's *Barbier de Seville,* three of *Norma,* and on closing night Auber's
Crown Diamonds, already sung in the city in English and now, for the
first time, in French.[16]

All the productions, like those of the company the previous year, seem to have been modest both scenically and musically, except that for *Lucie de Lammermoor* Planel included for his tenor and baritone the frequently cut Wolfscrag "challenge scene," and for *Crown Diamonds* he managed to recruit a female chorus.[17] Plainly, he and his artists had courage, for in a city as small as San Francisco to offer three performances of *Norma* immediately after Hayes and Bishop had staged five was risky. But they also must have had talent, for their *Norma* earned two repetitions. As always, the French community supported a French undertaking, and this second season of Planel's company, though little noted in the leading newspapers and journals, must be counted a success. In all, Cailly and the French company gave seven performances and introduced two operas to the city.

On the second night of the season Cailly sang some Verdi. The occasion was a benefit offered to her by the French volunteer fire company, Hook and Ladder, Lafayette No. 2, and as her final number the program promised the "Great Cavatina of the Opera Ernani." But even more interesting, earlier, as an interpolation in Paer's comic opera *Le Maître de chapelle,* she scheduled the "Celebrated Polecca of the Opera, *I Lombardi,* with variations expressly composed for her." This was the aria "Non fu sogno," and the variations, no doubt, were arranged by Planel. Because the benefit preceded Hayes's farewell recital, at which Coulon sang an aria from this opera, Cailly was the artist to introduce music of Verdi's *I Lombardi* to the city. But the newspapers took no notice of her: four steamers docked the day of her benefit, and the reports of their cargoes and the news they had brought from the distant world choked the papers the next morning.[18]

A more serious challenge to Bishop throughout this spring, though partially blunted by a difference in repertory, was offered by Anna Thillon, an English artist of international reputation (Fig. 8), who had arrived in the city on the last day of December 1853 accompanied by her husband and an unknown tenor, Stephen W. Leach. Thillon had a small, appealing voice of wide range, was pretty, with a winning personality, and in her chosen repertory was a match for Bishop, successfully sustaining a season of light opera in English from mid-

January through May 1854. She opened with Auber's *Crown Diamonds*, presenting it in an English version, with a small orchestra, led by George Loder from the piano, and all the secondary singers, except Leach, local artists.

The opera was one with which she had an association, for in Paris in 1841, at Auber's request, she had created the role of Christina, Queen of Portugal, and three years later had used it for her London debut. Now she returned to it for her first appearance in San Francisco, singing it five times. Continuing with her season of opera in English, she produced Donizetti's *Daughter of the Regiment* (5 performances), Auber's *Black Domino* (2), Bellini's *Sonnambula* (3), Balfe's *The Enchantress* (7), his *The Bohemian Girl* (5), and Rossini's *Cinderella* (4). Thillon's greatest triumphs were with the two Balfe operas, *The Enchantress*, which he had composed for her, and *The Bohemian Girl*, in which she invariably won rapturous applause for the aria "I dreamt I dwelt in marble halls."[19]

Then, as if to prove her versatility, she restaged *The Daughter of the Regiment* for two performances, presenting it now in its original French and using for the tenor and bass roles Laglaise and Coulon. According to the *Wide West*, it was "the best representation of the opera" the city had seen, partly because the singers had the style for the work and partly because Thillon restored a good deal of music that she had cut from her production in English.[20]

The cuts, most likely, did not originate with her. At this time, in both the United States and Great Britain, there was a strong though dying tradition of doing foreign-language operas in English versions, and these often differed greatly from the originals. Henry R. Bishop, for example, made a version of Rossini's *Barbiere* that substituted music of his own as well as of Paisiello for parts of Rossini's score. Another Englishman who made countless versions of opera and oratorio, Michael Rophino Lacy, created one amalgam entitled *The Israelites in Egypt; or, The Passage of the Red Sea*, which combined selections from Handel's *Israel in Egypt* with some from Rossini's *Mosè in Egitto*; Lacy's compilation of various Rossini scores into a *Cinderella* was also for many years extremely popular in the United States.[21]

GLEASON'S PICTORIAL

F. GLEASON, { MUSEUM BUILDING, TREMONT STREET. }   BOSTON, SATURDAY, FEBRUARY 28, 1852. $3.00 PER VOLUME. 10 Cts. SINGLE COPY. } NO. 9.—VOL. 2.

MADAME ANNA THILLON.

No actress since our recollection has produced such a *furore* as Madame Anna Thillon during her late engagement in this city at the Howard Athenæum. The pieces which she has appeared in have been "The Crown Diamonds," "The Black Domino," and "The Daughter of the Regiment;" this last piece having been originally written for her. She is the original *fille du regiment*, and to our mind she has never been surpassed in the character. Throughout her engagement here she has been most ably supported by Mr. Hudson, the Irish comedian, who is also a fine vocalist. During nearly all the time of her engagement in Boston, the tickets to the theatre have been sold at auction—the house bringing premiums as high as six hundred dollars on one occasion. Coming among us almost entirely unheralded, she has won a universal popularity. Never has any operatic singer of her class met with a more enthusiastic reception, or been so successful as she has been during her stay in this city. She has charmed all by the fascination of her beautiful style—so graceful, so natural, so expressive, and yet so powerful. Her delicious voice, says a contemporary, is music itself, and is only in harmony with the radiant intelligence that beams from her sylven face, and speaks more forcibly to the heart than any form of words of which human language is susceptible. The beauty of her countenance, not voluptuous, but indicative of passionate joy—her piquant naïveté of manner—her exquisite tones—her captivating gestures—her beautiful attitudes, and the indescribable charm of nature that plays around her like a halo of light, beguiling the audience into a momentary belief that their scenes are delighted with a reality, and not a mere dramatic representation on the stage, have been the theme of every tongue, and have won for this gifted lady an immense popularity. Night after night the house has been crowded to excess, and the plaudits have been, not merely the formal recognition of the presence of genius, but the warm and spontaneous effusions of the heart. She is one of those few artists that never weary by their performances, because they are true to nature, like a beautiful landscape, which imparts pleasure every time it is beheld. Hence the fact that she has performed so many as two hundred times in a single character, in London. In Paris, and in the British metropolis, she has been equally triumphant; and the critics of both countries have been unanimous in their judgment as to her incomparable charms, while the subtlety and versatility of those charms have defied their ingenuity to analyze them. It is not this or that feature in her performance, but the bud *ensemble*, like the statue of Venus de Medicis, that dazzles and captivates the spectator. Madame Thillon was born in Calcutta, of English parents, but was brought up in France from the age of fourteen. She made her *début* at

Clermont, in the opera of "Le Roseignol." She afterwards appeared in "Jean de Paris," in which she attracted the marked notice of the French critics and the public. This was the commencement of a glorious career in France, which was succeeded by an equally flattering one in England, having obtained an engagement at the Princess's Theatre in London, where she made her first appearance in "The Crown Diamonds," creating an excitement scarcely ever surpassed by the attending the performance of any other artist. Her success in France and England is crowned by her triumphs here, which, however, have only commenced, for there is a brilliant future before her. The artist that can produce such effects in the old world and in the new—in the three greatest countries on the face of the globe—differing in many respects in a most remarkable degree, but all unanimously concurring in their judgment in her favor—must be more than an ordinary woman. In truth, Madame Thillon possesses originality and genius of the very highest order, and her gifts have been cultivated with the most perfect finish. She is entirely unique, there being no other comic opera singer in the world like her. Far from having wearied the public, Madame Anna Thillon could still fill the Howard nightly for a month to come; but her engagements in other cities precluded her longer stay in Boston. However, we have the satisfaction of knowing that Mr. Marshall has entered into an engagement with the lady to return in this city after a brief absence, when our citizens will have the satisfaction of again enjoying her professional performances. This will be particularly interesting to some of our young gallants, who seemed to have totally lost their hearts and become slaves to her extraordinary beauty of person. In another part of the paper we give a likeness of Mr. Hudson, the excellent Irish comedian and vocalist, who has sustained Madame Thillon during her engagement at the Howard. Our artist has taken the engraving herewith presented from life, the lady having afforded him the necessary private sitting for the purpose, and our readers may be assured of its truthfulness, though to those who have seen her this assurance will be quite unnecessary. It is exceedingly agreeable to know that one who has won so much of popular esteem and favor is as worthy as she is beautiful, and that her private life is graced by all those sacred and happy associations that ennoble and purify the heart. It is to be regretted that it is too often the case, that artists who, in their profession and upon the stage, challenge our most earnest admiration, yet leave a blank in our estimation by evincing a character in their private lives that ruins all. Though a woman possess the beauty of an angel, though every movement be grace, and every feature loveliness, if boldness be written in her face, it blots out all the lines of beauty and shadows the fairest work of the Creator.

PORTRAIT OF MADAME ANNA THILLON.

These English versions unquestionably made an opera's music, or some of it, familiar. Henry Bishop's *Barber*, for instance, played every year in New York from 1819 through 1824; thus, when Manuel García and his company put on the first Italian-language performance of the opera in 1825, a large part of the audience probably was ready for it. But as Anna Thillon was beginning to discover, by the 1850s an increasing fraction of the audience wanted an opera as its composer intended it to be heard, or at least a closer approximation to it than the usual English version allowed.

Like the *Wide West*, which had complained forcefully of the cuts in *The Enchantress*, the *Alta California* condemned the Thillon version of *Cinderella* as more a play than an opera; and *Pioneer Magazine*, in an unsigned article on music in the city, angrily declared that she sang merely arias and scenes, never an entire work, and bluntly implied that she was now too old to sing a complete opera. Also, her orchestra was too small, and George Loder's effort at the piano to buttress its volume was "an utter abomination," spoiling the quality of the single-note instruments; the chorus, too, which probably numbered no more than the usual six or seven, was inadequate. All the visiting sopranos, moreover, shared the fault of not trying to unite their supporting singers into the opera: the productions, though staged and with costumes, were too much like a celebrity's concert, with assisting artists. The anonymous author closed with a warning: Audiences in San Francisco were not ignorant; "We have attended the opera in New York, Boston, New Orleans, Paris, London, Naples, everywhere—We are from all parts of the world, and we know what good music is, just as well as any community."[22]

As if in response to at least some of these complaints, Bishop and Bochsa in July announced a production of Weber's *Der Freischütz* that in several respects would prove extraordinary. She recently had completed a week's "season" of two operas: three performances of Donizetti's *Linda di Chamounix* in English and two of his *Lucrezia Borgia* in Italian, both works new to the city.[23] Though *Der Freischütz*, like many operas in this period, was slated to be followed by a farce, *The Governor's Wife*, and so presumably would be cut, Bishop and Bochsa nevertheless promised that it would be presented with an enlarged orchestra and chorus. The production would be not only the opera's local premiere but, although sung in English, the first German opera to be presented in the city. The language apparently posed no difficulties for the chorus, which, numbering thirty-three, was recruited chiefly from two German singing clubs, the Turn Gesangverein and the Sängerbund. Probably, as usual, there was no women's chorus, for the German clubs typically restricted membership to men.

The expansion of the orchestra to "upwards of thirty," with the increase trumpeted in the public announcements, was achieved by combining the Metropolitan's usual band of about fifteen with that of the Verandah Concert Society, which had volunteered its services for the production's run. At the fourth performance the count was reported to be thirty-two players. In New York at this time, an opera orchestra generally numbered about thirty-six; in Venice's small Teatro La Fenice, fifty-five; and in Milan's large La Scala, ninety. The *Freischütz* orchestra was a breakthrough in San Francisco's musical life, equally important for concert and opera, and credit for the advance should go to the man who organized, rehearsed, and conducted the orchestra, the harpist Bochsa.[24]

In September an orchestral group followed his example, announcing a series of concerts with a "Grand Orchestra of Thirty Musicians,[25] and at the end of that month Bishop and Bochsa would offer another operatic spectacle, *Judith*, with an enlarged orchestra. Gradually thereafter the number fell back to the usual fifteen, or at most twenty, whether for concert or opera. Nevertheless, a higher standard for sound had been set, and, when not met, the complaints of inadequacy were more frequent.

Another change, too, gained momentum from this *Freischütz* production. After the fifth performance, Bishop and Bochsa, with an eye on the box office and a flexibility unusual in opera, announced abruptly that the sixth would be sung in German. The shift in language presumably was no problem for Herr Mengis and the chorus, or for Bishop, who was famous for singing in all languages. But Julia Gould, who had been singing the second soprano role of Aennchen, evidently had no

German, and she was replaced by Von Gulpen. Thus, on 30 July, only five days after the opera had been sung in English, San Franciscans heard it in its original language—the city's first opera sung in German.[26]

In all, *Freischütz* had seven performances within twenty-two days, its success apparently leading Bochsa in October into one of those inexplicable failures that haunt the stage. With a chorus increased by recruits from the Turn Gesangverein and an orchestra presumably at least somewhat enlarged, he mounted another San Francisco premiere, Auber's grand opera *La Muette de Portici,* often known by its alternate title, *Masaniello.* Auber's works were popular in the city, and Bochsa no doubt expected the French community to turn out in force. But *La Muette,* or *The Dumb Girl of Portici* (it apparently was sung in this instance in English), is an oddity in that its heroine, being mute, requires not a singer, but a character dancer, and although Bochsa apparently cast the opera well, Bishop did not appear in it. Possibly her absence slowed ticket sales, or perhaps there was trouble with the accompanying farce, for *The Dumb Belle* was replaced abruptly by *Did You Ever Send Your Wife to San Jose?* Whatever the reason, the opera's five performances played to notably thin houses, causing the *Herald* to remark, "It is difficult to account for the unpopularity of this piece, as it is finely got up, abounds in excellent music, and is really well acted."[27]

Perhaps the explanation lay in surfeit. In these months, four sopranos and their assisting artists presented San Francisco with a more abundant feast of opera than New York could boast, and at least a part of their audience lost its appetite for "trills and *roulades.*" In the coming January the critic for *Pioneer Magazine* would complain: "From April to December last, Shakespeare with all his laurels on his brow, was banished. . . . Rossini, it is true, appeals to our tastes. But while these should be cultivated, it must be remembered that Shakespeare appeals to our intellect. However softening in its effects, however purifying and elevating may be Music, there is something ennobling in the Drama." And he rejoiced in the prospect of more drama, less music.[28]

But despite all this opera, by midsummer, when Thillon and Hayes had departed and Cailly, like Pellegrini, simply vanished, it was still true that the three celebrities, Thillon, Hayes, and Bishop, had sung not one note of Verdi. He was not in the repertories of the first two for good reason: his dramatic roles were too heavy for their light voices. But that was not true of Bishop, who had sung in his *I due Foscari* in Naples in 1845 and later that year had intrigued to obtain the title role for the premiere of *Alzira*.[29] Verdi, however, had refused to have her, and perhaps the rebuff rankled, for in her initial seasons in New York, in 1847 and 1848, she had ignored his music just as she was doing in San Francisco.

But if tit for tat was her game, in September she threw it over and announced as the chief work of her "fourth season" an opera, *Judith*, with music "selected and adapted by Mr. Bochsa from Verdi's far-famed sacred operas of Nabucco, I Lombardi, Joan of Arc. &c."[30] In the late 1840s, Bochsa had edited for Casa Ricordi, Verdi's publisher in Milan, selections for harp from all three of these operas, and in 1850, when he and Bishop were again in New York, he had created a pastiche, "a Grand Spectacle" of "the best musical gems of Verdi," which he had titled *Judith*.[31] Sung in English, with splendid scenery, a ballet, and a military band onstage, it had run for five nights at the Astor Place Opera House before being withdrawn in a quarrel with the management.

Presumably the New York and San Francisco productions were much the same. In San Francisco, at least, most of the music was taken from *Nabucco*,[32] and the story, so as to give Bishop the title role, was changed from Nebuchadnezzar's taking of Jerusalem to Judith's beheading of Holofernes. Bishop was praised in particular for her second-act aria, which perhaps was "Anch'io dischiuso"—though of course with a different text and most likely sung in English. She also was admired for her "brindisi," the "drinking" or "banquet song" from *Macbeth* and the only number of that opera to gain much popularity in the United States.

With regard to the "brindisi," however, the critic of the *Alta California* noted that in context, in *Macbeth*, the aria had greater impact. There, he said, it is sung by Lady Macbeth at a banquet to rally her husband's sagging spirit, and the music has an apt "scornful" edge; in *Judith*, where it also was sung at a banquet, it served merely to celebrate Judith's courage and beauty, and "it fails to elate." Neatly stated, that is the problem of any pastiche: the better suited the music is to its original purpose, the less well it can fit another.[33]

In San Francisco, Bochsa presented his "Grand Biblical Spectacle Opera" in six "tableaux," with a ballet inserted in the third and with the orchestra and presumably the chorus enlarged. If the numbers of performers did not match those of *Der Freischütz*, they evidently came close, and the production was staged with considerable panache and success. In all, by the city's standards, *Judith* had a long run—six performances in September, October, and November—and its second act, which seems not to have included the ballet, combined one evening with Flotow's *Martha*.[34]

Looking back, *Pioneer Magazine* remarked, "*Judith* was a mosaic, which would hardly stand before a critical attack. Yet it contained a great deal of most excellent music, and was adapted to the limited power of the company."[35] Aside from any virtues of the music, the adaptation to particular voices surely was the reason for the work's success. To support Bishop, Bochsa could recruit only the usual local artists, but he evidently had closely tailored the vocal lines to their talents. Pastiches such as his then were common, but they seldom outlived their initial run, or were intended to. This one, with productions in New York and San Francisco, and with Bochsa at the helm and Bishop singing, doubtless was more substantial musically and better performed than most. At least it gave San Franciscans for the first time in three and a half years—the first time since Pellegrini's single performance of *Ernani*—a chance to hear a full of evening of Verdi, and they responded with pleasure.

SIX

Ernani, Nabucco, I Lombardi, and *I due Foscari*

On 13 November 1854, the *Herald* carried an announcement that "The Italian Opera Company, lately arrived from Italy," would appear at the Metropolitan Theatre for fifteen nights and present a season of Italian opera.[1] Opening the next night with *Ernani* and playing through 14 December, the company offered a repertory of *Ernani* (4 performances), *Lucrezia Borgia* (3), *Nabucco* (3), *Maria di Rohan* (2), and *Il barbiere di Siviglia* (2). In addition, as part of an evening of excerpts, it also sang the first act of *La sonnambula.* With this season—five operas, two each by Verdi and Donizetti, one by Rossini, and an excerpt of Bellini—the relative popularity among the Italian composers begins to tilt in Verdi's favor, in part because Donizetti's *Maria di Rohan,* withdrawn after two hearings, was the only box-office failure. "We have little doubt," wrote the reviewer for the *Herald,* "that it would have drawn large houses for many nights, after the audience had once become familiarized with its music."[2] But unlike *Ernani* or *Nabucco,* except for a first-act aria sung by Hayes, *Maria di Rohan* arrived unheralded by concert excerpts.[3]

The company was the largest yet to visit San Francisco; but despite the eagerness of some local journalists to call it "complete," it was nothing of the sort.[4] In 1847, when the Italian company from Havana had toured New York, Boston, and Philadelphia, besides its leading singers it had included a mixed chorus, an orchestra, two conductors, scenery, and costumes—as one New York newspaper had exclaimed, "Everything, save a theatre."[5] By comparison, the company arriving in San Francisco was merely a troupe: a manager and six singers—three sopranos, two tenors, and a bass-baritone—without chorus, orchestra, or conductor. It did bring, however, costumes, which it announced were "remarkably rich, varied, and characteristic";[6] also a prompter, who seems to have been the husband of the seconda donna; and not one but two prima donnas, Clotilda Barili-Thorn and Marietta Bedei. In addition, traveling with Barili-Thorn, by whose name the troupe generally was known, was her young half-sister, Carlotta Patti, who would make her professional debut in San Francisco, as both pianist and singer. Left at home with Barili-Thorn's mother and step-father was a still younger half-sister, Adelina Patti, who later became one of the century's most famous divas.

To round out their forces the troupe hired George Loder as musical director, five more soloists, a small orchestra, and a men's chorus.[7] Apparently, a women's chorus could not be recruited. Among the singers added was the bass Leonardi, who at Lima in August 1853 had sung with Barili-Thorn in the local premiere of Verdi's *La battaglia di Legnano*. As the season in San Francisco progressed, he and the troupe's bass-baritone, Alessandro Lanzoni, were the artists who won the most applause, particularly in the two Verdi operas, a fact which may have confirmed for audiences that a part of what distinguished Verdi from Bellini or Donizetti was an emphasis on the lower range of the male voice.

Barili-Thorn, born into a family of Italian musicians, most of them singers, had made her professional debut in Italy at least as early as 1845, and two years later, while still not yet twenty, she had created a stir in New York. Remarkably pretty, she soon married a rich and socially prominent New Yorker, but continued to sing; and though her voice was considered to lack brilliance and power, it was much admired for its purity and range. As an actress, however, she was thought to be cold and tame. Unfortunately, while in San Francisco she seems to have suffered continually from a mild bronchitis and had to sing over what one critic called "the hoarseness which attacks all strangers on their arrival."[8]

In Italy, New York, Mexico City, and Lima she had grown up with Verdi's music, and though her voice was too light for much of it, she evidently understood its style. This seems to have been true also of her colleagues, especially perhaps of the baritone Alessandro Lanzoni, who, if identity of name is equivalent to identity of person, in Rome in 1849 had sung a small solo role under Verdi's direction at the rehearsals and early performances of *La battaglia di Legnano*. But more than just Barili-Thorn, Leonardi, or Lanzoni, the troupe as a whole consistently was praised for making of its productions something more than merely concerts in costume. Of the opening-night *Ernani*, with "augumented" chorus, the critic for *Wide West* concluded: "Taken as a whole, it is the best attempt at opera we have yet had."[9] And *Pioneer Magazine*, in summarizing the troupe's virtues, reported: "It is capable of presenting an opera without giving one part an undue preponderance over the others, or leaving the principal lacking the support necessary from the subordinate characters."[10] In San Francisco, with the Barili-Thorn season, opera as drama took a step forward.

Another advance appeared in the price of a box seat. On opening night, for all but the private boxes the company charged the Metropolitan's regular scale for opera: orchestra seats, $3; parquet and dress circle, $2; second and third tiers, $1. But for the boxes, where seats usually cost $3, the price was set at $9 to $25. The sharp price increase in the best seats, while the line was held on the others, reflected economic conditions in the state and city. For those who in one business or another had struck it rich in California, the times were still remarkably good, full of profit; but for others, those for whom the Gold Rush had not panned out, they were increasingly hard. Signs of an economic depression had begun to appear. Able-bodied men frequently could not find work, and on occasion banks or businesses failed. The golden days in which Catherine Hayes could parlay a small talent into a nest egg of $30,000 were fading. The surface mines, with their sudden wealth, were running out, and money now more frequently was made in trade, shipping, real estate, and farming. Harder to accumulate, it was more closely held, and in the future, at least in the arts, profits would be less extraordinary.

In several respects, Barili-Thorn's *Ernani* could not fail to improve on Pellegrini's. It had the larger chorus and orchestra, which now were becoming usual, and for the baritone role of Don Carlos it could cast a baritone, Lanzoni, in place of Von Gulpen, a mezzo-soprano, thus regaining for several scenes the desired weight and quality of voice. In other ways, however, it did no better, and perhaps worse. It, too, lacked a women's chorus, and Barili-Thorn had that "hoarseness," while the tenor, Carlo Scola, who in the title role was supposed to project manly pride, beauty, and daring, "falters in his steps, stands nerveless and unsteady, with knees inclining towards each other, and his whole system relaxed and feeble."[11]

Even so, the critic for the *Golden Era*, directing a backward kick at Anna Thillon, rejoiced that "on this occasion we had the pleasure of seeing George Loder once more at his post with the *baton*."[12] And according to the *Herald*, the introductory men's chorus to the first act, the finale to the second, and the finale to third, previously sung in English by the Pacific Musical Troupe, were all "startling bursts of magnificent music." In addition, Leonardi's voice, in the bass role of the Spanish grandee Don Ruy Gómez de Silva, had "all the depth and volume of a trombone, and when he chooses to give it play, it will drown both orchestra and chorus." And the reviewer had praise only slightly less fulsome for the baritone, Lanzoni.[13]

The *Alta California*, after commenting on Leonardi's "rich bass," went on to remark of the opera generally: "The music, like all of Verdi's is peculiar, and abounds in passages of great brilliancy and sweetness."[14] The critic, using "peculiar" in its sense of "individual," by juxtaposing "brilliancy" and "sweetness" points to another way in which Verdi's music sounded different to audiences accustomed to Bellini and Donizetti. Verdi's arias, in their slow-fast, soft-loud, grief-and-joy, were more sharply contrasted, both one to another and inwardly. An Italian critic of the day, comparing him to Donizetti, wrote that Verdi, "as the more passionate of the two, strives the more often to agitate and excite the listener, whereas Donizetti almost always wishes to please him."[15]

In the United States those who disliked Verdi's style, finding its shifts in mood abrupt, accused him of melodrama, of striving too hard for effect. One such was the New Yorker George Templeton Strong, who recorded in his diary after hearing several performances of *Ernani* that Verdi was like "an author who deals only in italics, large capitals, dashes, and interjection marks." But another contemporary, the Bostonian John S. Dwight, editor of the national weekly *Dwight's Journal of Music,* saw some merit in the style, a tighter musical structure, and a closer adherence to the drama's events and emotions. Though his feelings about Verdi's music were mixed, Dwight called it "as strong and exhilarating as October air after the sultry languor of Donizetti and the sweet, sentimental sameness of the Bellini melody."[16]

Verdi did not achieve that freshness and vigor by chance or unconsciously. As became known when the first large collection of his letters was published in 1913, he frequently wrote to his librettists asking for "contrast" or "variety" in the drama so that he might reflect it in the music.[17] In 1853, for example, he complained in a letter to a librettist, "To me, our opera nowadays sins in the direction of too great monotony." He was speaking of his own *Nabucco* and *I due Foscari,* but the comment could apply to *Norma* or *Sonnambula,* or even to *Lucia di Lammermoor.* "They have but one burden to their song," he added; "elevated, if you like, but always the same."[18] Far more than Bellini or Donizetti, he sought for his dramas variety and contrast, and by means of these to attain a feel of accelerating pace—all qualities that San Franciscans found increasingly attractive.

Indeed, *Ernani* proved so popular that the company extended its season, repeating the opera three times before the end of the year and then, with a change in cast, once again in January 1855, as well as performing Acts I and III in an evening of excerpts—all in all, a strong exposure in a city of no more than 40,000. Meanwhile, only three months after Bishop and Bochsa's *Judith,* Barili-Thorn staged three performances of *Nabucco.* Thus Verdi's music suddenly flooded the ears and minds of the city's music-lovers, who confirmed at the box office their liking for his style of romantic melodrama. Especially they responded to *Ernani,* an examination of the meaning of honor, in which a nobly born hero forced to turn bandit, having married the beautiful and loving Elvira, on his wedding night must redeem a pledge of suicide to his rival, Silva. Walt Whitman, who loved the opera for its "haughty attitudes" and "fiery breath," put the image of its final scene into his poem "Proud Music of the Storm":

> I see where Ernani walking the bridal garden,
> Amid the scent of night-roses, radiant, holding his bride by the hand,
> Hears the infernal call, the death-pledge of the horn.[19]

With these performances by the Barili-Thorn company *Ernani* began a run in San Francisco that in the next forty-four years, to the end of the century, would total 150 performances, making it a favorite among the city's opera-lovers. After 1862 it would rank second in popularity among Verdi's operas to *Il trovatore,* but in this first decade, if the frequent performance of complete acts in concert can weigh in the account, it was by far the most often performed (see Appendix F.)

The production of *Nabucco,* which followed one of *Lucrezia Borgia,* introduced the alternate prima donna, Marietta Bedei, as Abigaille, with Lanzoni as Nabucco, Leonardi as the Prophet Zaccaria, and Loder conducting. The *Pioneer* thought Bedei lacked power and brilliance but otherwise sang nicely, and it acknowledged that her second-act aria, presumably "Anch'io dischiuso," had excited the audience and "was beautifully executed." Of the opera itself it reported:

> "Nabucco" is similar in character to most of Verdi's operas; intricate concerted pieces of great artistic skill, and brilliant instrumentation, with a lack of beauty and melody. It was placed upon the stage with great completeness. . . . The choruses were the best part of this opera, and the triumphant march, played by the military band upon the stage, and the funeral march behind the scenes, had a grand effect. The part of Nabucco, presented by Lanzoni, was, however, the feature of the opera. In the last scene of the second act, when the king loses his throne and his reason—in the *aria* and prayer in the fourth act and in the last scene and *finale* of the fourth act, he was truly admirable.[20]

The reviewers of both the *Herald* and the *Alta California* agreed with their colleague, both mentioning the stage band, the choruses, Lanzoni's artistry, and one of them also praising a well-performed pas de deux inserted in the third act. As the dancers were those who had appeared in *Judith,* possibly the choreography was the same. In any case the opera, which played three nights to full houses, had a genuine success, not only as spectacle but as drama.[21]

Further, at the second and third performances the reviewers and audience began to notice more in the music than just the stage band, choruses, and dramatic scenes. On repeated hearings the critics for both the *Pioneer* and the *Alta California* were impressed by Fenena's prayer in the fourth act, "Oh, dischiuso è il firmamento!"[22] This aria for the second soprano is short, relatively easy to sing, and easy to overlook. But in time it would become sufficiently popular in the United States to be published separately as "To Me the Firmament Is Clouded." As Verdi's operas became more familiar, audiences began to hear in them, besides the "passages of great brilliancy" and the brass bands, his contrasting "sweetness."

Though the company's season appears to have been profitable, it had not reaped for its members the rewards expected, and they were reported to be "not so well pleased with their success as they anticipated."[23] Nevertheless, they decided to continue, and after a visit to Sacramento in early January, they returned to repeat *Lucrezia Borgia* and *Ernani,* with Mengis in the latter replacing Leonardi as Silva. Then, on the twenty-fifth of that month, the manager of the Metropolitan Theatre issued a bulletin of the theatre's plans for opera, which included future performances by the company.[24]

The business agreement between Barili-Thorn and the theatre's manager, Mrs. Catherine Sinclair, is not altogether clear, but the latter evidently functioned not only as the theatre's lessor but also as an impresario. It was she who had brought the Barili-Thorn troupe to California and created the company to support it, and presumably she gave the Italian singers some sort of financial guarantee in return for a hand in their repertory and scheduling. Whatever the terms of the agreement, her announcement was greeted generally with approval, and *Wide West* headlined an article on it entitled "Good News for the

Lovers of Music." By then, January 1855, Sinclair evidently had come
to agree with the journal's opinion that "in a community no larger than
our own, too frequent performances, especially of opera, are fatal to
success."[25] She therefore sought to reduce the number of performances, by combining Barili-Thorn's troupe with Bishop's, hoping no
doubt to cut costs, raise profits, and improve quality.

In addition, she had sent an agent to the East Coast to negotiate with
other artists, particularly with Louisa Pyne, an English soprano specializing in English operas and light operas in English versions. The
critic in *Wide West* looked forward to a season of Gay's *The Beggar's
Opera*, Wallace's *Maritana*, Auber's *Fra Diavolo* and *Crown Diamonds*,
Rooke's *Amilie*, Balfe's *Bohemian Girl*, and, finally, his *Enchantress*, "with
all the music, not the emasculated affair produced by Mme. Thillon."[26]
On the Italian side of her repertory Sinclair proposed to include at
least *La favorita, Lucia di Lammermoor, L'elisir d'amore, Il barbiere di Siviglia,
Don Giovanni*, and Mercadante's *Il bravo*.

In the end, the agent in the East failed to lure Louisa Pyne or an
alternative westward, and there was no season of English opera inter-
spersed with light French opera in English versions. Nonetheless,
though neither Bishop nor Barili-Thorn can have relished being
crushed together, however reasonable the scheme, Sinclair did manage
to present a number of Italian evenings in which forces were joined.
One method, a step backward for the development of opera as drama,
was to combine acts from different operas. Thus, on 28 January, she
produced a program consisting of an act from *Sonnambula* (Bishop), two
from *Lucrezia Borgia* (Barili-Thorn), Act II of *Der Freischütz* (Bishop),
a pas de deux, and "The Grand Operatic Ballet and Scenic Spectacle"
The Ice Witch.[27] Presumably, to keep the evening from becoming mon-
strously long, the acts were shortened, probably by cutting choral
numbers and arias for secondary characters.

With a production of *L'elisir d'amore*, however, there was a real
merging of the troupes. Bishop sang Adina; Mengis, Dr. Dulcamara;
and the Barili-Thorn troupe provided Scola and Lanzoni for
Nemorino and Belcore.[28] And then finally, on 8 March 1855, Sinclair
presented the city's premiere of *Don Giovanni*, with Bishop as Donna

Anna, Barili-Thorn as Zerlina, Lanzoni as Don Giovanni, Mengis as Leporello, and Bochsa conducting. An advertisement in the *Alta California* promised that besides the "three separate orchestras—as written in Mozart's original score" the production would be "the only time" that the two prima donnas would "sing together in the same opera."[29] Further, on opening night, to crown the excitement during the opera's ball scene, members of the audience, if masked and costumed, could dance onstage, and also after the performance.[30]

According to the *Herald,* the premiere sold out with nearly a thousand persons turned away, and the second and third performances seem to have played to full houses. But Sinclair did not extend the run. The opera, with six soloists and extra instrumentalists for the onstage orchestras, must have been expensive to produce, and profits in all ventures increasingly were squeezed. In January, Sinclair had reduced the cost of seats in the theatre's third tier from $1 to 50 cents, because of "the exigency of the times."[31]

Meanwhile, the two troupes continued from time to time to stage their own productions, a rivalry in which Bishop and Bochsa fared better than Barili-Thorn. Undaunted by the financial failure of *La Muette di Portici,* Bochsa, in early January, turned his attention to another grand opera from Paris, Meyerbeer's *Robert le diable,* which he planned to present in English, with Bishop singing the role of Isabella and himself conducting an expanded orchestra and greatly enlarged chorus. To that end, on 7 January 1855, he placed an advertisement in the *Alta California,* which he ran for three days:

> The immediate aid of THIRTY AMATEUR VOCALISTS wanted to join in Meyerbeer's magnificent invisible church choruses. No study by heart. Also six harpists (led by Mr. McKarkel) and a large Organ. Inquire of Mr. Bochsa, International Hotel.[32]

The need for aid truly was immediate, for he opened only five days later, by which time he was able to advertise "a full chorus—joined in the Invisible Church Chorale by a number of amateur vocalists" and also an "enlarged orchestra," including an organ.[33]

The opera, often said to be the first serious manifestation of musical romanticism on the French lyric stage, tells an improbable story of temptation by the devil, and its most famous scene, which some persons considered blasphemous, included a ballet of phantom nuns that is best described in language appropriate to the mid–nineteenth century:

> In the Sicilian convent graveyard where Robert's mother lies, dissolute dead nuns who once held profligate orgies there rise in hellish beauty and scanty winding sheets at [the devil's] command to tempt [Robert] with unholy dances (bassoons chuckle as the phantoms leave their graves); and when, casting off their cerements, they appear unveiled, their blandishments induce Robert to pluck the mystic branch.[34]

The opening night was sold out, and many persons were turned away. The next morning the critic for the *Alta California*, though not mentioning the orchestra, chorus, or ballet, was enthusiastic about the singers, particularly Bishop, who had been accompanied on the harp by Mr. W. McKarkel in the opera's most famous aria, Isabella's "Robert! toi que j'aime"—except, of course, it was sung in English.[35] Yet despite apparent success, by the fourth performance the house was no more than half full, and Bochsa stopped the run to revise the production.[36] After a few weeks he presented it again, this time in French, with Bishop singing both soprano roles and himself both conducting and playing the harp during "Robert! toi que j'aime." With the latter, according to *Wide West*, he and Bishop produced "a perfect *furore*."[37] Yet once again the production apparently failed to fill the house, and after a single repetition Bochsa withdrew it. Presumably his and Bishop's profit, if any, was small, for in a review of the final performance the *Alta California* remarked, "These are hard times, and of that there can be no better evidence than the Metropolitan presented last evening. The magnificent opera of *Robert the Devil* . . . has been brought out in a manner that would draw full houses in almost any large city in the world. Yet the house was thin last evening."[38]

The economic problems of the opera companies came to a head in the spring with Barili-Thorn's production of Verdi's *I Lombardi alla prima crociata* (The Lombards on the First Crusade; Fig. 9). Though two of the opera's arias had been sung in recitals, the full opera had not yet been heard in the city, and so the production would be a premiere. The opera, strangely, is the only one of Verdi's twenty-six to be based on an Italian literary work, and it tells the story of a fraternal feud in Milan that ends years later with a multitude of deaths in the Holy Land. Stretching in time over a generation in the family and in setting from Milan to Jerusalem, it lacks the concentration of *Nabucco,* though it shares much the same kind of music, marches, choruses, a prayer, and some intricate concerted numbers. In addition, *I Lombardi* has the distinction of being the first of Verdi's operas to be produced in the United States: an Italian company visiting New York presented it at Palmo's Opera House on 3 March 1847, and in that performance the leading soprano role, Giselda, was sung by nineteen-year-old Clotilda Barili, who now introduced the opera to San Francisco.

In New York the critics had greeted their first exposure to a full evening of Verdi with general dispraise: his melodies lacked "the catching popular qualities of a Bellini or a Donizetti," and his passion for instruments of brass and percussion" produced "mere noise without substance."[39] In San Francisco, despite a production advertised to have "a powerful chorus," "enlarged orchestra," and George Loder conducting, critical opinion of the music was lost in the explosion of a disagreement between Sinclair and the singers.[40]

The quarrel, originating in poor receipts at the box office, was fanned on Sinclair's side by costumes borrowed from her by the singers but not returned and by the seemingly unnecessary cost, in hard times, of a private carriage to transport Barili-Thorn between her hotel and the theatre. For their part, the singers protested a long delay in pay, and their simmering irritation flashed into anger on opening night of *I Lombardi,* 1 May 1855, when on surveying the house through the curtain they discovered many of the expensive seats empty, a sure sign of further delay. According to the *Alta California* the next morning:

There was a very fair and fashionable audience in waiting at the Metropolitan last evening considering the fact of the steamer's arrival late in the day,

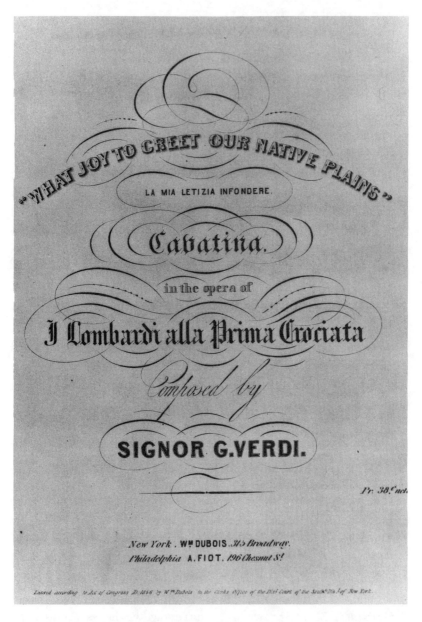

Fig. 9.   A title page for sheet music. (Pierpont Morgan Library, New York; George W. Martin Collection)

bringing the disastrous financial news. There was a long and vexatious delay, however, before the performance commenced, some of the Italian troupe being consistently sick, or miffed, or something else, so as to aggravate the audience to a most unbearable extent. If the Italians expect the people of San Francisco to sustain and patronize them, they should not thus trifle with their patience. The opera, when it did come, was well given, and well repaid the audience for waiting while some of the troupe were on a *strike*.[41]

Thus, with emphasis, the paper recorded what seems to have been the first strike by artists in San Francisco's musical history. The singers' tempers, however, did not cool, and before the next performance, scheduled for the evening of 3 May, Sinclair stepped before the curtain to address the audience:

Ladies and Gentlemen—I regret extremely that I am compelled to appear before you to make an announcement which I am sure will cause equal regret to you, as pain to us. The artists composing the Italian opera troupe positively refuse to sing, in consequence of the insufficiency of attendance here this evening, and I have assumed the unpleasant task of making this statement, in order to exonerate myself from any charge of willingly disappointing the public.[42]

She lamented that a depressed economy and the demands of artists made Italian opera unprofitable, but in place of Verdi's *I Lombardi* she was delighted to be able to offer the audience a drama company in Shakespeare's *Much Ado About Nothing.*

The singers replied two days later through the *Herald:*

The Italian Opera—Editor of the Herald: We, the undersigned, have been astonished to read in the two newspapers of this city, that we were ready to sing at the second performance of the "Lombardi" last Thursday. That report was not correct. We are tired of working for nothing. Will you have the kindness to insert these lines? Yours truly, Carlo Scola, A. Lanzoni.[43]

The next day in letters to the *Alta California,* Barili-Thorn restated the singers' grievances and Sinclair asked the public "to suspend their judgement" until she could "publish an exact statement of the receipts, expenses, and losses" incurred by the troupe's productions. The paper, however, chose not to withhold judgment and in that same issue fired a broadside against all Italian opera, insisting that it "cannot be supported here, and Mrs. Sinclair made a great mistake in attempting it. It was bound to ruin her and the theatre, as it has ruined every manager in the United States, who ever attempted it." In all respects the editorial blamed the singers, "foreign adventurers, with pretentious names and Italian airs," and it pointed out that Loder, the chorus, and the orchestra all "would have been willing to have gone on with the opera on Thursday night, so that the disappointment was in no respect to be attributed to them. They had been long enough in the country to have some respect for an American audience."[44]

Two days later Sinclair published her figures, revealing that the initial "Barzani" (*sic*) season of "16 nights" had lost $3,908, and the subsequent "Barili-Thorn" continuation that had begun in January had lost $9,977. She blamed the small audience for *I Lombardi,* at least in part, on "the disastrous commercial news received but a few hours before [curtain time]"—a reference to the failure of Page & Bacon, a bank in St. Louis to which many in San Francisco had ties. Published directly beneath her letter in the paper was another from L. T. Planel complaining that the theatre (that is, Sinclair) still had not paid him for the orchestral parts he had prepared for the opera.[45]

The row reached a resolution of sorts when the Barili-Thorn troupe broke its engagement with Sinclair and, replacing Loder with Rudolph Herold as its musical director, decamped with costumes and artists to the Union Theatre. There, finally, a second performance of *I Lombardi* was achieved, on 19 May. Again the critics for the *Herald* and the *Alta California* praised the opera and singers in general terms, with the latter paper devoting some of its remarks to the strike:

> On Saturday evening the old Union Theatre (now rechristened the Italian Opera House) was again thrown open to the public, the opera troupe lately engaged at the Metropolitan being the vocal corps for the occasion. This company have taken the Union and intend giving a series of operas there, commencing with *I Lombardi*. The house was tolerably filled, and the audience consisting for the greater part of French citizens, was one of the most enthusiastic and fashionable to be got together in the city. The

orchestra was very fine and elicited the warmest applause. Madame Thorne acquitted herself with great success.... Although the fiat of the San Francisco public has gone forth against the opera, yet this troupe may support themselves ably by a determination not again to disappoint their patrons and leave the stage in a huff when the boxes and parquette are not filled. A few nights of as excellent performances as were given on Saturday evening will do much towards reestablishing the corps upon their original footing with opera goers.[46]

The next evening the company gave *I Lombardi* a third performance, but apparently, unlike *Ernani* and *Nabucco,* it never filled the house. Evidently neither the music nor its performance were at fault, and it seems likely that the audience stayed away either out of anger with the singers or because of the increasing financial depression. Whatever the reason, in reporting the strike the critics failed to discuss the music.

Hardly a week later, on 26 May, the company presented still another Verdi opera, *I due Foscari,* which it had introduced to the city with two performances at the American Theatre in late March. The opera is based on Byron's play *The Two Foscari* and set entirely in Venice. Although Verdi composed it next after *Ernani,* it is quite different in style and story, more tightly constructed, more introspective, and more continually gloomy—to a point where, in his own judgment, it has "but one burden to its song": the destruction of a doge and his family on trumped-up charges of treason. Though frequently given in its day, the opera has not matched the continuing popularity of its predecessors, *Nabucco, I Lombardi,* and *Ernani,* perhaps because it lacks their grand marches and swinging choruses. Yet its music, in its concentration, has frequent moments of power. And it is this opera rather than any of its three predecessors that caused Donizetti to exclaim, "Frankly, this man is a genius. He finds it hard, it's true, to find the phrases, but when he has found them, he makes them stick in the ear like a haunting memory."[47]

The earlier performances had passed almost unnoted, though the first, on 23 March, was the opera's local premiere. Now in May, despite Lanzoni as the Doge, the critics still found nothing to say about the opera, and even its fourth performance, on 1 June, went without com-

ment.[48] Possibly the lack of attention was rooted in the move to the
Union Theatre, for thereafter the troupe and its activities received far
less publicity. Or perhaps it was a result of unfamiliarity, for even more
than *Maria di Rohan*, *I due Foscari* had arrived in the city unknown.

The company, however, was not yet finished with it. Somehow,
most likely through the underwriting of several rich patrons, the singers effected a reconciliation with the Metropolitan Theatre (Fig. 10).
Sinclair had retired as its manager on 9 June,[49] and her successor
promptly negotiated with the troupe for two performances. For the
first, announced as a benefit on 13 June for Barili-Thorn, the opera
chosen was *Ernani*, with Loder once again conducting.[50] For the second, a benefit on 16 June for Lanzoni, it was *I due Foscari*, followed by
the third act of *Ernani*—and on this occasion the critic of the *Alta
California* published a review.

> The opera of *I due Foscari* is less brilliant than *Ernani*, but it is, in our
> opinion, unrivalled by that or any other work of Verdi, known to us, in
> mingled sublimity and pathos. Francesco Foscari we consider one of the
> greatest, most impressive figures in the gallery of musical art—an immor-
> tal expression of princely and paternal grief. He is in music as the Laocoon
> in the Sculptor's art—those who have gazed upon the one—those who
> have listened to the passionate accents of the other—retain forever inef-
> faceable the memory of their sublime agony.[51]

The critic's metaphor of the elder Foscari as "a figure in the gallery
of musical art" points to a slight shift in Verdi's style taking place in
his early operas. In both *Nabucco* and *I Lombardi*, Verdi's third and
fourth operas and the first to win success outside of Italy, the chorus,
portraying respectively the Hebrew people and the Lombards, has an
exceptionally large role. In *Nabucco*, in fact, the opera's focus is as much
on the Hebrew people as on the King of the Assyrians. With *Ernani*,
which followed *I Lombardi*, the chorus is less important, and it becomes
still less so in the sixth opera, *I due Foscari*. Verdi continued to write
lovely music for his choral ensembles, but the chorus never again was
a protagonist. Musically, in these operas Verdi progressively becomes
more interested in creating human beings than in composing epic
dramas in which the chorus represents the people or the nation. Significantly, in his search for librettos he never seriously considered a

Fig. 10. Interior of the Metropolitan Theatre; published in the *Golden Era*, 18 June 1854. (California State Library, Sacramento)

myth; he wanted always real people in real situations. Shakespeare was his favorite playwright, and like Shakespeare in his plays Verdi in his operas would create a gallery of figures remarkable for the complexity of their humanity. Ultimately, that is where Verdi's greatness in opera abides.

In his gallery of figures perhaps the first portraits to show full mastery of rhythm, tone, and vocal color are those of Rigoletto, Azucena in *Il trovatore,* and Violetta in *La traviata,* and these lead on to the even more perfectly realized King Philip in *Don Carlos,* the revised Simon Boccanegra, Otello, and Falstaff. But every artist has early sketches that show promise, and chief of these for Verdi were his musical portraits of the two Macbeths. Even before them, though, for audiences with attentive ears and eyes, came Nabucco, humbled in his pride; the haughty and vengeful Silva in *Ernani;* the superstitious Attila; and the suffering Francesco Foscari.

The opera had been mounted only at the last moment as a replacement for Donizetti's *Maria di Rohan,* which had been advertised. The reason for the substitution was not disclosed, but presumably it suited Lanzoni, for his evidently powerful performance suggests that he liked the role. In any event, the *Alta California* critic judged that the change had lessened the audience "by perhaps one fourth" because "the majority of operagoers here prefer the sing-song of Verdi's immediate predecessor in celebrity to the majestic declamation of that great master."[52]

Nevertheless, though Verdi still trailed Donizetti in public esteem, signs of his growing popularity increasingly appeared, many of them outside the opera house. Earlier, in March, at another benefit performance for Barili-Thorn, her half-sister Carlotta Patti had chosen for her piano fantasy a set of variations on Verdi's opera *Il corsaro.*[53] Then on 10 July, at Barili-Thorn's "farewell" recital preceding her departure for South America, there was more Verdi. With Loder at the piano, she sang the cavatina from *Attila,* "Allor che i forti corrono," and the troupe's tenor, Scola, offered a "Song of Louisa Miller," almost certainly "Quando le sere al placido" and apparently the first music of this opera to be heard in the city.[54] The following month, at a performance of the Germania Concert Society, an ensemble of twenty, the concertmaster, performing as soloist, played a fantasia by Henri Vieuxtemps on themes from *I Lombardi;* this he repeated in November.[55]

Then there were the San Francisco Minstrels. The company frequently mocked the most popular operas with skits under such titles as *Mrs. Norma, The Child of the Regiment,* and *The Cat's in the Larder* (Rossini's *La gazza ladra,* or *The Thieving Magpie*). Now, to mark Barili-Thorn's farewell, they burlesqued "Italian Opera" with an extended caricature using chiefly the music of *Ernani* and Auber's *Fra Diavolo.* The program announced that the part of "Madame Clothilda Barilda Greasy" would be sung by "Signorina Camelinas"—a man, for the company had no women. "Campbell achieved a most extraordinary vocal feat," wrote the reviewer for the *Herald.* "His falsetto is a style of vocalism only to be compared to the powerful but soft tones of a female voice. The solo from *Ernani* is given apparently without the least exertion above the natural effort of the voice, and each note is clearly and distinctly sung." Of the comic routines the reviewer particularly liked "the ludicrous gesticulations of the conductor in handling the baton" and "the remarkable duel between the rival lovers," which exhibited "a wonderful deal of agility on the part of the combatants."[56]

Bishop, meanwhile, had been making a three-month tour of the mining towns; soon after her return, just before Barili-Thorn departed, she produced another San Francisco premiere, Rossini's *La gazza ladra*, for which she employed Lanzoni, Von Gulpen, and several secondary singers from the Barili-Thorn troupe who had remained in the city.[57] As a pendant to a subsequent performance of the opera she added, much to the delight of the critics, "a musical frolic": the first act of *Norma*, with herself singing Pollio, "a rakish and flirting Roman Consul à la Don Giovanni," Herr Mengis as Norma, two men as their children, and Lanzoni as Adalgisa. Unfortunately, though it is clear from the announcements that Bishop and Bochsa had hoped to play four or five repetitions of the double bill, only one was achieved because of Bochsa's increasing ill health.[58]

Nevertheless, refusing to be daunted, she and Bochsa next planned a production of *La Muette de Portici* in a more complete version then he had mounted the previous summer. This time Auber's grand opera would be sung not in English but in its original French and with Bishop in the only soprano role. Though the performance reportedly drew a good house and was received favorably, it was not repeated, again apparently because of Bochsa's health.[59] Instead, as a benefit for Bochsa, the two artists revived *Der Freischütz*, but in English and with an inferior cast. In anticipation the *Alta California*, no doubt in sincere admiration but also to help ticket sales by arousing sympathy, published an appreciation of Bochsa:

> For the last year and a half he has been laboring hard, and vainly, we are sorry to confess, to establish the Lyric Drama among us. He has had to contend with difficulties which would have arrested another at the outset. He has encountered and overcome them with a vivacity and determination

which show that while the bodily frame of the man has grown old, the spirit of art has been vigorous in the musician. He has great claims on lovers of music in San Francisco. Without his efforts they would have had nothing but the apologies for opera produced by Madame Thillon . . . and the limited and very unsatisfactory repertoire of the Italian troupe. . . . This, we believe, is to be the last night of the opera at the Metropolitan. Mr. Bochsa has not been making a fortune by his exertions, quite the contrary. . . . He is now an old man.[60]

He was sixty-six, which in San Francisco, where hardly a man was over forty, no doubt made him seem old indeed. His health, clearly, was failing, and in January 1856, soon after arriving in Australia, he died.

As predicted, the *Freischütz* performance was the last staged opera at the Metropolitan by Bishop and Bochsa; in fact, it was the last in the city until 1859. The public apparently had turned away from opera. On 6 July, at a benefit concert for Lanzoni, the house had been so empty that he "chose not to sing"; money was "refunded" and the "gas turned off." The critic for the *Alta California* concluded sadly, "It seems that the public just now is not in the musical vein—they must have novelties."[61]

By mid-August Bishop and Bochsa had announced their departure the following month for Australia, and the critic for the *Alta California* observed regretfully that the city's opera singers now were so dispersed that opera was no longer possible. In Bishop's last weeks, however, she sang several concerts with the Germania Society, and at one of these in late August, in Turn-Verein Hall on Bush Street, the program was unusually operatic. It featured a clarinet solo of Theme and Variations from *Tancredi;* the overture to *William Tell,* "played for the first time by the German Society" and destined to be the much-repeated orchestral hit of the season; and finally, the "Favorite Cavatina from Verdi's Ernani—sung for the first time by Madame Anna Bishop." Now even she, who except for *Judith* had ignored Verdi, acknowledged his rising popularity.[62]

At another concert with the German Society she sang "the celebrated 'Brindisi' from Verdi's Macbeth," apparently the only number from this opera to have much success in nineteenth-century America, while at a subsequent concert a second tenor from the Barili-Thorn troupe, Luigi Comassi, sang "the Grand Recitative and Aria" from the opera, presumably "Ah, la paterna mano."[63] Neither piece drew critical comment. But when Bishop, at still another Society concert, repeated the cavatina from *Ernani,* the reviewer for the *Herald* exclaimed that she was "capital" in it, singing "with her usual power and abandon" and "drawing down vehement encores."[64]

At her farewell concert with the Society, on 27 September, she sang nothing of Verdi but offered selections from *Sonnambula* and *Linda di Chamounix,* the "Casta diva" from *Norma,* "a pot pourri of Mexican airs," and "Home, Sweet Home." In the news item announcing the concert the *Herald* regretted that on her departure, "for the first in many months' time our city will be perfectly destitute of a first class operatic singer."[65]

Two months later in another news item it further lamented,

> The musical taste of the people of this city is lethargic, difficult to move in the first instance and more difficult to please in the second. None have felt this probably more keenly than Madame Bishop, one of the most prominent of the limited number of lady vocalists that there are in the world, and who was forced to quit our shores, at all events if not destitute still badly deficient in this world's goods. Barili-Thorn and the Opera Troupe are another case in point.[66]

In addition the writer might have mentioned Mrs. Sinclair, who, because of her losses in opera, had been forced to give up her lease on the Metropolitan Theatre and quit the role of impresario.

Bishop's importance in the history of music in San Francisco—of music in general, not merely of opera—is suggested in a review of the Germania Concert Society:

> The orchestra [eighteen men and a conductor] . . . did capitally, and are lacking only in one particular—strength in the stringed department. A couple of first violins and another double bass, in addition to their present forces, would aid matters materially, already improved by the introduction for the first time at these delightful concerts, of timpani or kettledrums. . . . [The *William Tell* Overture] was the finest orchestral feat, if we may except the "Freischütz" that we have listened to in San Francisco.[67]

Bishop and Bochsa together had produced the *Freischütz* whose orchestra more than a year later, and indeed for several years to come, provided the model by which orchestras were judged. Similarly, for the heavier, dramatic operas, though not for the light or sentimental, the memory of her voice and artistry furnished the criteria to measure the power, brilliance, accuracy, and agility of others. And in addition to opera she had sung, and sung well, such works as Haydn's *The Seasons* and *The Creation* and Rossini's *Stabat Mater.*

Nonetheless, though she widened her operatic repertory while in San Francisco, for the most part it remained old-fashioned. Despite her success with *Judith,* with which she also had won good reviews in New York, for almost a year she did nothing to exploit the operas that underlay that pastiche, not even by singing their popular arias in concert. Though she must have known from her years in Italy, and by word from Europe as well as New York, that Verdi was the rising man in Italian opera, she continued to produce only the works of Bellini, Donizetti, and Rossini. Meanwhile the Barili-Thorn troupe had arrived, and to it must go the credit for giving the city the opportunity to hear a representative selection of Verdi's early operas: *Ernani, Nabucco, I Lombardi,* and *I due Foscari.* For the immediate years ahead, Bishop set the standard of performance; Barili-Thorn, the direction of the repertory.

SEVEN

Economic Decline, *Il trovatore* in Excerpts, and the Vigilantes of 1856

San Francisco's economic depression of 1854–55 was slow to lift, and in the spring of 1856 it suddenly transformed into a startling political and moral upheaval. Though in its first year it had affected the arts only slightly, it soon thereafter became a brake, particularly on opera, which was both complicated and costly to produce. By August 1855, the month of Bishop and Bochsa's last productions, the number of operas presented was decreasing, and by year's end it had dropped almost to zero. Soon opera-lovers were looking back on the days of Barili-Thorn, Thillon, and Bishop as a golden age.

The gravity of the depression can be seen in the number of business failures. According to one historian, "In 1854 came the crisis. Three hundred out of about a thousand business houses shut down. Seventy-seven filed petitions in insolvency with liabilities for many millions of dollars. In 1855 one hundred and ninety-seven additional firms and several banking houses went under."[1] In 1856 the number of failures again increased, but the losses lessened; and most historians agree that economic improvement, though unrecognized, had begun.[2]

But to those then living in the city the turnaround was not so clear, and to many the depression began to seem a moral as well as economic failure. The fever for quick wealth from whatever source continued, though its chief manifestation was changing.

In the early years of the Gold Rush men had mined the surface of the land, using a technique called "placer mining," and fortunes had been made by individuals who, with little more than a pick, pan, and shovel, had hurried into the Wilderness to stake a claim and try their luck. Behind them, on the city's doorstep, they left a disturbing reminder of their haste to be rich: by December 1850 the harbor was littered with 451 abandoned ships.[3] In the mining fields the destruction of the countryside, for those sensitive to it, was equally appalling. The miner E. Gould Buffum, for one, wrote in 1850: "Two years have entirely changed the character of the whole mining region at present discovered. Over this immense territory, where the smiling earth covered and concealed her vast treasures, the pick and the shovel have created canals, gorges, and pits, that resemble the labours of giants." No miner bothered to pick up litter or restore the land to its natural contours, and in time much of the debris and topsoil would drain into creeks and rivers, eventually closing some to fish and navigation. And as ever more powerful tools for mining were introduced, the destruction and pollution increased.[4]

By 1856 the first "pick-and-shovel" phase of the Gold Rush was all but over. Most of the land now was claimed, and individuals were giving way to companies that practiced "quartz mining," which required mechanized tools to probe for lodes of gold far below the land's surface. An individual still might strike it rich, but he was increasingly likely to make his money not by mining the lode himself but by selling it to a corporation. Land speculation, long a plague in the city, now infected the interior as a battle over mineral rights.

The rough behavior for which California was notorious perhaps had moderated, but certainly less than the state's boosters liked to claim. In May 1855, the state legislature passed a law to prohibit gambling, and the famous El Dorado Casino was advertised for rent, but as the *Bulletin* noted, "The only effect . . . seems to have been to drive gamblers to the second and third stories." There was still a startling amount of drinking, and even the city's chroniclers, who tried always to look on the good side, admitted: "No place in the world contains any thing like the number of mere drinking-houses in proportion to the population."

With the drinking and drunkenness there was much brawling; and in the words of an English mining engineer: "Smoking and spitting every-where—one cannot walk in the salon [on the Sacramento steamer] without kicking over 'spitoons,' as the receiver is called, the very sight of which invites a discharge from an American mouth."[5]

The violence in daily life was as strong as ever. In the State Assembly most members routinely attended armed with guns and knives. In the theatres the audience's language often was loud and coarse, brawling was common, and a court case reveals that as late as 1859 ushers still sometimes used "slungshots"—a mass of metal or stone fitted onto a handle and used as a weapon—to control the unruly. Pistols were worn in theatres; in 1856, in the American, a man who continually annoyed a lady by "crowding past her seat" tried to shoot her escort, who had protested. Outdoors, street fights, often with fatalities, occurred almost every day. In August 1855, an argument at a polling booth in the center of town quickly became an affray of six men stabbing and shooting. The mining camps were famous for their lynchings; and San Francisco was known for its homicides and suicides, said by 1854 to total, respectively, 4,200 and 1,200. And these numbers seem low, for almost every day the newspapers reported more of all three.[6]

Some of the violence had its comic side, such as "the Bateman case," in which a playwright's husband, H. L. Bateman, angered by a critic's review of his wife's play, struck the critic in the face, drew a gun, fired, and missed. Taken to court, he won the judge's sympathy for having to endure the article's abusive tone but was fined $300 for seeking revenge in the public streets.[7]

The fine was unusual. Dueling, which was common and increasing, had popular support and was indulged by state officials. In May 1854, after one of Anna Thillon's performances of *La Fille du régiment,* the *Alta California* reported, "During the first act . . . two gentlemen, one an ex-member of the Legislature, had an interesting little fist fight in one of the orchestra boxes, by which the whole house was thrown in disorder, and the performance delayed for a few minutes when the parties were separated by a mutual friend."[8]

The origin of the brawl, it later was revealed, lay in Mr. George

Hunt's feet, which at the time were resting on a chair that Mr. N. Hubert, a former member of the State Assembly, wished to occupy. The men failed to negotiate the removal of the feet, or to settle the ensuing quarrel, and a few days later they met to fight with pistols at ten paces. Mr. Hubert had as his second a former Speaker of the Assembly; Mr. Hunt's second presumably was at least a gentleman. Mr. Hubert shot and killed Mr. Hunt. The *Alta California* observed that the issue of a warrant against Hubert for murder was quite useless until the legislature by statute prohibited dueling. Under common law in California, no jury would convict.[9]

Yet despite the smoking, spitting, gambling, and brawling in the theatres, entertainment of all kinds flourished in San Francisco. Even opera for eighteen months had stirred a remarkable response, and some of the cause doubtless lies in the peculiarities of the city's population. Frank Soulé, a contemporary journalist, in 1854 estimated total inhabitants at over 50,000 persons, a figure most historians consider at least 10 percent too high. Still, Soulé's proportions may be close to correct: he counted the number of men at 39,000, women at 8,000, and children at 3,000. In a typical city, of course, the women and children greatly outnumber the men.[10]

San Francisco thus was a city in which few had reason to stay home at night. As families then typically had five or six children, in the city there probably were no more than 700 families; and of an elder, grandparent generation there was none. Roughly 80 percent of the population was men, most of them single, under forty, and with money to spend. In the circumstance, the arts flourished, and not only opera. The amount of Shakespeare, Sheridan, Goldsmith, and other playwrights staged is equally remarkable, and there was also a great deal of pantomime and dance as well as resident and visiting minstrel companies. Against so much competition, to say nothing of the circuses and sporting events, the support for opera is astonishing. Besides its expense, it is burdened with some unique problems, such as the frequent foreign language; and it requires of its audience close attention, or the music will be missed and the words, even if translated, not understood. It also demands some acquaintance with music, for its vocal forms seldom are the simplest. Yet opera thrived, possibly in part because of its natural tendency to extravagance and melodrama. In these qualities the men saw, perhaps, the kinds of lives they were leading, lives filled with pledges and betrayals, sudden reversals of fortune, occasional displays of exemplary virtue or hideous vice, and the possibility always of violence. In such an atmosphere it is not surprising that opera in general, and Verdi's in particular, because of their masculine tone, their frequent and angry confrontations, and their underlying melancholy that ends so often in death, should find a sympathetic audience.

The French immigrant de Russailh noted the difficulties many men had in adjusting to the city's peculiar, fevered life. "I have seen men go mad, and many others lose hope and drink themselves to death, finding no better end for their troubles. I've known some who were reduced by discouragement and boredom to such a condition of bestial torpor that they were utterly incapable of the slightest effort." After one of the city's many fires he saw a man who had lost everything shoot himself; and another man first shot his wife and child and then himself.[11]

For many more than the suicides, it seems, the dream of California turned sour. The editors of the *Golden Era* noted sadly that although immigrants to the state in 1854 had numbered about 92,000, those departing had totaled 40,000. And in May 1855 *Wide West* commented, "The emigration from this state for some time past has been confessedly greater than the accessions to its population." Searching for the reason, the journal concluded: "Men have become so reckless in their pursuit of wealth in this country that each is now afraid to trust the other; the result is that the prudent are taking their departure." Among them were George Loder, who had conducted so many of the operas, and Mrs. Sinclair, who had produced them. By the spring of 1856 both had followed Bishop and Bochsa to Australia.[12]

Yet in many ways San Francisco steadily was improving the quality of its life. Though its political and judicial systems generally were held to be corrupt, dominated by a group of ex-Tammany Democrats from New York City, men who were said to mine their fortunes out of graft, the structures of government were in place and capable of reform. The city's architecture had improved; more houses now were built of brick or stone, and fires were rarer and less devastating. The streets, at least in the center of town, had been paved or planked, and some even offered sidewalks. They also were better lighted. On the evening of 11 February 1854 the first gas lamps were lit, and coal gas soon was replacing oil and candles as the chief source of illumination. Within weeks the Metropolitan Theatre had converted to gas, and most new buildings used it from the start. In the world's big industrial cities— New York, Paris, or London—gas had been common for decades, though in Milan, as late as 1855, most streets still had only the dim light of oil.[13]

In San Francisco's theatres the arrival of gas apparently did little to change the local customs of stage lighting or the audience's expectations. At the Opéra, in Paris, the introduction of gas, at the premiere of *Robert le diable* on 21 November 1831, had caused a sensation. In the cloister scene, the setting for the ballet of the phantom nuns, the gaslight, whiter than the usual candlelight and therefore better able to simulate the moon, had been projected downward by reflectors from chandeliers of gas jets above and behind the cloister's arches, thus imitating the fall of moonlight into a room. To the audience accustomed to see sets lit primarily from the front, chiefly by oil or candles in the footlights, the cooler, whiter light and the projection of shadows forward and down the stage rather than backward and up had been a stunning innovation, a long step toward realism in theatrical settings. But there are no reports in San Francisco of such imaginative use of the new light, and probably the theatres lacked the equipment to produce such effects. For the San Francisco theatres gas meant primarily a more evenly distributed light, in part because gas jets, unlike candles, needed no tending after being lit and so could be more widely dispersed in the wings and above the stage. Consequently the intensity of the grotesque shadows cast by strong oil or candle footlights was lessened, and singers and actors with makeup could achieve a more natural appearance. As before, however, the auditorium remained fully lit throughout the performance.

The soprano who to some extent succeeded to Bishop's place in the city in the autumn of 1855, arriving only a month after her predecessor's departure, was by comparison quite unknown. Indeed, there is almost a gypsy quality to Drusilla Garbato and her husband, Luigi, who served as her conductor and manager. Apparently they came alone, without any assisting artists, any store of costumes, or any advance publicity, and so by way of advertisement her husband invited a hundred or more music-lovers to a rehearsal for her first recital. Among those attending was the critic for the *Alta California.*

> At 12 o'clock after one or two very spirited overtures, Signora Garbato appeared on the stage, and executed several selections from opera. . . . She has a voice in which the peculiar qualities of the contralto and so-prano are united with very remarkable effect. . . . [She is] yet young, rather inclined to *embonpoint,* with a pleasing and vivacious expression. . . . Besides she has a very arch and *taking* smile, not altogether affected, which at times lights up her expressive face, and which, with concert dress and the friendly gas, is destined to create a fluttering beneath the waistcoat of many a musical enthusiast. Her style is pure, but florid; and the voice, particularly in the upper register, fresh, and the notes richly and heartily delivered.[14]

A few days later, still trying to describe her particular vocal quality, he would add in a review: "There is a richness about her voice (a mezzo-soprano) and a freedom from any straining for effect."[15]

Though she advertised herself as a "prima donna from La Scala at Milan," as well as from almost every other important Italian or Spanish house,[16] and so presumably had some training and experience, her voice seems to have been something of a puzzle for American critics. She first sang in the United States in Boston in the summer of 1854. Apparently she, her husband, and perhaps one or two other singers had landed in New York City intending to go straight to California but, lacking the money, had arranged instead a quick season in Boston; there she sang in *Ernani, Lucia di Lammermoor,* and *Sonnambula* and was reviewed by the magisterial John Sullivan Dwight.

The Elvira [*Ernani*] of Signora Garbato had great faults with some good and useful qualities. Her power of execution is considerable, but she constantly exaggerates in tone and manner, overdoing pathos until it touches no responsive fibre. Indeed she is a fair example of the false style of soprano singing which now reigns in Italy, and which is due to overforcing in the zeal to sing the Verdi music, whereby the voice runs out into extremes, of screaming high tones, and coarse and mannish low tones, while the middle shrinks and becomes more and more characterless and feeble. Welcome the recent signs of a return in Italy to Rossini and true singing![17]

Dwight's stress on the range, high and low, that Verdi demanded of his sopranos suggests one way in which Verdi's vocal writing seemed to contemporaries to differ from that of the earlier composers. He stretched the voice to its extremes. This in itself was not new; there always had been high and low notes. But among earlier composers these usually had been notes sung in passing, touched only lightly, often more of a musical flourish than a dramatic expression. Verdi, however, asked of his sopranos at the top and bottom of their range a more forceful utterance. To many ears the unexpected weight and resonance that he sought in these notes sounded ugly, especially when sung in competition with Verdi's louder orchestration. Undeniably, the increased intensity that he sought changed the quality of the vocal sound, and many singers, critics, and vocal coaches feared that it would damage the voice.[18]

Yet Dwight in his review was untypically ambivalent, as if not altogether settled in his opinion either of Garbato's technique or of Verdi's music. Of her performance as Lucia he wrote: "[She] had nothing of the maiden-like appearance of Lucia . . . and screamed through much of the music; yet parts of it, especially the caressing strains in the mad scene were sung finely."[19] And of Verdi, despite his misgivings, he concluded, "There is vigor in Ernani, and the music contains many touches of fine dramatic power."[20]

Possibly Dwight's reluctance to dismiss Garbato's voice outright as inadequate, poorly trained, or ugly reflects a suspicion on his part that though he preferred a different style of singing, her voice and style were, in fact, suited to the new sort of musical melodrama Verdi was introducing, one that asked for full tone and emphasis at the extremities of the voice. In any case that seems to have been the response of the critic of the *San Francisco Herald* after hearing her in several concerts:

> Of all the various solos that Verdi has given to the musical world in these later years the most brilliant as well as the most arduous, the most celebrated also, and which will constitute in future time one of the few compositions *par excellence,* that will hold him up to fame as a musical composer, is the "Ernani, involami" in the First Act of the opera *Ernani.* The powers of Barili-Thorn were scarcely adequate to the requirements of this solo, whose brilliant intricacies were no more than mastered by Madame Bishop, who in turn was wanting in that sympathy and perfect abandon so necessary to the full and perfect rendition of the aria. Madame Garbato, who though doubtless sure to prove a favorite in the opera, is not, we imagine, in her true element in a concert room, went through the composition with great power and effect.[21]

It is ironic that the Act III finale for baritone and chorus, which had done the most to make *Ernani* popular in San Francisco, as well as all the arias from other Verdi operas that basses and baritones had introduced to the city, should be so firmly swept aside to crown the opera's soprano aria as Verdi's greatest. One reason may be that *Ernani* contains such abundant riches that only upon repeated hearings will they all be revealed—and now it was the turn of the soprano cavatina, "Ernani, involami," to be remarked. Or perhaps the aria now had been sung by enough sopranos that the music itself, rather than the singer, could become the object of admiration. But another reason doubtless lies in the importance of the singer's voice and style. The English Anna Bishop, with a high, clear, bright, but somewhat inexpressive voice, no doubt could simulate Latin "abandon"; but when measured against one who perhaps came by it naturally and could express it in more colorful tones she seemed, in memory, less exciting. From the descriptions, Garbato seems to have been the first true Verdian dramatic soprano to reach the city, and her loyalty to Verdi in her opening programs suggest that she felt most at home in his music.

She made her debut on 3 November 1855, backed by a group called the Philharmonic Concert Society, conducted by her husband. The program opened with the overture to *Nabucco,* continued with the soprano's romanza from Act I of Donizetti's *Lucrezia Borgia,* and, as the finale before the intermission, presented the Anvil Chorus from *Il trovatore,* the first of that opera's music to be heard in San Francisco. After the break she continued with its Act IV, scene 1: including both the Miserere, in which the soprano, at the foot of the castle tower, vows to save the tenor imprisoned within, and the subsequent "Grand Duo" with the baritone (Herr Mengis), in which, as a last resort, she offers herself to that hated man in return for the tenor's life. Musically, the scene opens with her aria of sweet despair, turning ominously solemn as monks offstage begin their chant for the condemned tenor—Miserere: Have mercy, Lord, on a body soon to die. Then, the baritone having entered, the music crackles with a fierce energy as the soprano proposes her bargain, and she and the baritone set its terms. Finally, the bargain accepted and the tenor's freedom promised, the soprano and baritone, though diversely inspired, close the scene with bursts of ecstatic joy.

By universal agreement the music is some of the greatest that Verdi composed; yet the reviewers for the *Herald* and the *Alta California,* while praising Garbato, have not a word to say of it, except that it suited her voice.[22] In all, in November she gave five concerts, scheduling the cavatina from *Ernani* three times, the Miserere three times, and the Anvil Chorus, advertised as with "about a thousand hammers," three times. And the critics never discussed the music.[23] Unhappily for Garbato, the audiences, though appreciative, were often sparse; and worse, by the fourth concert, on 22 November, everyone's attention had focused elsewhere. A quarrel in a theatre had burgeoned into an ugly crime that was beginning to threaten the stability of the city.

On Thursday evening, 15 November 1855, General William H. Richardson, thirty-three years old, the U.S. Marshall for the Northern District of California and with a distinguished record in the state's government, took his wife and her friend Mrs. Whiting to the American Theatre to see an evening of pantomime and dance, chiefly *The Red Gnome,* a fairy extravaganza, and *Nicodemus,* the story of an unfortunate fisherman. Not long after the program began the Richardson ladies, seated in the gallery, began to feel uncomfortable; a man on the orchestra floor was staring at them. Angered by the persistence of the staring, Gen. Richardson went down to the floor to remonstrate with the man and learned from him that the Richardson ladies were not the object of interest: directly behind them sat Arabella Ryan, Madam of the city's most famous whorehouse and a personification of vice in the city. By the custom of the day, her escort, Charles Cora, a forty-three-year-old professional gambler, formerly of Genoa, should have secreted her in a private box adjoining the stage or at the rear of the orchestra. The gallery, open and visible in the continuously lit auditorium, was for respectable people.

Summoning the management, Richardson returned to the gallery, and Cora was asked to remove himself and the offensive woman. He refused. There were harsh words, heard by many in the gallery, and the Richardson party left. The public nature of the dispute suggested the possibility of a duel, and the goings and comings of both men were watched with interest. On each of the next two days the men were seen talking, but, in the opinion of witnesses, they parted amicably. On the third day, at 7:00 P.M. in Clay Street, near Montgomery, Cora shot Richardson dead. Though Cora subsequently claimed he fired in self-defense, witnesses on the street reported that Richardson did not have a gun in hand.

Cora immediately was arrested and placed in jail. He seemed quite confident, however, that he soon would be free, and so pervasive was the belief in the corruption of the municipal government—the sheriff reputedly had paid $100,000 for his four-year post—that many persons thought it certain. Someone rang the city's "Monumental" bell, citizens gathered at the Oriental Hotel, and there were speeches calling for another Vigilance Committee like that of 1851, which had reformed the city's government by hanging or exiling the most venal and violent of its corrupters. In the end, no Vigilance Committee was organized; but the meeting sent a troop of fifty men to surround the jail, to prevent Cora's escape.

In the midst of these troubles a new voice began to make itself heard. In October a newspaper, the *Daily Evening Bulletin,* had begun publication with a Scotsman as editor, James King of William, whose name in old Scots style proclaimed his father. King, who had failed twice in recent years as a banker, was married, with six children, and in his new role as editor he proposed to sweep the city clean and make it habitable for decent, family people. To that end he wrote his columns with all the self-righteous zeal and acid of John Knox harrowing the ungodly in sixteenth-century Edinburgh. Soon after Richardson's murder King published an editorial, "Theatres and Ladies," in which he asked: "Now is it not about time for every respectable married man in this city to determine in his own mind not to frequent any theatre or other place of public amusement unless some substantial guaranty be offered by the proprietors that these disgusting prostitutes be excluded therefrom?"[24]

When the proprietors ignored his request for some guaranty, he kept attention focused on them until the manager of the Metropolitan Theatre felt it expedient to write an open letter to the paper, assuring King that "an officer is stationed at the door to prohibit improper females from going to any part of the house, save the boxes assigned to them." How the officer distinguished between proper and improper was not disclosed.[25]

The theatres, however, soon were a minor issue compared to the trial of Cora, which threatened to turn into a farce. The court clerks made errors in the papers that held up the proceedings, witnesses left the jurisdiction, and finally, after the trial in mid-January, the jury failed to agree and was discharged. It was said to have divided four for murder, six for manslaughter, and two for acquittal—ten to two, but the two forced a new trial. King prophesied that Cora never would be hanged. "Rejoice ye gamblers and harlots! . . . Cora has escaped this time on the testimony of gamblers. . . . Weep, ye honest men of San Francisco! Weep for the fame of the fair city ye have built!"[26]

That winter of 1855–56 was a difficult season for drama and music in San Francisco. A sense of defeat permeated much of the city, and audiences patronized mostly the lighter entertainments, the comedies, farces, song recitals, and minstrel shows. Garbato, despite her critical success with operatic arias, choruses, and scenes, was unable to create a demand for fully staged opera, not even for *Il trovatore*, and when in February she sang a benefit for the Lafayette Hook and Ladder Company No. 2, she found it appropriate to sing only lighter music, a program entirely of Italian and Spanish songs. Two years earlier for the same audience, Clarisse Cailly had scheduled several opera arias, including two by Verdi.[27]

Still more unhappily, Garbato and other artists now gradually lost what little attention the newspapers and journals previously had given them as more and more space was devoted to the political and moral campaigns that King and the *Bulletin* kept astir. In January, in a single-sentence news item, the *Alta California* dismissively stated: "Signora Garbato is in the city, occasionally singing at concerts." In February it reviewed the first subscription concert of the Germania Concert Society, at which she sang three selections, but merely reported the event's occurrence without identifying even one of the works performed. The following month, after a benefit at which she was scheduled to sing Bellini's "Casta diva" and a new Spanish song, the newspaper remarked on the number of ladies in the audience but observed that it had "no room to particularize the different pieces executed."[28]

Meanwhile the number of orchestral concerts dwindled, and apparently no operas at all were presented. Thus in the winter of 1855–56, as the second half of the Gold Rush decade began, Verdi's tally of operas fully produced remained where Bishop and Barili-Thorn had left it: *Ernani* (7 performances), the pastiche *Judith* (6), *Foscari* (5), *Nabucco* (3), and *Lombardi* (3).

The city's political and judicial affairs, however, continued turbulent.[29] The jury's inability to reach a decision did not free Cora, who was held for retrial, and James King and the *Bulletin* kept up their crusade to convict him. In the paper King had found a pulpit, and in discovering his voice he tasted power, for it soon was evident that he expressed the feelings of many of the city's residents, perhaps even the majority. These people, predominantly Protestant and from the South or New England, felt they were governed by the dregs of New York City's Tammany politicians, most of whom were Catholic and Irish, and some of whom were criminals. The Tammany crowd, it was alleged, controlled the polling booths, public office, and judicial system by corruption and intimidation; to many San Franciscans these professional politicians seemed to have become a class apart, impervious to reform. And along with the political corruption went moral degeneracy. Besides the gambling, and the dueling, and the homicides, there was the ubiquitous prostitution. In the small city the whorehouses were in the center of town, most of them on Dupont and connecting streets, a section where many people lived and where everyone sooner or later came on business. Some whores simply chalked their hours and prices on their doors and when scolded were cheeky, and the toughs they attracted were often threatening. The wives and mothers in the city, as well as most of the clerics and their congregations, adopted the *Bulletin* as their spokesman and enlisted vociferously in its editor's crusade.

Meanwhile King continued to publish periodic denouncements of dueling along with editorials on such subjects as "Men and Principles" and "The Moral Responsibility of Lawyers," even as he conducted a charitable appeal for "The Orphans" and gave the city excellent coverage of foreign and domestic news. But municipal and moral reform were his chief aims, and to them he returned again and again. Finally, on 14 May, though warned by the city supervisor, James P. Casey, not to do so, King published Casey's New York prison record. That afternoon, in daylight, in the street, Casey shot him. Six days later King died.

Within hours of the shooting, the business leaders of the city had met in Turn-Verein Hall and voted to organize San Francisco's Second Vigilance Committee, under the leadership of thirty-two-year-old William T. Coleman (named after the Swiss revolutionary William Tell). Formation of the Committee with intent to unseat the government was treason against both the city and state, and to defend itself if attacked, as well as to control the streets, its members and supporters promptly seized whatever arms they could find, including some cannon. A call went out for volunteers to serve in a citizens' army; the response was prompt and sufficient to form twenty-six companies of a hundred men each under five officers, and these began to patrol the streets. The French asked and were allowed to form their own units under French-speaking officers. Ultimately about 8,000 men served in the force, which was financed by dues and voluntary contributions. As one of its first acts the Committee transferred both Casey and Cora from the sheriff's jail to its headquarters, a defensible, downtown building now christened Fort Gunnybags. As soon as the volunteers were organized, the Committee seized the city's criminal and police jurisdiction, leaving much of the civil administration to elected officials.

Not everyone approved. Many lawyers were troubled by a resort to violence when the courts were open and undisturbed in the exercise of their jurisdictions. Many politicians, too, whether out of interest or principle, were opposed to the Committee, and three of the four most important newspapers initially censured it. King's paper, the *Bulletin,* not surprisingly was in full support, but the *Alta California* and the *Chronicle* vacillated. The staff at the former reportedly one day had prepared two articles, one favoring, one opposing the Committee; after a visit from some vigilantes, it published the one favorable. The *Chronicle* held out longer against similar pressure and ultimately was ruined by the consequent loss of public support. The *Herald* steadfastly opposed the Committee, and in retaliation businessmen burned copies in the street before its office, withdrew their advertisements, stopped their subscriptions, and urged or forced others to follow their lead. They soon had reduced one of the city's leading papers to a sheet of small significance.

Some clerics, too, were not entirely at ease with the seizure of government. One who preached against it was asked by members of his church to end his opposition; he refused and was burned in effigy. In most areas of the city popular pressure on men to back the vigilantes was strong, and where it alone was not powerful enough to win support, the Committee, by its acts, coerced many into silence.

Both the city and state governments opposed the rebellion and tried at first to persuade the Committee to back down. When talk failed, the state governor, J. Neely Johnson, who was only twenty-eight, threatened to call out the local militia, which was commanded by a thirty-six-year-old West Point graduate who was now a banker, William Tecumseh Sherman, later of Civil War fame. But there was a problem. The militia, which in any case might not have obeyed orders, had insufficient arms, and Sherman estimated that to overpower the vigilantes he would need, besides muskets, several pieces of artillery and an armed ship to control the harbor. The commander of the U.S. Army arsenal at Benicia, the only source of such weapons, faced with the likelihood of civil war, hesitated and then refused the requisition. Sherman, who had spoken forcefully for action against the rebels, resigned; his replacement dithered and, ultimately, did nothing.

The Committee held trials, and these were swift, without right of appeal, and, of course, in violation of state and federal law. On 22 May Cora and Casey, both convicted of murder, were hanged. Before then, Cora, on the urging of his priest, married Belle Ryan. Two other men were hanged for murder, twenty-five were deported for lesser crimes, a few others were ordered to leave the city, and some 800 departed voluntarily. Then, on 21 August, following a parade of its troops, the Committee disbanded and returned the city's criminal and police jurisdiction to the municipal government.

It is not easy to measure and judge the episode. In the next few years it became clear that the upheaval had accomplished a political revolution of sorts, though some historians argue that the improvements could have been won at the ballot box, without recourse to rebellion and its attendant injuries. As moral reformers, the vigilantes accomplished almost nothing—perhaps because in their origin and practices they were themselves so morally flawed. Possibly no community so lacking in wives, children, and grandparents can reform itself. In any case, along with its reputation for extraordinary vitality the city continued to be notorious for its vice and violence.

Sherman, whose integrity the *Evening Bulletin* and *Alta California* had tried to impugn, later wrote scathingly of the press's role in fostering treason. The *Alta California* insisted that the leaders of the Committee were men "of sense and discretion," whose sole purpose was "to purify

our city, to check the reign of violence, lawlessness and bloodshed."
But to those who supported the vigilantes, who willingly subordinated
the rule of law to the rule of men, Sherman directed this question:
"Their success has given great stimulus to a dangerous principle, that
would at any time justify the mob in seizing all the power of government; and who is to say that the Vigilance Committee may not be
composed of the worst, instead of the best, elements of a community?"[30]

It is equally hard to gauge the episode's effect on the arts, but it
plainly was considerable. On 28 April the *Alta California* reported:
"Theatrical affairs seem to have reached almost a dead stand-still in
this city. The two beautiful theatres, the Metropolitan and the American, are closed, the former being about to undergo the changes necessary for the accommodation of a Circus Company.... Some of the best
actors in the State are in the interior towns, or are travelling."[31]

No doubt many artists thought it the season to be out of town,
among them, seemingly, Garbato. Of actors touring the interior one
was Catherine Sinclair, who, after a successful ten months on the stage,
was about to depart for Australia. Also leaving for Australia were the
scene painter at the Metropolitan, the leader of its house orchestra, and
its leading actress. George Loder, who had been reduced to conducting
a weeklong Ladies Festival, which seems to have been a sort of indoor
garden party with refreshments, soon followed them, as did also two
of the better French singers, the tenor Laglaise and the baritone Coulon. It would take time for newcomers to replace the talent that,
because of the economic depression and the vigilantes, left the city.[32]

The Minstrels kept performing but apparently, whether or not
voluntarily, dropped political comment from their skits. A popular
actress, Mrs. George Chapman, instead of mounting a play at the
Musical Hall, offered a program of readings from *Hiawatha;* presumably expenses were small and the poem noncontroversial. Not long
after the hangings, however, in the final week of May, Edwin Booth
appeared at the Metropolitan in a production of Bulwer-Lytton's *Ri-
chelieu.* The *Wide West* praised Booth highly but found the supporting
company, with few exceptions, poor.[33]

Serious music of all kinds suffered more than theatre, though as much perhaps from the economic depression as the state of rebellion. Orchestral music, using the smaller halls and based almost entirely on local concert societies, was less hard hit than opera, which tended to rely on visiting troupes and celebrity singers. But what soprano in Mexico City, Lima, or New York, on reading of events in San Francisco, would not postpone her visit? What local impresario, faced with hard times and a part of the potential audience on any night patrolling the streets, would not delay mounting a production or importing singers?

In late May at the Metropolitan, a troupe of Spanish singers presented a single performance of a comic opera, *Tío Canillitas* (Uncle Smallshins), with music taken mostly from *La Manola, Vito Vito,* and *La Fille du régiment.* The *Wide West* was scathing:

> The dancing that should have occurred in the piece was omitted. The male singers attached to the company are very poor, not as good in fact as some of the French and Germans attached to the chorus. We would suggest to this company that, if they wish to produce a favorable impression in the community, they should add to their number Signora Garbato, whose execution of Andalusian ballads has hitherto been so much admired. We are not certain, however, that the lady is in the city; if so, they would do well to secure her services.[34]

Garbato had arrived in San Francisco at an unfortunate time. Though acknowledged to be the city's leading soprano for all of the year she was there, November 1855 through October 1856, by May, when the vigilantes exploded into armed rebellion, she and her art had become so irrelevant to daily life that even the largest newspaper could not report her whereabouts. Though surely she had the desire to appear in staged performances of opera, she apparently never did, not even in one of Verdi, to whose style she was so well suited. And after her departure, several years would be required before opera could regain a secure place in San Francisco's musical life. Then, with *Rigoletto, Il trovatore,* and *La traviata* as his new works, Verdi would draw abreast of Donizetti and surpass Rossini and Bellini in popularity.[35]

PART II

EIGHT

Maguire, His Opera House, and the Bianchis

On 15 October 1856, two months after the Vigilance Committee had disbanded, its self-appointed work done, Thomas Maguire, the owner of San Francisco Hall and its resident company, the San Francisco Minstrels, began work to improve his theatre. His action was both a sign of the return to normal city government and a promise of better times in the city's depleted cultural life.

Maguire (Fig. 11) was a flamboyant man, and he went about his improvements in his usual eye-catching manner. To widen the auditorium by fifteen feet, increase the area backstage, and introduce gas throughout, he started his carpenters and masons to work even as the Minstrels continued their nightly performances. At the end of a week he sent the Minstrels on tour while the workmen knocked down the old walls inside the shell of the new and reconstructed the interior. Six weeks later where San Francisco Hall had stood, on the north side of Washington between Montgomery and Kearny streets, he opened to the public for inspection a wholly new theatre named "Maguire's New Opera House," which he inaugurated on 29 November with a performance by the Minstrels, whose company he had increased to fifteen. When the men were on tour, Maguire booked plays, concerts, lectures, and revues for the hall, and he looked forward to a day when he could

Fig. 11.   Thomas Maguire. (The Bancroft Library, University of California, Berkeley)

produce Italian or "white" opera in addition to the "black" of the Minstrels. In only a few years he would achieve that aim, producing in his own house, by then enlarged once again, the longest seasons of opera San Francisco yet had seen and presenting among the many new operas the local premieres of *Rigoletto* and *Il trovatore*.[1]

Maguire, who ultimately built twelve theatres in California and for his activities as an impresario became a national figure, brought with him from New York a passion for opera. Though his forays into producing it more than once impoverished him, his loyalty to his vision of what the opera should be—not only the art but also the theatre housing it—never wavered. After one season he is said to have remarked, "I lost thirty thousand dollars; but didn't I give them opera—eh?" He seems never to have considered whether producing it, or building and decorating theatres to house it, was financially wise, only whether he had sufficient money. And though he died poor, he seems not to have cared; he had lived richly.[2]

He arrived in San Francisco in September 1849, accompanied by his wife, Emma, known as "Little Em," and by his fifty-year-old father, who died the next year; and soon, at some undetermined time, a brother, John, came out to join him. John, who seems to have been younger than Tom, was a quieter man but always helpful to his brother.

Tom Maguire was a fine figure of a man and in flush years always well tailored and with a diamond stickpin; but he also was quick to anger, to strike a blow, or to spit in a man's face. He was said to have been a carriage driver in New York, a bartender in the Park Theatre, and a hanger-on of Tammany Hall; also to be unable to read or write. The first three reports are likely, but the illiteracy seems doubtful, though he relied greatly on his wife and secretaries for his correspondence. In any case, he was fearless, and after his death a friend who had known him in both New York and San Francisco described in a letter to a newspaper seeing Tom Maguire in the Parker House saloon "stand off Bob Edwards, a young Philadelphia desperado, who had killed several men. Edwards stood with his six-shooter pointed at Maguire, who showed no fear, until a policeman came in and arrested

Edwards for killing a Mexican out at the Mission. . . . In 1853," he continued, "Maguire faced Vi Turner, a desperate sport, and bitterly cursed him on the corner of Washington and Montgomery Streets. There was no back-down in Tom Maguire."[3]

Certainly, he was a man for San Francisco, and in the hurly-burly of the Gold Rush years he found congenial soil in which to root his talents. Within a year of his arrival, with the aid of "Little Em," who was said to be smart at business, he owned a piece, and perhaps more, of the Parker House, one of the city's finest gambling saloons.

In October 1850, indulging his passion for theatre and music, Maguire built in the loft above his saloon the first Jenny Lind Theatre, the one in which Von Gulpen introduced what seems to have been the first aria of Verdi sung by a professional artist in San Francisco, "Ernani, involami." When fire on 4 May 1851 destroyed this theatre, within six weeks he rebuilt the Parker House and, on its upper floor, a second Jenny Lind Theatre. Before the workmen's scaffolding was down, however, this saloon and theatre also burned to the ground. He had no acquaintance with Jenny Lind, and she never sang in San Francisco, but evidently she represented for him the ultimate in glamor and artistry. So he built a third Jenny Lind Theatre, larger, more opulent, standing on its own lot, and made of Australian sandstone rather than wood (see Appendix B.)

Yet despite appearances by such celebrities as Junius Brutus Booth and his sons Junius and Edwin, Maguire could not keep the theatre's 2,000 seats filled, and expenses continually outran receipts. Finally, making use of political friendships originating in New York, he sold the theatre for $200,000 to the City Council for use as a City Hall. The bargain caused a tremendous scandal, with charges of graft, but the sale was not upset, and by the autumn of 1852 Maguire had paid off the last of his creditors. Thereafter for several years he tended his saloon and gaming tables, recouping his fortune.

During the economic depression of 1854–56 he found a way to reenter the production of drama and music. In the spring of 1855 the owners of San Francisco Hall and of the Minstrels failed, and Maguire bought them out, though not until the autumn did he begin to advertise himself as the new owner. Nevertheless, he started at once to add a bit of variety to the minstrel shows, and his love of opera soon revealed his hand in the repertory. In midsummer the Minstrels began a series of opera burlesques, for which Maguire augmented the company with a popular singer, Mrs. Julia Gould Collins, and hired a conductor, George Loder, to improve the musical arrangements and performances. That summer, in addition to their burlesque on Italian opera based on *Ernani* and *Fra Diavolo*, the Minstrels announced *The Virginny Girl (Bohemian Girl)*, *Skin-de-Hell (Cinderella)*, *Norma*, and *Child of the Regiment*.[4]

Throughout most of 1856, however, like most persons in the theatre, Maguire kept an eye on the Vigilance Committee and acted cautiously. He had the Minstrels march in the funeral procession of James King of William "with band and muffled instruments"; he paid for the uniforms for a quasi-military volunteer company, the "Minstrel Guards"; and he donated a $300 gold watch as a prize for marksmanship. He had need of such gestures, for the sale of the third Jenny Lind Theatre to the city still raised angry charges of political corruption, and among his old Tammany friends was one, David Broderick, who, though he escaped the Committee's purges, was a leader of the Tammany politicians. Worse still for Maguire, in September 1856 he lost his temper with a bill collector, mauled the man, and, flourishing a knife, threatened to kill him if the sum due was not forgiven. Brought to court for assault, Maguire was fined $150; it was after this bad publicity that he offered to buy uniforms for the "Minstrel Guards."[5]

The next month he rebuilt his theatre (Fig. 12). The dimensions of the "opera house" when complete were: width, 55 feet; length, 137; and height, 50—still small by today's standards. The stage was 35 feet deep, with an enclosure before it, apparently at floor level, for the orchestra. On either side of the stage, before the proscenium but onstage, was a box, with another above it, all highly ornamented with gilded mouldings and drapes of red and gold. The predominant color of the auditorium was white, set off by red and gold, and from the ceiling hung a gas chandelier with twenty burners. For ventilation Maguire rejected a mechanical fan as too noisy for drama and music and relied on two

Fig. 12.   Maguire's Opera House. (The Bancroft Library, University of California, Berkeley)

windows high on each side wall. These, in an era when men drank and
smoked in the balcony and seldom washed before arriving, proved
inadequate.

The orchestra floor seated 700, and the single, deep gallery, 400.
The latter's front curved gracefully from wall to wall, and its seating,
undivided into boxes, was in continuous rows, broken only by aisles
and without columns to spoil the sight lines. At its lowest it dipped to
within ten or eleven feet above the seats beneath; but according to a
reporter for the *Bulletin*, the auditorium's appearance was "airy" and
"pleasing."[6]

There remains to be described the treatment of the drop curtain, in
these years in San Francisco often a sore subject. Indeed, even the
posters outside theatres could arouse comment. One old pioneer

turned journalist, on a saunter up Clay Street to admire the shops, stopped in astonishment before the placard of the Adelphi Theatre: "What the deuce is this, with a huge picture in front, representing boys and girls, who look just as if they couldn't help it, all painted up for war, or some sort of frolicking, rigged out with flags, and covered with gridirons. It looks mightily as if paint was plenty, and taste and art scarce."[7]

Inside the theatres, opinions of taste and art frequently focused on the drop curtains, which offered local painters their largest areas for display. The first American Theatre, which opened in October 1851, won admiration for its appointments but no specific notice of its curtain. The third American Theatre, inaugurated in March 1859, escaped censure by presenting "a fancy Italian landscape, with the ruins of a temple, some trees and shrubbery, a distant mountain and a few figures—a pretty design."[8]

The curtain of the second American, however, caused instant protest at its debut in December 1854. The critic for the *Pioneer* described it as "a sad hodge-podge, made up of a representation of the Golden Gate, a far suggestion of a clipper ship, a steamship, such as we venture to say has not its counterpart upon the surface of the Pacific, Atlantic, Indian or Frozen oceans, two pillars, and between them a melancholy Washington upon a pedestal." Adopting the view of a colleague on *Wide West*, he ascribed Washington's despondency to an ill-painted cannon that pressed on his foot. But that was merely the start of the artist's failure. "The entire painting *means* nothing," the critic lamented. "But there it is, and, if we are to judge anything from the past, there it will be, with its fellow at the Metropolitan, for the next two years—a species of chronic intermittent eyesore, visiting the community five times nightly."[9]

A year or two later the theatre's manager attempted to replace the "eyesore," but did no better. The new curtain carried business advertisements, as sometimes was done in Europe, but on its debut the audience reacted so violently, hissing, booing, and shouting, that the curtain had to be discarded. Finally, in the spring of 1859, when the theatre once again was remodeled, the management reached a truce with its public: the curtain portrayed the ruins of a Greek temple.

Evidently in these years San Franciscans wanted their curtains to bear an allegorical meaning or, at least, a classical scene.[10]

Where others had failed, Maguire and his painter for the New Opera House succeeded. The reporter for the *Bulletin* described the curtain as "a very large and fine one, [which] represents the sea-born city of Venice with its domes, towers and palaces. One of the great canals is seen in front, with barques and gondolas floating upon it. In the foreground is the marble porch of a palace, with columns and tapestries; and there are not wanting the figures of high born ladies and gallant chevaliers."[11]

This was a vision, perhaps, of how San Franciscans liked to think of themselves and the city they were building. Their city was Mediterranean in its light, air, and seascape, and also in its countryside, in the vineyards of the Napa and Sonoma valleys and in the flocks of sheep and herds of cattle grazing on the foothills of the distant mountains. More specifically, the city was Venetian in its cosmopolitan mixture of peoples and in the seaborne commerce that tied it to the great emporiums of the world. And then there were the high-born ladies and gallant chevaliers.[12]

It is a maxim of theatrical lighting that an attractive curtain, warmly lit, will rouse in a gathering audience a feeling of congeniality and anticipation, and this was especially true in the nineteenth century when going to the theatre or opera was as much a social as a cultural event. Evidently Maguire's curtain, which he advertised as an inducement to patrons, contributed to the affection that audiences soon developed for his opera house.[13]

Yet with so many of the better singers and the conductor George Loder departed for Australia, no operas other than burlesques and comedy skits were presented in San Francisco in 1857; it was a year in which walking marathons became the rage. Even so, Verdi was not entirely forgotten. From time to time the burlesque of Italian opera, with music from *Ernani,* was revived, and in midsummer the *Golden Era* found it newsworthy to report: "Verdi has made so much money by his operas that he recently bought real estate, in the vicinity of Parma, to the amount of 400,000 francs, for cash." The amount no doubt was large, but in a city only partially recovered from an economic slump, it seems to have been the "for cash" that was most notable.[14]

Meanwhile, in the spring, Maguire, accompanied by "Little Em," had traveled to New York and then on to London to see what celebrities they could lure to San Francisco. With theatrical stars they had some success, but not with singers. Throughout the winter of 1857–58, then, the opera house presented a great variety of drama, lectures, and spectacles, but of music only the Minstrels, who were joined from time to time by guests, male and female, to present the opera burlesques and comedies.

Maguire, however, increasingly was recognized as the city's most important impresario, and it became his habit to conduct his business in the street, splendidly dressed and standing usually before his opera house or in the main plaza, Portsmouth Square. One day, in the street before the opera house, he was approached by Mrs. Crabtree, the mother of Lotta M. Crabtree, who was on the threshold of becoming the country's most famous and enduring child star, singing and dancing her way into everyone's heart for the next forty years. Mrs. Crabtree suggested an engagement for Lotta at Maguire's prestigious house, which he refused, supposedly with a harsh comment on Lotta's talents. The child's doting father thereupon pulled out his revolver, fired, and grazed Maguire's arm. Maguire turned and strolled off.[15]

An event of greater importance to him occurred while he was in Europe. On 15 August 1857, the Metropolitan Theatre, the house most closely associated with opera, burned. It had fallen on hard times, but its removal, which left only the American Theatre as a major house for drama or music, was an obvious benefit to Maguire. In April 1858, therefore, he once again enlarged his opera house, this time raising the roof in order to add a second gallery, deepening the stage ten feet, and—presumably a necessary capitulation in the larger house—installing mechanical ventilating fans. When the theatre reopened, its capacity had increased from 1,100 to 1,700.[16]

The upper gallery, called "the Family Circle," had its own entrance from the street, as did the now lower gallery, "the Dress Circle." The latter was still the section of the house most favored by ladies, in part

because the downstairs lobby opened directly into Maguire's neighboring saloon, "The Snug," where Maguire's brother John presided. It
was a "reasonable-rate" saloon, selling drinks for one bit, 12½ cents,
and featuring high-quality brandy and rum, particularly a nectarinish
drink called a "Rum Shrub." Behind it were the game rooms. Before,
after, and during intermissions, male members of the audience gathered in the saloon, and some also went into the back rooms to gamble.
Like Domenico Barbaia, the great Italian impresario of the early nineteenth century who supported his opera productions at Milan and
Naples with income from the gaming tables then permitted in the
opera houses, Maguire underwrote his ventures into drama and opera
with profits from "The Snug."[17]

But Maguire, lacking singers, could not produce opera on money
alone, just as singers without money and backing—Garbato, for one—
could not. Somehow the artists and the money had to be brought
together, either by someone's intent or, on occasion, by someone's luck.
In Maguire's case there was luck.[18]

On 15 October 1858 there arrived in San Francisco an Italian tenor,
Eugenio Bianchi, and his wife, Giovanna, a soprano (Figs. 13 and 14).
They had come from Mazatlán, a Pacific port of Mexico, with six other
passengers on a very small, very slow Italian schooner, the *Giulietta*.
(The *John L. Stephens*, which docked the next day, carried 1,400 passengers and steamed from Panama in roughly half the time the schooner
had taken to sail half the distance.) The two artists landed without
advance publicity, for unlike Bishop, Hayes, or Biscaccianti, neither
Bianchi was famous or great, or destined to become so. They apparently had sung with credit both in Italy and in Mexico, where they had
met and married and where, in Mexico City on 10 January 1857, he had
sung in the local premiere of *Macbeth*. Later, in 1860–61, they would
have a great success in Australia, but except for that venture across
the Pacific, once arrived in San Francisco they made their careers
there, much honored in the city but with reputations extending little
beyond it.[19]

Onstage they both lacked somewhat in presence; he appeared
"sturdy and rather fussy," and she, "stout." He was "somewhat clumsy"

Fig. 13.   Eugenio Bianchi. (SF Performing Arts Library)

Fig. 14. Giovanna Bianchi. (SF Performing Arts Library)

in his stage movements, and so was she. His voice, however, was exceptionally warm, pure, and sympathetic, and the critic for the *Alta California*, having attended a rehearsal before the first concert, announced in anticipation that Bianchi was "the finest tenor we have ever yet heard in California." Her voice, apparently, was less appealing: according to one critic, she had a "gushing style of doing things, and she takes the eyes if not the ears by storm."[20] Yet it seems she was at least adequate vocally, and better as an actress; and with Maguire's backing the couple instantly revived the city's appetite for opera, repeating the steps toward staged productions taken by their predecessors, but now more quickly. In six months they were presenting operas fully costumed and staged, with a well-rehearsed company, enlarged orchestra, and conductor.

They introduced themselves to the city in the usual way, with a concert, but aided by Maguire were able to enlist in support forces larger and more sophisticated than those the Pellegrinis had been able to muster in 1851. Now instead of an orchestra of ten or twelve, there was one of twenty or even twenty-five; and instead of the first violinist conducting from his chair and, most likely, being unused to directing singers, there was an experienced conductor, Rudolph Herold, who was familiar with the hired orchestra. Further, though the Bianchis were unknown, they were the first operatic artists of any quality to appear in the city in two years, and to greet them on the evening of 23 October, only eight days after they landed, an eager audience jammed the house. The next morning the *Alta California* reviewed the performance at length, incidentally having much to say about Verdi.

OPERATIC CONCERT—The introduction of the new aspirants to public favor, Signor and Signora Bianchi, at Maguire's Opera House, last evening, must have been gratifying in the highest degree to the performers themselves. The audience was in the highest degree select and numerous, and the demonstrations of applause decided and by no means stinted in respect to quantity. The programme of the evening was made up almost exclusively of that high florid style of music peculiarly characteristic of the modern school—a style which, for the time it is calculated to display and exert the voice to its utmost capacities, is pretty certain to work retribution in the end, by cracking or breaking it. Verdi commenced the programme, and Verdi ended it. He came in with the Trovatore and went out with I Lombardi, about two as complete specimens of musical acrobatism as ever were written. However, after all, it will not do to speak disparagingly of this professor of the spasmodic Italian style, for, in reality, he is the only composer of the age. Not but that Rossini, Meyerbeer, Balfe and others, are living, but they are not writing, and Verdi is the only industrious, enthusiastic student of his art of the day—regularly bringing forth his operatic conceptions each year, and continually adding fresh stores to the repertoire of Europe. We do not think it was necessary, last evening, that the dish of melody served up should have been so exclusively sauced from the Verdi caster. It is, beyond a doubt, the popular, or at least the fashionable style of music of the day, but it requires too much action. Signora Bianchi, who has naturally a fine soprano voice, had to exert herself too much. She labored to please her audience, and certainly succeeded to her heart's content, at least if tumultuous applause be any symptom of approval. Notwithstanding this, however, it is almost impossible to found a positive opinion as to her powers. Hereafter, something of the older masters will test the matter sufficiently—something of Mozart, or of Van Webber [sic], or of Rossini. Signor Bianchi is certainly the finest tenor we have ever had in the state. His voice is agreeable and clear, and remarkably sympathetic. All who have heard [Lorenzo] Salvi, the greatest tenor that ever visited America, can at once perceive marked resemblances in that silvery lightness of tone so eminently possessed by Signor Bianchi. Mr. Koppits, during part 1st, played one of his delightful flute solos—a fantasie on theses from La Fille du Regiment. It was an exquisite piece of instrumentation and his unequalled modulations and trills excited warm plaudits. We cannot conclude without a tribute to the excellence of the orchestra, under the leadership of Mr. Herrold [sic]. It is so long since we have had any musical treat of this kind, that it was doubly grateful. The force was composed of the old Germania, long so popular in this city; and a couple of light, brilliant overtures added much to the general enjoyment.[21]

With such a review, and with an audience storming the doors for more such concerts, Maguire negotiated a long-term contract with the Bianchis, fitting them into his schedule wherever he could. Starting with their third concert, moreover, he presented them in costume, with "scenic effects"; he hired a chorus; and he enlarged the orchestra, the Minstrels' band joining the "old Germania," thus swelling the number of players, in all likelihood, to well over thirty. Not since the days of Bishop and Bochsa's *Freischütz* had the city heard such a glorious sound.[22] Yet "Notwithstanding the immense outlay," he promised, "Prices will NOT be raised!" And true to his word, he kept them at $1 for the orchestra, parquet, and boxes, 50 cents for the dress circle, and 25 cents for the top gallery—the lowest prices yet charged in the city for opera. Happily, considering the crowded houses, he recently had installed six new ventilators in the outer walls between the dress circle and upper gallery, and as the *Alta California* reported, "The air in the space between these two tiers is now kept constantly fresh and pure."[23]

The opening program was so successful, presenting four arias, a duet, and a trio from six Verdi operas,[24] that the Bianchis apparently did not change it until the third concert—the first with costumes, chorus, and enlarged orchestra—for which occasion they apparently programmed selections from *Lucia di Lammermoor* and *Lucrezia Borgia*, by Donizetti, and from *Trovatore*.[25] At the sixth concert, on 11 November, they again changed the program, singing one aria by Donizetti and four numbers of Verdi. She sang an aria from "Verdi's new opera" *Luisa Miller*, which, because not discussed by the critics, cannot be identified. He sang a "Grand Aria" for tenor and chorus from *Attila*, almost surely the tenor's cavatina "Ella in poter del barbaro!" Together they sang the "Grand Duo" from *Rigoletto*, "Signor ne Principe"—possibly the first music of this opera to be heard in the city. Then, with a local French bass-baritone and the chorus, they closed with the final act of *Ernani* entire.[26]

On 18 November, for their eighth concert, they changed the program again, and along with some arias by Donizetti presented the audience with what seems to have been a local premiere, some music from *La traviata*. He sang a "Cavatina," most likely "De' miei bollenti spiriti," and together, as their finale, they offered a "Duo," probably "Parigi, o cara," which they repeated three nights later. On neither occasion, alas, did the critics discuss the music.[27]

In other programs they sang still more Verdi. In their first and tenth concerts they had presented a "Grand Duo" from *I masnadieri*, surely "T'abbraccio, o Carlo" and apparently the first of this opera's music to be heard in the city. Then in the fourteenth concert, on 9 December, he and the chorus for the first time offered the opera's opening scene, "O mio castel paterno." Again, though, the critics are silent about the music.[28]

Meanwhile, in addition to a repetition of his cavatina with chorus from *Attila,* they added a duet from that opera, "Sì, quell'io son, ravvisami," and closed their concert of 26 November with Acts III and IV of *Ernani*—half that opera. Two days later, with a different program, they presented from *Trovatore* the Miserere and all of Act II, scene 1, including the Anvil Chorus; and then, in their final two concerts, besides selections from *I masnadieri,* they sang the entire first and third acts of Bellini's *Norma.*[29]

In all, in a period of fifty-eight days they gave sixteen concerts, fourteen of them in costume with some sort of minimal scenery, and of these at least half included complete scenes or acts of operas. As the critic for the *Alta California* exclaimed in delight and astonishment, the programs had proved "vastly popular" and drew the largest crowds "ever seen in the opera house." The 1,700-seat theatre apparently was never less than sold out; thus, by rough estimate, at the end of the Bianchis' "season" some 27,000 tickets had been sold for opera, in a city of about 45,000![30]

If the Bianchis were exhausted, they were allowed only a short respite, for Maguire had booked them on a tour, starting in Sacramento, where he controlled the two big theatres and where the state legislature would be in session in January. On the sixth of that month at the Forrest Theatre, "the largest and most fashionable audience of the season" heard an "operatic entertainment" that "was one of the most brilliant and successful ever given by the Bianchi." Presumably in the spring, on the Bianchis' return to San Francisco, the city once again, after a break of almost four years, would have fully staged productions of operas, with Verdi the favored composer.[31]

NINE

Il trovatore Premiered;
Ernani Revived

In April 1859, when the Bianchis had returned from their tour and started rehearsals for an opera season in May, Maguire repainted the interior of his opera house, covering the ceiling with cupids and angels, the front of the dress circle "with highly colored flowers and birds," and adding over the proscenium arch "the Chariot of Phoebus, and above that the Heraldic Eagle, with flags and general national trophy." Whatever the intended meaning of the symbols, they also signified that Maguire's alternation of minstrels, drama, comedy, and opera had found favor in the city and he had prospered. The refurbishing, he proclaimed in advertisements, was done "in the rich and glorious style of the reign of Louis XV."[1]

Two weeks later and after several days of anticipatory news stories, the Bianchis announced for the opening night of their season, 5 May, their first staged production of an entire opera, *Il trovatore*. The orchestra, they promised, would be "large and carefully selected," the costumes and scenery new, the chorus "full and efficient," and the opera played "without cutting."[2] In fact, as reviews later revealed, they skimped on the chorus and made large cuts. Nevertheless, on 5 May 1859, at Maguire's Opera House, was presented the local premiere of the opera that quickly became San Francisco's favorite for the next fifty years. Because of their own and Garbato's missionary work much of the music was familiar to audiences, and they were able to sell ten performances to full houses, six within the fortnight at Maguire's, three more in July at the larger American Theatre (cap. 2,000), and one, again at the American, in September. Meanwhile, in May they also produced *Ernani* at Maguire's, and in August, at the American, the local premieres of *La traviata* and *Attila*.

Throughout this parade of performances the newspaper critics seldom have much to say of Verdi's music, yet two of them occasionally make interesting comments, and though they never sign their reports, they soon begin to display individual sensibilities, frequently stressing different aspects of what they see and hear. Possibly the critic for the *Bulletin* was James Nisbet, a Scot, the paper's supervising editor and reputedly in charge of its news and literary departments. He also supposedly wrote the theatrical notices, but inasmuch as nothing yet discovered ties him to the music reviews, it seems better to consider their author still unknown, as is the critic for the *Alta California*.[3]

Certainly, given the social customs of the time and the city's peculiar demography, both journalists were men; and, happily, both were knowledgeable about opera. One, the critic for the *Alta California*, is an enthusiast, who sometimes in his excitement for an artist or the music loses his footing. He was the one so taken by Garbato's smile. The other, on the *Bulletin*, writes for a paper devoted almost entirely to political and economic news, and sometimes his pieces have about them an air of assignment: he enjoys music, but his chief interest is elsewhere. If he can obtain the libretto of an opera before its premiere, he will publish a synopsis of it; and he will attend the first performance, but seldom the second, or third, and, unlike his colleague, never a rehearsal. He writes with precision—and with buckets of cold water nearby to douse unwarranted enthusiasm.

The critic of the *Alta California*, in contrast, writes with the wide swings of praise and condemnation that often bespeak the passionately engaged, and, loving opera, he is constantly in the opera house. True to character, he attended the first four performances of *Trovatore* and reviewed each, revising his opinions slightly as he saw and heard the familiar concert excerpts now set in context and acted as well as sung. Following the premiere, he declared:

> The general verdict of the times is that Il Trovatore is the finest of all of Verdi's operas. The treatment of the subject is much more comprehensive than that which he has bestowed on any of his other works. More study has been devoted to making the principal parts distinctive, and a greater number of such characters throng the opera than usual. . . . The leading business of the opera is done by Manrico, the Trovatore. All of the finest melodies of the piece are written for this part.[4]

Today, surely, many opera lovers would dispute that all the best melodies are given to the tenor, the Troubadour, and the critic himself soon modified his conclusion. Nevertheless, it is notable that what struck him most powerfully on first sight and hearing of a staged production of the opera was the music for the title role. Possibly he inclined to that view because of the impact of Bianchi's voice, the best in the cast, or because some of the mezzo-soprano's part had been cut, but whatever his reasons, he probably stated the reaction of most people coming to the opera for the first time, when it was fresh and new. Today, when it has the stale familiarity of a classic, audiences are trained, perhaps over-trained, by critics and teachers to focus their attention and praise on the music for the mezzo-soprano, the gypsy Azucena, in part because, allegedly more than the tenor's, it bears in its fluidity and responsiveness to her thoughts the seeds of Verdi's future style. Yet despite Verdi's predominant interest in the gypsy's character and conflicting passions, frankly declared in a letter to his librettist,[5] he gave to the tenor not only the opera's title, but also more songs and arias than any other character received, a prominent part in the finales of all four acts, and the only solo aria to close an act. It is not surprising, therefore, that throughout the nineteenth century most of the melodies that went into barrel organs and music boxes, with the exception of the Anvil Chorus, were the tenor's; and of them perhaps the most popular was his cry of despair from the prison tower, during the Miserere, "Ah, che la morte" ("How slow is death in coming to one who wants to die; Leonora, farewell!"). Verdi, of course, cannot have known how audiences today would see and hear *Il trovatore,* particularly those acquainted with his later operas, but he seems to have gauged correctly how his contemporaries would view it.

After the opera's second night the critic chose to praise as "the gem of the evening" the duet for Azucena and Manrico in the final scene. Mother and son are in the tower, awaiting execution, and as the duet's climax Azucena, recalling their happiness in earlier times, sings, "Ai nostri monti" ("Home to our mountains, let us return"), joined in the closing bars by Manrico. A yearning for "the old home" presumably had meaning for many in San Francisco, and with this second performance, according to the critic, the audience began to respond to Azucena and her music.[6]

In this review the critic also pointed out that Maguire had begun to alternate the Minstrels with the Bianchis: "African one night; Italian, the next.... Those who wish to compare the two classes of opera—the foreign and the domestic—have a good opportunity now."

Following his third exposure to the opera, he wrote of the evenness of Verdi's inspiration. "There is such a profuse sprinkling of operatic gems all through the four acts, something handsome being appropriated to each performer, that the ear of the listener is charmed with a succession of pleasant things."[7]

Only after the fourth performance did he begin to criticize the artists. The chorus, which had no women and probably only eight men, in particular drew his fire. It "was merely passable on the first night and ever since has been deteriorating rapidly." The trouble was "sheer carelessness"; the "Anvil Chorus of last evening was execrable," and the other choruses "lacked spirit and unity, which is the more inexcusable as the duties of this branch are quite light." In his anger at the chorus he may have underestimated the weight of its duties; in *Trovatore* it has an important role, not altogether easy to sing.[8]

The critic for the *Bulletin* reviewed only the first performance, but he wrote, most unusually for him, almost two-thirds of a column, perhaps in part because this was the city's first fully staged production of a serious opera in almost four years. In the course of what he had to say he reveals much about the production of an opera in San

Francisco in 1859, as well as a bit about the social customs of the day. For instance, he comments, "The theatre was densely crowded; and much of the parquette was filled with ladies, who could not obtain seats in the dress circle." It seems that, as a result of the gradual improvement in the audience's behavior, in part because of the numbering of seats and because of gas replacing candles in the auditorium's chandelier so that there was no longer the hazard of dripping wax, respectable women and their escorts were beginning to take seats on the parquet or orchestra floor; and the overflow of ladies from the dress circle to the parquet at the premiere of *Trovatore* signals the slow rise in respectability, and price, of what used to be "the pit."⁹

On the difficulties of casting an opera in San Francisco, with plain reference to this premiere he remarked: "Italian opera here has many disadvantages to contend against. Generally speaking, it is impossible to muster a chorus of female voices; then, the chorus of male voices is German, while the principal solo singers are Italian, French, German, Spanish, or English, as the good fortune of the time may have it, and all are mingled together in the same piece." In fact, this first *Trovatore* lacked a women's chorus, had a men's chorus of Germans, numbering apparently only eight, and a cast in which the tenor and soprano were Italian, the mezzo-soprano and bass, French, as was also the conductor, and the baritone was English. (And as evidence that Italian opera was not yet an American tradition, note that the critic does not include Americans among the potential soloists.)

The orchestra, too, was a problem: "[Though many] players in this city are indeed excellent musicians, they seldom perform in large numbers together, and from want of constant practice, cannot give that nicety and completeness of harmonious action" achieved by orchestras "in the great cities of Europe and the United States." But in San Francisco, he observed, audiences were content with less. "A very hungry man is not fastidious as to the character of the victuals that satisfy his appetite."

Unlike his colleague on the *Alta California*, the *Bulletin* critic considered that the soprano had "the great work of the piece," evidently the Miserere, which Signora Bianchi had performed "effectively," though "her voice is not the most soft and sympathetic." The opera's final scene, however, impressed him still more, especially the contrasting vocal lines of the trio as the dying Leonora urges Manrico to escape, even as he mistakenly berates her for betraying him, while beside them Azucena "dreams on her restless couch of her mountain home and the olden joys that will never, never again return." Stirred by the character and portrayal of Azucena, he quoted in his review a stanza of her song in Italian and then translated it into English.

The opera's music no doubt was the chief cause of its success, but surely also partly responsible were its visual images, now offered to the city for the first time. These, at their simplest, portray a campfire in the mountains, a setting familiar to every miner, and, at their most romantic, a tableau of a bride left at the church door (if Verdi's stage directions are followed) as the groom and his men rush off to save his mother: "I was her son before I loved you."

In addition, there are some scenes that can be grasped fully only if staged. For example, the trio in the final scene that so moved the critic for the *Bulletin* presents a confused, exhausted Azucena, heedless of the soprano close by who is sinking to the floor in death while the tenor hurls at her his charge of betrayal. The unnatural disjunction of Azucena from the passionate drama taking place beside her must be seen; a singer's voice or position on the concert stage, even a turned back, will not convey it. Similarly, an audience must see the soprano become prone—Verdi's word—in the horizontal position that everyone instinctively recognizes as a sign of death, even as the tenor behind her stands vertical, the position of life. Sung as a concert excerpt, with the soprano and tenor side by side, and both upright, the trio cannot stir as deep a response as it may in a theatre.

About some other aspects of the production, however, the reviewer for the *Bulletin* was not so happy. Bianchi's Manrico "was nothing as a piece of acting," though his singing was "very fine"; and the "wooden-jointed" Germans parading about as soldiers at the start of Act III were simply "ludicrous."

We may add, that the costumes, scenery and stage appointments generally, were of a magnificent description; and having done so . . . we think that a few critical, if not disparaging remarks, may be ventured upon. We must protest against that horrid bell introduced in the first scene and again in the Miserere. Surely an instrument of purer and clearer tone can be found. . . . And *apropos* of bells, an improvement would be effected by dispensing with the cow-bell used to signal the orchestra into their places, preparatory to calling up the curtain. The ordinary stage bell . . . would answer the purpose quite as well. Then for Heaven's sake, let the property-man remove the trade-labels from the anvils.

Even the clothing of the orchestra members was noted, and judged. Apparently the men usually wore whatever they pleased, but for this premiere, exhibiting "good taste," they had made an effort: "All had on white vests—except one grim old Frenchman" who in place of "his dingy waistcoat" might better have substituted "a reasonably clean white shirt."

Finally, turning his eye on the audience, the critic observed that "a large proportion" of it was composed of "foreigners—Italians, Frenchmen, Germans, etc." who "listened with proper decorum." Unfortunately, there were others, presumably many of them Americans, who "attend the opera merely for the purpose of seeing and being seen," who talked and whispered through much of the music, and whose "ill-timed applause was permitted in several instances to lose us the best effect of some of the gems of the evening."

There are some traditions of audience reaction to *Il trovatore* that, though arguments based on them are exceedingly tenuous, may hint at the nationalities of the two critics. Because of the political situation in Italy in this decade, when the Italians, led by Cavour and Garibaldi, were seeking ways to oust the Austrian armies of occupation, Italian audiences found patriotic allusions in Manrico's music. Prime Minister Cavour, for example, though reputedly a monotone, was said to have memorized a stanza of Manrico's most famous aria, "Di quella pira" ("From this fire"), which the tenor sings on hearing that his mother— for whom Italians understood Italy—was about to be burned at the stake. "Unfortunate mother," he cries, "I hasten to save you, or at least to die with you." And when Cavour learned that the Austrians had fallen into his diplomatic trap and attacked the Italians, drawing France into the war on the Italian side, reportedly in his excitement and pleasure he droned, "Di quella pira," meaning "From this fire" Italians will make a free and independent Italy.[10]

The critic for the *Alta California,* who at the premiere of *Trovatore* thought Manrico had all the best tunes, was sensitive to these patriotic allusions, more so than the writer for the *Bulletin,* as will be apparent in the two men's remarks on *Attila.* He also, unlike his colleague, apparently spoke Italian, did not mind obstreperous applause, responded strongly to the lead singers, and remarked only rarely, this instance notwithstanding, on the quality of the chorus and of the orchestra. It would be too much to assume that he was an Italian immigrant to the city, but he approached opera with an Italian sensibility.

The man on the *Bulletin,* conversely, seems Anglo-Saxon or Teutonic in background, and here *Trovatore* supposedly provide a distinction. According to some singers, English audiences, with their tradition of support for the underdog, respond most warmly to Azucena when, chained and condemned by the baritone to burn at the stake, she furiously turns on him, warning of God's anger. The Germans, on the other hand, with their extraordinary respect for unsatisfied longing, or *Sehnsucht,* expressed in literature as well as song, are said to be most moved by her yearning to return with Manrico to the mountains, those mountains that are home and to which they "will never, never again return." The critic did not mention the first aria—possibly it was cut—but waxed rhapsodic over the second. Whether or not he was a German, his response to opera seems more Germanic than Italian, and perhaps more Germanic than English.[11]

To follow the six performances of *Trovatore* the Bianchis had scheduled five of *Ernani* (Fig. 15), but the first two were canceled because of the baritone's illness. The last also was dropped, possibly for the same reason. The artist, Stephen W. Leach, had sung Di Luna without impressing either critic, perhaps because already ill, and he did no better with Don Carlo in the two performances of *Ernani*—although on opening night the finale to Act III, for baritone and chorus, as usual "was vehemently applauded and had to be repeated."[12]

The opera by now was an old favorite, and the critic for the *Alta*

California, lamenting the canceled performances, stated baldly in his review of the second and last, "No opera has acquired a greater degree of popularity than this superb composition of Verdi; and . . . there is no perceptible diminution in the interest and delight it affords to all lovers of music."[13]

The man at the *Bulletin,* in reviewing the first night of *Ernani,* wrote mostly about the chorus or its absence.

> A large portion of the music is so beautiful that even indifferently rendered it is sure to please. The want of a female chorus is still more felt here than in the case of Il Trovatore. The eight German male voices that form the chorus are powerful enough for the small house [cap. 1,700], but they are coarse; and the audience long in vain for the variety and sweetness of the proper swell of female voices. As it is, there is a monotony and harshness in the chorus that is very, very far from giving one a true idea of *Italian* opera. We trust that the new English Opera troupe [which had announced a season of opera] will bear this in mind, and at whatever cost, contrive to produce at least half-a dozen female choiristers in their pieces. The Barili-Thorn troupe of 1854–55 managed to bring out that moderate number. The opening drinking number [the bandits' chorus, which was very popular during these decades] . . . and the celebrated closing scene and chorus of the 3rd act . . . were very fairly executed. The last produced an *encore.* The portion of the trio of the second Act, sung by Signor and Signora Bianchi, "La vendetta piu tremenda," was given with great spirit, which at once ensured a senseless repetition of the passage. Signora Bianchi, if she does not deeply move the musical sensibilities of her audience, has a faculty of uttering occasionally some passionate shrieks and noises that much affect the enthusiastic.[14]

After this second performance of *Ernani,* on 20 May, the Bianchis abruptly closed their "season" of Italian opera, and for reasons not entirely clear. The critic for the *Alta California* reported that they wanted more time to rehearse their next season, which would be given at the American Theatre starting in late June, and possibly would include productions of *Lucrezia Borgia, Linda di Chamounix,* and *Semiramide.* But in June Maguire sued Bianchi to recover some operatic scores, and the litigation revealed that a final break between the two men had occurred as early as 23 May. Maguire pursued his claim in a

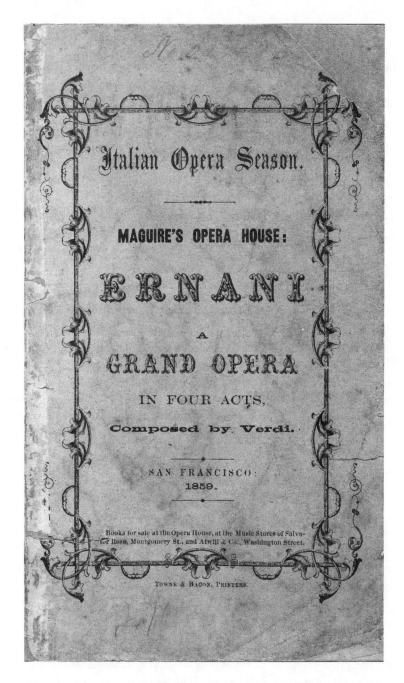

Fig. 15. A libretto for the Bianchis' opening season at Maguire's Opera House, containing a synopsis of the opera and its text in English. Performances were on 19 and 20 May 1859. (The Bancroft Library, University of California, Berkeley)

leisurely fashion, allowing Bianchi to use the scores while the suit continued, but the legal action, which seems ultimately to have been settled out of court, suggests on both sides a large failure of trust and sympathy.[15]

Maguire, like Sinclair before him, sought to vary serious Italian opera with lighter English opera and English versions of French and Italian comedies and romances, and to that end he had brought to the city—or perhaps merely was blessed by chance a second time—a troupe of five singers, a conductor, and a manager who called themselves the New Orleans English Opera Troupe. They arrived in the midst of the Bianchis' season, and immediately Maguire put the new artists into rehearsal with a chorus and orchestra, no doubt raiding those that were already singing and playing for the Bianchis. And it seems likely that disputes arose between the groups over dates of performance and hours for rehearsal, with Maguire backing the newcomers.

He presented them for the first time at his opera house on 27 May, in an English version of *La sonnambula*. The performance, supposedly because of the soloists' opening-night nerves, came close to disaster, and the audience's reception was "harsh and ungentlemanly."[16] A second performance, however, went better, and with a production of Rossini's *Barber of Seville* the company had such a success that the critic for the *Alta California* quite forgot his attachment to Verdi (or perhaps that day a substitute wrote for him).

> Recently we have been so deluged with music of the modern Italian school that this introduction to the cheering, sparkling genius of the greatest of living composers was particularly refreshing. Compared with the astonishing *"embarrass des richesse"* of the score of this opera . . .—compared with all this, we ask, how poverty-stricken, attenuated and dull are the Trovatores, the Traviatas and all else pertaining to that dismal and spasmodic composer M. Verdi![17]

Throughout June the English Opera Troupe, changing its opera almost nightly, played a repertory reminiscent of Anna Thillon's in 1854: Balfe's *Bohemian Girl*, Auber's *Crown Diamonds* and *Fra Diavolo*,

Donizetti's *Don Pasquale*, and Rossini's *Cinderella*, "with excerpts from *William Tell* and *Mosè in Egitto* etc." Besides giving the operas in English and sometimes in curious versions, the Troupe frequently cast its slim-figured contralto, Georgia Hodson, in the tenor roles, such as Almaviva in the *Barber* and Thaddeus in the *Bohemian Girl.* Yet despite the odd casting—in those days not so unusual as it would be now—the audiences evidently were responsive and the houses full, if perhaps not quite so crowded as in May for the Bianchis.

The latter, meanwhile, continuing to rehearse for their season at the American Theatre and having broken with Maguire, had begun to act as their own producers. In a quarrel with their mezzo-soprano, Mme Jenny Feret, they lost both her and her husband, Mons. [Ferdinand?] Feret, who had conducted *Trovatore* and *Ernani.*[18] Yet they managed to find replacements and to open at the American on 27 June with Donizetti's *Lucrezia Borgia,* enjoying a great success, in part because they had increased the chorus of men and women's voices to eighteen. Not since the days of Bishop and Bochsa's *Robert le diable* and *Der Freischütz* had the city heard such a large mixed chorus in opera, or, reportedly, one so mellifluous. The critic for the *Bulletin* observed: "[It] seems to be composed of Frenchmen and Italians. Their voices are clearer, sweeter and more harmonious, and their action more graceful and spirited than are those of the German chorus to which of late the public have been accustomed."[19]

The Bianchis' "season," which ran through 18 July, included five performances of *Lucrezia Borgia,* four of *Norma,* a benefit night with selections from *Norma, Ernani,* and *Attila,* and, as their final opera, three performances of *Trovatore,* which showed no sign of losing its appeal. On opening night it "drew a crowded and fashionable audience," which demanded and received repetitions of popular numbers.[20]

Then, as if in response to the challenge of the Bianchis' independence, Maguire, on the evening following their final performance of *Trovatore,* brought back his English Opera Troupe from a two-week season in Sacramento and reintroduced them to San Francisco with a *Trovatore* sung in English.[21] The next morning's review in the *Alta California* reveals that the Bianchis in their production, besides skipping the chorus of nuns, or perhaps giving it to the men to sing, had made other large cuts. "We are pleased to observe," purred the critic, "that the duettino at the end of the third act, between Leonora and Manrico, and the duet between Azucena and Manrico, in the second act, omitted in the Italian opera were given in full."[22]

The first is the short section, twenty-two bars between the tenor's arias "Ah si, ben mio" and "Di quella pira," in which Leonora and Manrico, moving slowly toward the chapel in which they are about to be married, sing of their love. The second, "Mal reggendo," is Manrico's account of his hesitation to kill the baritone, Di Luna, and Azucena's pressing him never again to fail in this aim. The first, though the opera's only love duet, is musically perhaps a small matter; the second—most likely cut because of the loss of the experienced mezzo-soprano—is one of the opera's most impressive duets.

The most startling aspect of the Troupe's production, however, was that the contralto Georgia Hodson sang Manrico, a role that, in its vigor and forcefulness, was far more "heroic" than the other tenor parts she had taken. Yet such casting apparently was customary, for during the Troupe's tour of the East in 1858 Hodson had sung Manrico in Charleston, S.C., Memphis, and Chicago, and probably in many other cities unrecorded. But she took San Francisco by surprise. "Miss Hodson astonished us in Manrico," exclaimed the *Alta California* critic. "That a lady should sing this music at all is wonderful, but to sing as Miss Hodson does, in the original keys, and precisely as a man is 'passing strange.'"[23] On the whole he liked the performance, yet he had nothing to say about hearing it in English; and though the production apparently was a success, the English Troupe did not repeat it but went back to their previous repertory, adding to it *The Daughter of the Regiment, Der Freischütz* (in English), *The Beggar's Opera*, Boieldieu's *John of Paris*, and Bishop's *Rob Roy*, a pastiche of Scottish numbers.

The success of *Il trovatore* in San Francisco during that summer of 1859 was extraordinary, a phenomenon. In July a visiting Spanish drama company even hurried onto the stage a performance of the underlying play by Antonio García Gutiérrez, *El trovador* (1836).[24] And in September the Bianchis, as part of a "farewell" season of benefits, revived the opera once again. In all, it had eleven performances in five months, selling roughly 20,000 tickets to a population of about 55,000. Just as 1854 was the year when every theatergoer in the city saw a dramatization of *Uncle Tom's Cabin*, so 1859 was the year when every music-lover went to *Il trovatore*, some two, three, or four times. No other Verdi opera in its first season, not even *Ernani*, had enjoyed such a success in San Francisco, and none in the future, not even *Aida* in 1877, would match it. Curiously, the one to come closest was not *La traviata* in 1859 or *Rigoletto* in 1860 but, in 1865, *Ballo in maschera*.

There can be no exact explanation of why the people of a city take one opera to heart and not another. Parisians, for instance, in the second half of the nineteenth century clearly developed a special fondness for *La traviata*. In that case, of course, some reasons are obvious. Not only is the opera set in Paris, but the underlying book and play are French and deeply imbued with French culture. Violetta and her circle, the *demi-monde* of kept women, in many cities and countries had no counterpart. She and her story could exist only in Paris, and Parisians, on going to *Traviata*, recognized their own world.

In much the same way, perhaps, San Franciscans, until after the great fire and earthquake of 1906, saw themselves in *Il trovatore*. In Europe in the mid–nineteenth century, Spain, the opera's locale, was a remote country, not yet touched by the industrial revolution, and artists of the romantic age often used it as a setting because the emotions of the people were thought to be undiminished by the civilization of cities; the emotions were larger, purer, more violent and varied, and more openly expressed. This surely is the reason that Victor Hugo and Prosper Mérimée turned to Spain for their settings of *Hernani* and *Carmen* and why Verdi and Bizet were drawn to those works. In turning Gutiérrez's already flamboyant play into an opera, Verdi enlarged the emotions still further, expressing them in extravagant sounds and exciting rhythms. The opera in its masculine tone, its violence, its nostalgia, its inherent melancholy, and its exalted portrayal of the hero and heroine all fit San Francisco as it was in 1859, and as its people continued to think of themselves for the next forty years. In every decade until 1900 *Il trovatore* was usually on the boards eight or nine of the ten years, and only once, because of cancellations, as few as seven. It was by far the most frequently performed of all operas, not only of Verdi but of any composer, of any nationality.[25] It suited the city, and San Franciscans took it for their own.

TEN

The Bianchis Produce
La traviata and *Attila*

By mid-July 1859, when the New Orleans English Opera Troupe returned from a short season in Sacramento, the quarrel between Maguire and the Bianchis evidently had hardened into a permanent break, for when Maguire gave himself a benefit at his opera house, on 22 July, the Bianchis, though in San Francisco, were not on the program. Whether the decision was theirs or Maguire's, an easy chance for reconciliation was not taken. The Bianchis continued their new alliance with the American Theatre, and Maguire again presented the Troupe at his opera house, where until mid-August it delighted the public by performing almost every night a different opera, usually an English work or one in an English version. Then, after a short rest, it again departed for "the interior."[1]

For the Bianchis, one result of their break with Maguire was that they were shut out of touring: he controlled the chief theatres in Sacramento and in several smaller towns. Nevertheless, they were able to use the periods between their "seasons," always scheduled for the Troupe's absence, to rehearse whatever new works they planned. On 6 August, then, a news item in the *Alta California* reported as the likely selections for their "second" season at the American Donizetti's *La favorita* and Verdi's *La traviata, Attila,* and *Macbeth*—an ambitious program, for all three Verdi operas would be local premieres, new to the chorus, orchestra, and secondary soloists as well as to the public.[2]

In this decade the gap between so-called serious and light opera was widening as the division in repertory between companies who sang predominantly Italian or German opera as opposed to English slowly increased. Both Anna Bishop and the Barili-Thorn troupe had been more "serious" than Anna Thillon in their choice of operas and fidelity to the scores, and between the Bianchis and the English Troupe the differences became still more marked. The English operas and versions of operas, the latter usually by Henry Bishop or Rophino Lacy, had much spoken dialogue, and the music often was composed or rearranged to be incidental to the play. A work's crucial scenes, even its climax, for instance, would be spoken, not sung. John Pepusch's *Beggar's Opera* was one model, and in Bishop's version of Mozart's *Marriage of Figaro*, for example, neither the Count, the Countess, nor Figaro sang, whereas the slightly inebriated gardener, a tiny part in Mozart, was allowed several interpolated popular songs.[3] Obviously, such operas or versions depended greatly for success on the personalities of the leading singers or actors, and, because demanding so much less musically of the chorus, orchestra, and singers, they were much more easily alternated, or hastily substituted, than the operas of Verdi, Donizetti, or Bellini.

In addition, Italian composers, with Verdi their leader (Fig. 16), were writing increasingly complicated scores. In Verdi's case, the operas grew longer, their musical ideas were more subtly worked out, and the orchestration became more sophisticated. Not only did he begin to use new and unusual instruments—in *Macbeth*, to obtain hollow or eerie sounds, he called for an English horn, bass clarinet, and a contrabassoon, the last a rarity in opera orchestras—but also in this era the instruments themselves, such as the flute and clarinet, had their mechanisms improved, making possible more notes and more difficult passages. Further, with experience, Verdi continually made better use of the instruments. In *Attila* (1846), in the overture and in the introduction to the soprano's aria, Act I, he for the first time writes passages for strings that suggest the intensity he developed further in *La traviata*

Fig. 16.   Verdi in 1859.

(1853), *La forza del destino* (1862), and *Aida* (1871). In *Macbeth* (1847), following the discovery of the murder of King Duncan, he has twenty-
seven bars of hushed singing for six soloists and chorus accompanied
only by timpani, which provide the rhythmic motif on which the
singers proceed; and in the Sleepwalking scene he scores an accompaniment for English horn and clarinet that requires flawless precision.
Without rehearsal neither scene will come off, and the Bianchis, to

present a season of three or four contemporary Italian operas, probably had to rehearse as much as or more than did the English Troupe to present a season of ten or twelve of its sort of opera.

For an American impresario, therefore, Italian opera, always a risky venture compared to English, was becoming more so, for if one Italian production failed at the box office, a large investment of time and money was lost, whereas if an English opera or version did not succeed, it could be swept instantly from the boards and a new one offered the next night. Maguire, no doubt, was eager to present Italian opera; it was musically more interesting, it had the greater prestige. But as a gambler he must have recognized that between the Bianchis and the English Troupe, the latter was the safer bet.

On 6 August, the *Alta California* reported that the Bianchis had *Traviata* and *Attila* ready and *Favorita* and *Macbeth* "in a forward state." Then, five days later, it announced that the Bianchis would open their season on 13 August with *Traviata,* "an opera founded on a plot similar to Camille. The music," it continued, "is exceedingly brilliant, being of a lighter character than most of this composer's works, and it abounds in a host of gems, which will soon become popular."[4]

The reference to the opera's underlying play, *La Dame aux camélias* (1852), known in the United States as *Camille,* was not a bit of pedantry. The city in the past four years had seen at least six productions of it, most of them opening to heated discussions of the play's morality. Should audiences of respectable men and women weep for the death of a prostitute, however great her self-sacrifice? Was death not the just penalty for her sin? The *Bulletin* continually attacked the play, scolded any actress who performed it, and, by uniting American Puritans with Scottish Presbyterians and Calvinists, might have managed to ban it if the city's French, German, and Italian immigrants had not been so numerous.

The *Bulletin,* however, voiced a view widely held, and with a single exception all the productions that played in San Francisco in this decade prettified the plot. The first to arrive, starring Jean Davenport, changed the heroine from a kept woman, a courtesan, to a coquette, allowing audiences to weep for the death of a woman who had taken only a single, retrievable step toward damnation. The French Society of San Francisco, scorning American prudery, produced the play as Alexandre Dumas, *fils,* had written it, but all American stagings in some degree continued to mute the plot and language, blurring implications. After so much discussion, though, most audiences must have been able to see through any veils, and in 1857 Matilda Heron, performing the play relatively unchanged (mostly she added moralistic speeches), had a triumph. Thus the way was prepared for *La traviata.*[5]

The Bianchis, announcing their second season at the American Theatre with a flourish, listed as their initial productions two performances of *Traviata,* to be followed immediately by two of *Attila;* presumably *La favorita* and *Macbeth* would come later. Anticipating full houses, the Bianchis explained that "in order to accommodate the ladies, and place the Theatre on the proper Opera House footing, the entire Parquette has been thrown into Orchestra Seats"—or, differently phrased, seats on the orchestra floor now would cost more. As if in recompense, however, they promised for both operas a chorus that would include women, a slightly enlarged orchestra, and "entire new costumes, properties and effects."[6] And with an eye on the political situation in Italy, where Italians aided by the French had managed to free half the country from the Austrians, they added to *Attila* on the advertisement a subtitle, *Or Italy Free!*[7]

Though the critics for the *Alta California* and the *Evening Bulletin* both liked *Traviata,* neither they nor the public welcomed it as warmly as they had *Trovatore,* and in its first year, 1859, instead of eleven performances it achieved only four. The critic for the *Bulletin* particularly admired the music of the final act from "Addio, del passato" to the end, and, despite somewhat disparaging remarks concerning Signora Bianchi's talents, acknowledged that the "plaintive accents and subdued affecting character of her acting throughout deeply impressed this audience." Yet he seems uncertain what to say of the opera itself and swiftly closed, "Such a work should be heard frequently to enable the amateur to appreciate the music."[8]

His colleague on the *Alta California* was no more specific. After the first performance he managed only to comment, "The opera was La

Traviata (The Lost One), an opera full of grief of the purest music." And after the second, "The music is light, sparkling, aye Camille-ish is the word, and where the serious and the joyous mingle, there are but few human chords which do not beat in unison therewith." Although the house was not as "packed as it should have been," he hoped for a third performance, and when one was announced he urged, "The opera is a concord of sweet sounds . . . a great work and should be heard by everyone."[9]

The opera seems to have puzzled critics and public alike. Anyone could see that its style was different from that of *Ernani* and *Trovatore,* but with only a slight experience of *I due Foscari* and none at all of *Luisa Miller* or *Stiffelio,* both of which had carried further the domestic intimacy of *Foscari,* no one had ready the terms on which to take *Traviata* or to describe it. And first attempts were made more difficult, perhaps, by drawbacks in the production.

Ideally, an orchestra of twenty-five or thirty is too small for a theatre seating 2,000. The players, to increase volume, have to "force," and blending becomes difficult; further, at the extremes of soft or loud, the orchestra tends to sound either thin or blaring. In Italy at this time opera houses of roughly 1,400 would have had close to sixty players, and, paradoxical though it may seem, the larger orchestra would have an easier time sounding both subdued and full-voiced without losing quality of tone. Maguire's house, with a capacity of 1,700, was not available to the Bianchis, but it would have been better for *Traviata.* The opera's intimacy would have carried more easily.[10]

Further, despite the additional choristers, the first-act chorus of departing guests was cut, along with other numbers not identified, and Verdi's careful alternation of solo and ensemble scenes, particularly in the first act, may have been spoiled. Also the orchestra, though enlarged, cannot have been enlarged enough. The Bianchis promised many additional players, even naming in their advertisements two of the city's best-known violinists, E. Hasslocher and Charles Schultz, who would join the strings; for *Traviata,* more than any other opera Verdi had yet composed, needs a large string section to provide a warm, intense sound. But however many players were added, the violins probably totaled no more than ten or twelve. Verdi did not specify the number he wanted, but a typical Italian house of this period would have provided fourteen first and ten second violins.[11] It is most unlikely, therefore, that the orchestra achieved the intensity of string sound that Verdi sought, and possibly that failure explains why the critic for the *Bulletin* thought the last act's beauty began only with "Addio, del passato." Only then does a voice, as opposed to strings, begin to dominate.

Finally, though *La Dame aux camélias* and its American versions were presented, as Dumas *fils* intended, as a drama of contemporary life, the opera at this time always was staged, contrary to Verdi's intent, in the costumes of Paris, 1700. Before the opera's premiere in Venice, on 6 March 1853, Verdi had fought hard for costumes in the fashions of the day and lost—just as ten years earlier, in Paris, Donizetti had fought and lost over his comedy *Don Pasquale*. In these years the idea of a contemporary setting and costumes for an opera was revolutionary. The directors of the Teatro la Fenice, in Venice, could not imagine an opera in modern dress; to them, to the singers, to the public, opera was historical, costume drama.[12]

Even in Paris, where everyone had seen *La Dame aux camélias*, the opera was set back a century and a half, and the early vocal scores, whether French or Italian, usually state its "epoch" as "circa 1700." Not until the turn of the century would opera companies in Europe and the United States begin to clothe their productions in the proper period, 1845–50.[13] Thus, in 1859, what San Franciscans saw was a musical drama in which the men wore wigs, breeches, and carried swords, just as in *Ernani* or *Trovatore*, but behaved quite differently. In a sense the tenor and baritone could be said to fight over a woman, yet neither drew a sword or even threatened the other; and the scene of greatest violence was not, as was usual in romantic drama, between two men, but between a man and a woman. Likewise the music, instead of being extroverted and full of bluster, as in *Ernani* and *Trovatore*, was introspective and attenuated. To many in the audience, therefore, what the eye saw and the ear heard may have seemed oddly matched, and certainly less well matched than in the spoken theatre. But whatever the cause, many seats were empty, and applause, compared to that for *Trovatore*, was light.

The man at the *Alta California,* for one, was eager to get on with the season, and he devoted most of his final review of *Traviata* to the next premiere.

> Tonight Attila is to be produced. This opera differs from all of Verdi's compositions, being sublime in the extreme, bordering more on the grandeur of Norma, without assimilating thereto, than any opera extant. The public has already enjoyed glimpses of its great beauties in the several morceaux the Bianchis have rendered at their concerts, and we can safely predict a great success therefor. The subject being historical—the invasion of Italy by the Hunnish horde, coupled with the European embroglio about Italy—renders its presentation at this moment of greater interest than usual. In its patriotic sentiment, and it abounds in telling hits, the friends of liberty will find much to excite their enthusiasm, whilst the lovers of the noble and generous in nature will also discover that the author has endowed Attila with more than the usual allotment of virtues.[14]

His anticipatory enthusiasm for *Attila,* so much greater than for *Traviata,* reflects the standing of the two operas at the time. The latter had failed at its premiere, been withdrawn for a year, and only recently begun its rise to fame, whereas in this decade *Attila* (1846), as the frequent excerpts of it sung and played in San Francisco attest, was one of Verdi's most popular operas. And it continued so until about 1870, when it began to fade from the repertory, disappearing altogether about 1900; but then after 1950, as a series of distinguished basses took it up—it is Verdi's only opera in which a bass has the title role—productions of *Attila* again became fairly common.

Besides stirring choral numbers and vigorous solos for the principals, the opera offers three spectacular scenes: Attila at the sack of Aquileia, the founding of Venice by Aquileian refugees, and the historic confrontation of Attila and Pope Leo I, in which the latter forbids an attack on Rome. In addition, there is the superb double aria for baritone, already described, and Attila has a powerful scene in which he wakes from a nightmare that forecasts his meeting with the pope. The dream, he at first admits, strangely terrified him; but then he firmly rejects his fears. The Verdi scholar Julian Budden, in assessing the opera and comparing it to others of its era, concluded: "It could well have been judged nasty, brutish and short. But at least it contains no superfluous tissue; it never sinks beneath its own weight."[15]

After the first performance, the critic for the *Alta California*, reporting the opera to be "the greatest lyric triumph" of the Bianchis' seasons thus far, jumped quickly from elation, to pride, to shame, ending with a sudden plunge into Latin and biblical rhetoric.

> We were little prepared after the great success of La Traviata to find a successor which would even surpass the predecessor, but such is the fact, and it is a matter of considerable pride that we can boast of such event, as San Franciscans, while at the same time, a blush of shame tinges our cheeks, when we reflect that but half the auditory of the American Theatre was filled. Where is the musical taste of our community, if it cannot be evidenced to at least a generous support of such worthy and meritorious artists as Signora and Signor Bianchi. Tastes may differ, but we think Attila to be the most brilliant of the repertoire thus far presented. It abounds with melody—infectious and spirit-stirring melody—and was rendered in a style worthy the repute of the Bianchis. Chorus, mise en scene, costumes and accessories were complete, nothing was wanted to render it a success. ... With this material [the Bianchi company] we have heard *eight* different operas, all given in a style which may well compare, taking things into consideration, with the infancy of the opera in New York. The opera is in its infancy here, but its tottering steps must be guided, it needs sustenance and encouragement, and if such is not meted out the Bianchis, then let San Francisco hide its head, and go weep, for it is but an *omnium gatherum* of fortune hunters, and the arts have no place with Mammon.[16]

The critic for the *Bulletin* was more judicious, though he, too, was pulled by the opera into a literary flourish of the sort he usually avoided. Starting with an account of how critics for many years had condemned Verdi's operas as too brassy, noisy, and martial, yet conceding the popularity of the music, he stated firmly that Verdi had developed his taste and genius, and *Traviata* and *Trovatore* "at once elevated him in the estimation of the most fastidious and exacting of the connoisseurs." Then, the standard of excellence set, he turned to *Attila*.

It evidently was one of those early operas "which had stirred up the bile of the critics." Yet there were parts he admired:

Those grand bursts of harmony that close the different acts, the effect of which is artfully enhanced by the previous declamation and passionate singing of principal personages, wonderfully affects the fancy of the audience. They are like the long role of a stormy sea upon a sandy shore, where the heavy fall of the breakers is incessant. The imagination runs riot in the harmonious uproar; and although the sounds are inarticulate to one who knows not the foreign language that is sung, yet there is a music and a rapture in such a union of human voices as there is, according to the poet, by the side of the ocean.[17]

He noted that the Italians in the audience had "very heartily and loudly applauded" more than once when the opera lent itself to patriotic sentiment, such as the moment when Attila gives Odabella, the soprano, a sword and she declares that she will use it to free her country. At this moment, the critic remarked, some Italians in the upper galleries had been moved "even to tears." But it was difficult, he complained, to identify the opera's most effective passages when no libretto, either in Italian or English, had been made available.[18] The chorus, for once, was "admirable," and the orchestra as good as could be "expected of one of its size."

With regard to the singers, he touched on several failings that surely had a part in deciding the opera's fate in San Francisco, failings that his colleague, so eager for a success, ignored. The artist who sang Attila, Stephen W. Leach, was "scarcely competent to do justice" to the role, which needs a bass voice such as San Franciscans in 1854 had enjoyed in Francesco Leonardi, a voice with "all the depth and volume of a trombone" and which in full play could "drown both orchestra and chorus."[19] Leach, whom Anna Thillon had brought with her to sing the tenor roles in her English opera repertory, apparently was a utility artist, with a voice of no particular quality. As needed, presumably with a little transposition here and there, he could sing tenor, bass, or baritone, but none with great success. In Italian opera, as opposed to English, whatever the range of his role, he invariably was "over-parted," hence disappointing.[20] And Bianchi had a similar failure in casting the baritone role of the Roman general Ezio. Like Pellegrini with *Ernani* in 1851, he evidently could find no true baritone for the part and gave it to a mezzo-soprano, Mme E. Kammerer. But she, according to the reviewer, had "too weak a voice, and is too inexperienced in music and stage business to give satisfaction in her somewhat important role."[21]

Even after the second performance, the *Alta California* reviewer could see no shortcomings in the production. "We really do not know how to account for the apathy so apparent in our public, and unless they shake off the shame, they will assuredly lose the opera. Attila was well sung, notwithstanding the dispiriting appearance of the house, and was warmly appreciated and applauded by those present."[22]

The critic for the *Golden Era* agreed on the opera's merits, and like his colleagues, he, too, was stirred by its performance to literary and aquatic allusions.

"Attila" is in every respect a startling production—calling into service the best efforts of the singers and orchestra. It is what may be called a regular "brass-band" chef d'oeuvre. While the noise and clatter of the numerous orchestra distract the tender sensibilities of the ear, the sweet voices of the hero and heroine (Signor and Signora Bianchi) fill the space with bewitching and harmonious strains. We will not indulge in the usual "learned critique" upon the performance. Suffice it to say, that it was really gorgeous in every respect. As the instruments of the orchestra "rose in voluptuous swell," we could see (in our mind's eye, Horatio) the hosts of Alaric and Attila, "like a mighty river breaking its boundaries, sweeping across the fertile and smiling valleys of classic Italy."[23]

Nevertheless, despite the enthusiasm of the critics and the opera's similarity in style to *Ernani* and *Il trovatore*, it was "lost" to San Francisco for the next three years, and along with it *Macbeth* and *La favorita*, for after this second performance, on 19 August, the Bianchis broke off their season and did not announce another. Probably the chief reason was the weakness of both *Traviata* and *Attila* at the box office. In addition, though, a partial cause was surely the difficulty in casting *Attila* and, presumably, *Macbeth*, which also calls for a strong baritone (Macbeth) and bass (Banquo). In both these operas the tenor role, which Bianchi could sing splendidly, is the least important of tenor, baritone, and bass, and the latter two he could not cast to strength. If in his double capacity of singer and impresario he was to avoid the financial disaster that had overtaken Barili-Thorn and Sinclair, he had to stop offering ill-cast, new productions. On his return to San Francisco in 1862, when he brought with him a competent baritone and bass, he promptly revived *Attila* and gave the San Francisco premiere of *Macbeth*. (For reviews of the latter, see Appendix E.)

Still, considering the critical acclaim for *Attila*, its unsold seats are surprising, and the most important cause may have been simple surfeit. San Francisco was a small city, roughly 55,000, and night after night for three months its music-lovers had been offered opera. To fill every seat every night, some 160,000 tickets would have to be sold. In light of that figure, a weakness at the box office in the fourth month is perhaps not so surprising.

There is some evidence—merely the newspaper reference quoted below—that the Bianchis, like the Biscacciantis before them, tried to find subscribers to underwrite further seasons of Italian opera. In Europe, of course, most of the opera houses with resident companies were supported in part by royal patronage or groups of aristocrats or businessmen. In the United States, where such traditions and institutions were lacking, impresarios and singers constantly sought as an alternative some sort of subscription system.

In their search for subscribers, however, the Bianchis doubtless were hindered by their break with Maguire. He owned the city's best theatre for opera, controlled the possibility of touring, and was certain to oppose anyone who produced opera without him—all reasons that, perhaps, can be read between the lines of a valedictory article about the Bianchis, published in the *Alta California* as they prepared a "farewell" performance of *Trovatore*.

FAREWELL BENEFIT TO THE BIANCHIS: —Signor and Signora Bianchi are about to leave our State for Australia, and previous to their departure, they propose to take a farewell benefit at the American Theatre on Saturday evening. Their departure will be a serious loss to the cause of music in San Francisco, and will be the source of corresponding regret to its friends. Signor Bianchi is a true artist. He understands both the theory and practice of music. His fine tenor voice, his thorough musical education, and his talent for his art befit him to appear with credit on any stage. But his value to our musical community depended almost as much on his other faculties—his ability as a manager and his understanding of all the complex machinery in the production of difficult operas. Signora Bianchi, although not the equal of her husband as a musician, was still a valuable addition to our musical talent. The attempt to establish the Italian opera by subscription failed for various reasons, and Signor Bianchi desires to try his fortune in other fields. Perhaps he will return to us before long. The home of the artist is in the country which pays him best. Signor and Signora Bianchi are popular personally as well as musically, and no doubt their benefit will be attended, as it should be, by a full and fashionable house.[24]

In the fashion of popular artists, the Bianchis, before departing, gave several more farewell performances. In a program dedicated by the Germans of the city to the explorer and natural scientist Alexander von Humboldt, who had died in May, they were soloists in Mozart's *Requiem,* and they also sang in performances of *Lucrezia Borgia* and *La traviata.* For the last, their final "adieux," the American Theatre reportedly "was a perfect jam." Then they were gone, leaving behind a record of extraordinary effort on behalf of opera and the memory that it was they who had introduced the city to *Trovatore* and *Traviata.*[25]

ELEVEN

Theatrical Scenery and Styles; *Traviata* and the New Realism

One aspect of opera production in San Francisco seldom mentioned by contemporary critics is the setting—scenery, costumes, and lighting. In these years, in any theatre in any city of the United States, no production of a play or opera had a unified interpretation imposed on it by a stage director; that post, and its authority, as yet did not exist. The concept first appeared in the legitimate theatre in Germany in the late 1860s, and it had a second, spontaneous birth in the United States in the early 1870s.[1] Before then, and even for many years after, stage rehearsals of a play or opera, if held at all, were directed by the stage manager or prompter with a promptbook, who did little more than indicate entrances and exits while making sure that necessary props, a candle or a sword, were in hand. If the play was new and the author present, he might determine the movements and "business"; if the play was old, the actors would follow tradition, or ignore it; and among themselves they might agree or disagree, each frequently following his or her own ideas on pace, style, and emphasis. In performances of Shakespeare, the most popular scenes generally were those of violence, comedy, or the famous speeches, which most of the audience knew by heart and which for the actors became, like opera arias, a chance for the display of individual artistry. Shakespeare in these days was pri-

marily melodrama and rhetoric, and in the delivery of either there was
not much subtlety.[2]

In opera, because of the added complication of music, there was
even less discipline, though Verdi, whenever he was involved in a
production, attempted to impose it. In 1869, writing to a librettist, he
stated his ideal, a plea for the composer as stage director: "In short,
everybody would have to follow me. A single will would have to rule
throughout: my own. That may seem rather tyrannical to you, and
perhaps it is. But if the work is an organic whole, it is built on a single
idea and everything must contribute to the achievement of this unity."[3]
In Italy, with each success, he increased his ability to impose his will;
but in Paris, no. After 1867, because of his distress with the rehearsals
of *Don Carlos* at the Opéra, he refused to compose again for that theatre,
and twenty years later, when he was all-powerful, in his contract with
La Scala for *Otello* he reserved the right to cancel the premiere even
after the dress rehearsal.[4]

In 1859, however, his guiding hand did not reach as far as San
Francisco, and in some respects, no doubt, the Bianchis' productions
would have distressed him. He would have been infuriated by their
cuts, and have considered their orchestras of thirty or less too small for
a theatre seating 2,000. Yet he would have been pleased that they
employed a conductor rather than relying on the first violinist to lead
from his chair. In Italian opera houses, it seems, a standing conductor
with a baton was not "regularly employed until the mid-1860s, and
even then the practice spread slowly."[5] As for the Bianchis' scenery,
costumes, and lighting, so far as these can be determined, Verdi probably would have found them no better or worse than those in any
provincial Italian opera house.

Scenery, in these days before photography had nurtured a desire for
realism in settings, usually consisted of a painted backdrop and two
pairs of "wings." The latter, set toward the front and middle of the
stage and parallel to the backdrop, would hang or stand on either side
of the playing area, protruding into it only a yard or two. For example,
the backdrop might portray a castle in the distance, and as that picture's frame, the "wings" would represent the trunks of large trees,

suggesting a park; and the scene would serve either for the murder of Banquo in Verdi's *Macbeth* or for the opening of Donizetti's *Lucia di Lammermoor*. In the spring of 1908, when Giulio Gatti-Casazza arrived in New York to become the Metropolitan Opera's manager, he was given a showing of the company's scenery stored in a warehouse. One setting, which he thought rather "ugly" and so inquired as to its use, represented a courtyard with a door opening onto the sea; and it served for the first acts of Thomas's *Mignon* and Verdi's *Otello*.[6]

Fifty years earlier, in San Francisco and the smaller California cities and towns, most theatres owned a number of such generalized scenes—a great hall, a prison, a chapel, mountains, the sea, a forest— and any company renting the theatre could use them. In the spring and summer of 1855, for instance, L. P. Frisbie of Nevada City, advertising the availability of his new theatre (cap. 500), stressed that along with it he was offering for hire "a new stock of Scenery," a collection of such scenes.[7] It seems likely, therefore, that when a critic of that decade writes of "newly painted" scenery for an opera's revival, in most cases he means only that an old backdrop has been retouched, with perhaps the addition of a vine over a doorway, flowers along a wall, or a distant boat in a seascape. Scenery was a pretty picture or perhaps a display of the painter's skill in false perspective, *trompe-l'oeil*, but generic rather than specific, and never abstract. As for furniture or heavier architectural pieces onstage, these were kept to a minimum; wherever possible, paint substituted for three-dimensional structures.

Because in the United States scenery was still the least part of an operatic production, no one, critics or artists, talk much of it. The Bianchis, in announcing their new productions, emphasize instead "new costumes, properties, and effects"—the last meaning such *coups de théâtre* as pistol explosions, blood on the shirt or hands, or thunder and lightning. Small troupes like the Bianchis' or the New Orleans English Opera Troupe did not tour with scenery, and so when Maguire presented first one and then the other group in *Trovatore*, in all probability each used his theatre's backdrops and wings. If the same music, why not the same castle?

With costumes, however, the leading singers invariably provided their own, and these, packed carefully and trunked from town to town, usually were highly individual and frequently sumptuous. In San Francisco in 1854, for example, Anna Bishop's "gorgeous warrior costume" for *Tancredi* probably had a chest plate and greaves of polished mail, a skirt of gilded chain-mail, a handsomely painted shield, and a helmet with at least three white plumes—and doubtless this was only one of many splendid habits. Though five years later the Bianchis' "new costumes" were not sufficiently stunning to win description in reviews, their productions may have been the better for it dramatically, and certainly their costumes would have differed from those of the New Orleans Troupe. In that regard prima donnas and tenors were as uncompromising as their purses could afford.

For the secondary singers and chorus, needless to say, the costumes were less sumptuous, and probably those in use in San Francisco in these years were no better, and perhaps worse, than those available at the Academy of Music in New York. There the theatre offered companies a choice of three styles, called "Paysannes," "Norma," and "Rich." The "Paysannes" were peasantlike, the "Norma," faintly classical, and the "Rich," vaguely Louis XIV; and they were combined or altered as required.[8]

Needless to say, leading singers made no effort to accommodate their costumes to those of the chorus. For *La traviata*, for instance, in which the chorus would be wearing "Rich," Clara Louise Kellogg pursued her own ideas. "I liked surprising the public with new and startling effects. I argued that Violetta would probably love curious and exotic combinations, so I dressed her first act in a gown of rose pink and pale primrose yellow. Odd? Yes; of course it was odd. But the colour scheme, bizarre as it was, always looked to my mind and the minds of other persons altogether enchanting."[9]

Similarly, few singers sought to match costumes with scenery. If the set showed snow on the ground, and the soprano fancied a cotton dress, she wore it. In an opera house where the auditorium remained lit throughout the performance and where artists, for the most part, sang directly to the audience from the front of the stage, ideas of illusion, when compared to those held today, were primitive.

Some of Verdi's operas play more easily than others in such haphazard settings. For example, *Ernani* and *Trovatore*—operas of swirling capes, indignation, and bravura singing—can seem relatively at home, whereas *Traviata* will not. The play that Verdi saw in Paris in 1852 and the opera he fashioned from it are both touched by a new style of realism then entering the theatre.

The story was contemporary, and audiences, who were increasingly fascinated by the exactness of detail that photography had begun to make common, soon wanted theatre scenery, especially for contemporary plays, to approach reality in the same way. By 1860 the art of scenic design was beginning to inch away from painted backdrops and wings to a concept of the "box set," in which three walls of a room are presented onstage, with the fourth, figuratively of glass, between the stage and the audience. The three walls have the appearance of solidity, and the room is fully furnished, down to the carpet and doormat.

The movement toward such settings was slow in the theatre, and slower still in opera, and Verdi perhaps was not fully aware of its implications. Yet the principles of the new concept, clear enough in the underlying play, inform the opera. In *La traviata*, all the scenes are set indoors; the first presents, or should, a seated dinner party in a luxuriously appointed house, and the last, a bedroom in that same house stripped of all but the most necessary furniture, a room whose bareness is part of the story. The opera is of a sort that gains impact when the walls seem real, the doors through them are functional, and the doorknobs are in place and visible. The fact that it did not have such scenery or even contemporary costumes at its premieres in Venice and San Francisco perhaps partially explains the puzzlement with which at first it was received in both cities. In these respects it was an opera ahead of its time.

How the Bianchis lit their productions must also be determined from general history rather than from any specific description. Certainly the medium was gas, which, though easier to control than candles or oil lamps, was not very different in effect. The major revolution in theatrical lighting came with electricity—greater intensity and color as well as control—and did not begin until the 1880s.

Maguire's Opera House, to which the American Theatre presumably was similar, had a gas chandelier of twenty burners in its auditorium, and there would have been additional gas jets either just inside or on the front of the boxes and on the sides and back walls of the balconies. Over the stage there also would have been a chandelier, perhaps slightly smaller than the one in the auditorium. Perhaps, too, at medium height there were a few burners on gas pipes concealed behind the wings. Yet even with gas, as with candles, the chief source of light onstage was the "glaring footlights." To counteract the extreme shadows that these threw on singers' faces, the stage chandelier remained lit throughout the performance, its light directed downward by glass reflectors. Its effect, however, was diluted by the habit of actors and singers to wear hats onstage, in part to avoid accidents. At the Union Theatre in San Francisco, for instance, on 17 July 1854, Laura Keene, the actress and manager of her own company, was cut about the head and face when glass fell on her from the stage chandelier.[10]

Although candles sometimes were dimmed by surrounding them with opaque cylinders, the bottomless cans were difficult to raise and lower, and gas offered an advantage in being easy to turn up or down. Further, the gas circuits, whether footlights, chandeliers, or sections of them, could be controlled separately from a "gas-board," usually managed by the prompter. But to extinguish and then relight gas burners during a scene required a sophisticated, expensive "sparking" mechanism probably not available in San Francisco in 1859. In the city's era of gas, therefore, though light in the auditorium of theatres could be dimmed, it usually was kept bright enough, as the Richardson-Cora incident reveals, for members of the audience to see one another clearly; and during an opera they easily could follow the plot and words in a libretto. Onstage, to indicate darkness the actor or singer would carry a candle or lantern; the convention was understood and accepted.

As might be expected of a man who wanted to control every aspect of an opera's production, Verdi took an interest in costumes and scenery. Before the premiere of *Attila* he wrote to a friend in Rome, an artist: "I know that in the Vatican, either in tapestries or in one of

Raphael's frescoes, there must occur the meeting of Attila and St. Leo. Now, I need a costume sketch of the Attila. Jot it down for me with a few strokes of the pen, and then make a note for me of the colors, with words and numbers. Above all, I need the hairdress."[11]

In this opera also, more than in any previous, he tried to make use of scenic effects that would combine nature with music. The Huns, he knew, lived in the forests and open air, and so, in contrast to *Traviata,* the only one of his operas with every scene indoors, *Attila* is the only one with every scene outdoors. In the Prologue a scene opens with a violent storm over the Venetian lagoon; then, as the tempest dies, the sun rises: Verdi wanted the lighting onstage to brighten in pace with the dawn in the music. In the first act, for a moment of repose, he offered a quiet forest, with moonlight reflected in a stream; and later, during a nocturnal, outdoor banquet, he wanted gusts of wind suddenly to extinguish all the torches, which he directed in the opera's score to be "a hundred flames issuing from huge trunks of oak-trees treated for the purpose."

From reports of the premiere at Venice, the dawn was a great success, but because of some material used in the torches, on being extinguished they stank horribly. At La Scala nine months later, however, apparently every scenic effect misfired. An eyewitness reported, "The sun rose onstage before signaled in the orchestra. The sea, instead of wind-swept and tossing, was calm, without a white-cap; there were hermits without huts, and priests without altars, and in the banquet scene Attila held a feast at night without visible lights or torches, and when the wind blew up, the sky continued clear and serene, just as on a beautiful spring day." Verdi was furious.[12]

In San Francisco, despite the combined scenic and musical dawn being in these years a famous feature of the opera, the Bianchis in their lighting apparently did not attempt it, for no reviewer mentions it; nor is there any description of any other of the opera's intended scenic effects. Though the American Theatre, with gas, was ahead of Italian theatres of the 1840s, in its stage machinery and lighting equipment, apparently, it was behind—except that some of the pantomime-ballet productions appear to have been very elaborate. Perhaps the Bianchis simply found the scenic effects too expensive to stage. Their absence, however, must have lessened slightly the opera's impact, for they are built into the music. Today, of course, after the hurricane Verdi let loose in *Otello* (1887), the musical storm in *Attila* seems paltry, and the dawn, naive.

In still another respect *Attila* and *Traviata* provide a remarkable contrast and reveal the direction in which Verdi was moving with his art, and with him, theatre practice in general. *Attila* is of the old, clutch-and-stagger style of drama—big gestures, bold statements, and every emotion played as an outsized passion; *Traviata* and its underlying play *La Dame aux camélias*, or *Camille*, point toward a subtler school of singing and acting that over many years quite changed the experience of theatre and opera.

Though the American actress Matilda Heron had success with a number of roles, notably Shakespeare's Juliet, she had a triumph as Marguerite in *Camille*, and as the noble courtesan she swept back and forth across the country, astonishing audiences with what seemed a new, natural style of acting. One of those whom she deeply impressed was the soprano Clara Louise Kellogg, who later modeled her Violetta in *Traviata* on what she had seen in Heron's *Camille*.[13]

In San Francisco the editors of the city's *Annals* wrote of Heron's impact on the theatre there:

Her chief merit was found in her perfect naturalness of manner; the total absence of those screamings, rantings, and gesticulations which have grown up rank and deep-rooted weeds on the dramatic field. It is this feature that causes the superficial looker-on to regard her efforts with indifference; that failed to gain for her a merited éclat from the less critical people of the East; that excited the admiration of Californians. It is a human being that performs—not an unnatural contortion; the characters represented appear before you—the author's ideas, interpreted and embellished by the *artiste's* genius. Miss Heron has thus been an eminent reformer of the California stage. Actors and actresses have subdued their rantings under her influence, and adopted a more life-like style of performing. Hence, the vast improvements in theatrical representations in this city, even in mediocre plays. Audiences have something at which to listen; attention is riveted on the play. The peanut eaters of the upper circles, and the gentlemanly loafers of the parquet, have been subdued into gentility; the quiet decorum of the parlor has supplanted the noisy bustle of the circus; even riotous applause is regarded as innappropriate.[14]

The change, though perhaps started by Heron, was slow to take hold, particularly in northern California, where *Trovatore*, with its bold, extroverted style, was such a favorite. For in 1875, when the great American stage manager and director Augustin Daly brought his company to San Francisco, he wrote back to his brother: "The press here still growl & call our acting tame and colorless— The fact is acting out here is all 15 yrs. behind the age. The thunder & lightning & absurd farce acting of our boyhood era."[15] Nevertheless, Heron in *Camille* was an artist in a play that accelerated a change in styles of acting and in an audience's perception of what was good theatre; and Verdi's *Traviata* had a comparable role in bringing on a similar change in Italian opera, though here change came even more slowly.

In *La traviata*, as compared to *Attila*, or even *Ernani* and *Il trovatore*, Verdi offered fewer opportunities to the "peanut eaters" and the "gentlemanly loafers" to burst into extravagant applause, hooting, stomping, and disrupting the performance with calls for repetitions. The story, in its unbroken focus on Violetta, is both more simple and more somber than those of the other operas, and in its psychological probings of her thoughts and feelings it demands closer attention from an audience, fostering an atmosphere of quiet and concentration. In *Attila*, for example, no scene continues as long as the interview between Violetta and Germont *père*—in which the mood of each constantly shifts—or is musically so interesting. By the time of *Trovatore* and *Traviata* Verdi was composing operas more integrated and complicated than *Ernani* and *Attila*, more difficult to perform, and seeking from the audience a deeper, more thoughtful response to the music.

To some extent the change can be followed in what the public in San Francisco admired in *La traviata*. Initially, according to a critic for the *Alta California*, the opera's "gems" were "Libiamo" (the drinking song), "Sempre libera," "Di Provenza," and, from the last act, Violetta's outburst "Gran Dio! morir sì giovine."[16] Each of these is composed in a style quite conventional for the 1850s, and not one occurs in what today would be called the heart of the opera, Violetta's extended duet with Germont *père*. Only gradually, therefore, did the public begin to appreciate the sequence of Violetta's responses to the remorseless argument of Germont *père:* "Non sapete," "Così alla misera," "Dite alla giovine," and finally, "Morrò! Morrò!"

This shift toward greater integration of the music with the drama and toward a more restrained style of presentation would not be to everyone's taste. Though the music-lovers of the public, including most critics, might rejoice at the direction taken, there were others in any audience for whom an opera could become too musical. What was wanted in an evening's entertainment, such might say, was excitement, color, and fun, wrapped in a good story, lavish costumes, a number of popular tunes well sung or played, and followed by a farce or burlesque to send the audience home laughing.

In this decade in San Francisco, although the French, Italian, and German immigrants supported opera more than the Americans, there was essentially a single audience in the city. Everyone went to every sort of entertainment—opera, drama, minstrel shows, mime, ballet, and circuses—and within the audience there were no sharp divisions of taste reflecting differences in class or culture. There was consequently no division between popular and serious music. What was popular was merely what was most often sung or played, or sold best in the stores, whether for use at home, in the theatres, or in the saloons. In all probability in these years, the most popular songs were drawn from Bellini's *Sonnambula.* The arias and choruses were available in every conceivable kind of arrangement and simplification, of which the most frequently encountered was the opera's finale, "Ah, non giunge," or, in its most common English version, "Ah, don't mingle." Many other operas ranked only slightly lower, among them Rossini's *Barber of Seville* and *Cinderella,* Donizetti's *Daughter of the Regiment* and *Lucia di Lammermoor,* and then, catching up fast, Verdi's *Ernani* and *Trovatore.*[17]

Historians date the beginning of the division between popular and serious music to the 1860s,[18] and the first signs of it in San Francisco appear in these last years of the 1850s. The Bianchis now struggle constantly to improve their productions of Italian operas; they rehearse longer than was common at the time, enlarge the orchestra and chorus, hire the best available conductor, and sing the opera in its original language. To a music-lover all their actions were admirable, and their productions, no doubt, were more true to the composer's intent and more musical than those of their rival, the New Orleans English Opera Troupe. Yet it seems likely that for the less musical of the audience, the Bianchi productions, just because of the foreign language and the greater abundance and complication of the music, proved less interesting, less entertaining. As differences in approach to the music in hand began to sharpen, the single, general audience began to splinter.

A reflection of the fact can be seen in a difference between the Bianchis and Anna Bishop, a singer less attuned to Verdi and his contemporary composers. Born in 1810 and roughly fifteen years older than either Bianchi, Bishop sang opera in the original language, but she also often, and typically when introducing an audience to an opera, sang in English versions; and further, by performing in burlesques and farces where she mingled opera with topical jokes and popular songs, she made the music and forms of opera seem familiar. With the Bianchis and the English Opera Troupe, however, the division between serious and light opera becomes more marked, a portent of opera's increasing limitation to "serious" music and gradual loss of much popular support.

TWELVE

A Duel, and a Period of Operatic Doldrums

The ethos of an age is reflected in its rhetoric—"I must draw your blood, victim of my contempt," snarls the baritone to the tenor in Act I of *Il trovatore*—and to a greater extent than sometimes is realized the extravagance of operatic melodrama in the mid–nineteenth century had its counterpart in daily life, especially in a new, frontier society. In San Francisco in the 1850s, life and opera often mimicked each other, with any difference all but disappearing.

One such instance, an event that in its consequences severely shook the moral sensibilities of Californians, occurred shortly before the Bianchis departed for Australia in early October 1859. Though the episode involved fewer persons than the vigilante uprising and resulted in only one death, it had a more immediate and profound effect on the people's tolerance for violence in daily life and led gradually to a change in public attitudes and habits.

The initial incident was a duel between one of California's U.S. senators, David C. Broderick, and the chief justice of its supreme court, David S. Terry, who quit his position to issue the challenge. Broderick, while sitting with a friend at the breakfast table of a San Francisco hotel and glancing through a newspaper, had made a disparaging remark about Terry, which was overheard by one of the judge's friends. Said Broderick, after reading a political attack on him by Terry: "I have always said Terry was the only honest man on the Supreme Court, but I take it back." Most contemporaries thought the remark mild and a duel unnecessary, the sort of quarrel that friends of the parties should be able to settle.

Broderick, though he had fought a duel in 1852, was not known as a man of violence, and although Terry had the reputation of one, as a judge on California's highest court he had sworn to uphold the state's laws, including those against dueling. Further, in 1856 both men actively had opposed the vigilantes' disregard for law. Yet Terry proved intractable. Resigning from the court, he demanded satisfaction, his reasons seeming to lie less in the words uttered than in his own and Broderick's personalities and in the issues and practices of the day.

Broderick, of Irish background and a stonecutter by trade, had emigrated from New York City in 1849 and begun at once to apply to San Francisco the political tactics and organization he had observed in New York's Tammany Hall. Finally, by 1856, having molded a personal following into an effective party, he achieved the post he most wanted, U.S. senator. Yet though a skillful politician, he apparently had a cool, secretive manner that many found unsympathetic. And some men, among them apparently Terry, hated him. His best friends in San Francisco were the Maguires, possibly the only persons to whom he revealed himself, and when in the city he often stayed with them in their apartment over the opera house.[1]

Terry, a Texan, was a politician of a different sort. Outgoing, hot-blooded, touchy about honor, in the 1850s, when politicians in particular seemed addicted to duels, he was the more typical figure. Stephen J. Field records that in the State Assembly during the early years of the decade, more than two-thirds of the thirty-six members would come to meetings armed, frequently with both knives and guns, and sometimes before speaking a member would lay his pistols on his desk, ostentatiously cocking them. In such an atmosphere debate was difficult; words, even innocuous words, if spoken in opposition sometimes were deemed personally offensive, and affairs of honor became common. Yet despite the law against duels politicians never were prosecuted for participating in them, whether as principals or seconds.[2]

Besides the conflict of personalities, however, there lay beneath

Terry's challenge a difference in politics, a reflection of the troubles
that shortly would divide the United States into North and South and
erupt, in April 1861, into civil war. Terry, a southerner, was a leader of
the emerging southern faction of the Democratic party in California,
Broderick, of the northern; and if Terry could remove Broderick from
the Senate, a southern sympathizer might be appointed to finish Broderick's term. Whether or not Terry had considered the idea, others had;
and the dying Broderick named it as the reason for his death.

In retrospect, the duel seems an instance of life imitating art, the
clichés of romantic drama and opera suddenly turned to shocking
reality, with Terry, the implacable challenger, ranting about honor,
refusing to be reconciled, forcing the duel on his opponent, and ready
to provide the pistols. Three years later, substituting swords for pistols,
Verdi would put a similar scene on the stage in the final act of *La forza
del destino.*

When the last effort at reconciliation had failed, the duel's time and
place, weapons, and conditions were set: 6:00 A.M., 11 September 1859,
on a field at the Davis Ranch in San Mateo County, just beyond the
San Francisco city limits; the weapons, Terry's eight-inch Belgium
pistols, both with hair trigger; and the distance, ten paces. Date and
place were widely known, and soon after the parties with their seconds
and surgeons had assembled and were marking the field, the chief of
San Francisco police appeared and, with a warrant endorsed by a
magistrate of San Mateo County, arrested the duelers. Huge crowds
were on hand at City Hall to see them brought in. But because no shot
had been fired, there was no violation of the law, and they were
released.[3]

Two days later, in a valley considerably farther from the city, the
duel was fought, with some seventy-five spectators on hand. Either
because of Broderick's inexperience or owing to some defect in the
pistol's trigger, it misfired as he raised his arm, and the bullet hit the
ground about fifteen feet from Terry. The crowd waited to see whether
Terry, honor satisfied, might not fire into the air. Instead he took
careful aim at the stationary Broderick and hit him just above the heart.
Some seventy-two hours later, Broderick died.[4]

In the final act of *Ernani,* when the vengeful Silva summons the hero to the only deed that can preserve his honor, suicide, Ernani cries in despair, "Ah! The tiger seeks his prey!" With similar rhetoric the *Alta California* mourned Broderick in a black-bordered editorial, beginning: "The lion hunt is over. The jackals that long hung howling on his track are at rest after their feast of blood." Yet the paper conceded that Terry had acted within the dueling code; and until the code emphatically was rejected by the public exercising its will through the state legislature, nothing could be done. The *Bulletin,* in contrast, called forthrightly for the existing law to be enforced and for Terry and the seconds of both parties to be sent to the penitentiary.[5]

Then, as winter came and went, Californians watched the spectacle of Terry's non-trial.

The legislature, ignoring the public's anger, approved the duel by shifting jurisdiction over it from the court of sessions to the district court, which was more susceptible to manipulation. Terry's lawyers thereupon successfully petitioned to remove the case from San Mateo to Marin County, where presumably they thought local feeling against Terry was less strong; and further, they successfully petitioned to have the local Marin County judge replaced by one of Terry's judicial cronies, Judge J. T. Hardy. Finally came the appointed day, with the witnesses for the prosecution scheduled to sail from San Francisco for Marin County early in the morning. According to the historian H. H. Bancroft, events went as follows: "The day is fixed for trial, the hour has arrived; the witnesses from San Francisco who should have been present are becalmed upon the bay; the court waits, and drinks, and smokes, and swears a little; then the prosecuting attorney moves a *nolle prosequi*"—and before the case could be stated, it was dismissed.[6]

Terry apparently thought that would be the end of the affair, but he should have considered the words with which a chorus in Act I of *I Lombardi* drives a murderer from the community: "Go! On your forehead God brands the fatal mark of Cain. . . . Though you roam through fields of flowers, in grottos, through forests, over mountains, your head will be always bloody, and a demon forever at your back."

Terry joined the Confederate forces during the Civil War but was relegated to duty behind the lines and won no glory. Later he returned to California, resumed the practice of law, and tried in 1880 to reenter politics by running for the post of presidential elector on the Democratic ticket. All his associates on the ticket were elected, but he was not. Evidently the public's memory was long and unforgiving, and under the weight of its continuing censure Terry became ever more disreputable in his person and practices. In 1889, he announced publicly that he would assassinate a U.S. Supreme Court justice, Stephen J. Field, who had ruled against him in a lawsuit. He overtook Field in the breakfast room of the railroad station at Lathrop, California. Field, who was accompanied for protection by a U.S. marshal, was seated, eating, and Terry, coming up behind him, struck him twice on the head; then, ignoring an order to stop, he was shot dead by the marshal. Though Terry had no gun on him, he was carrying a knife.

By 1889, when Verdi's most recent opera was *Otello* (1887), to many operagoers *I Lombardi* seemed dated, an opera no longer in style; and to many Californians Terry, in the year of his death, seemed an anachronism, a man who had outlived his time. The Broderick-Terry duel, in September 1859, with the aborted trial in the following winter and spring, was a watershed in California life and custom. After it, although the killings, suicides, and brawls continued as before, dueling went out of fashion, and there was not another instance of it between men who were prominent. And in time, along with dueling, the violence in daily life, including misbehavior in the theatres, also gradually diminished. There were, of course, many contributing reasons; but the duel marks the start of that change.

With the departure of the Bianchis in October 1859 the amount and quality of opera staged in San Francisco began to decline. Early that month Jenny Feret, the French mezzo-soprano who had scored a success as Azucena in the Bianchis' *Trovatore,* announced that she, her husband, and others of their community would stage at the American Theatre Ferdinando Paer's comic opera *Le Maître de chapelle,* performed in May 1854 by Cailly and the Planel company. A local musical society, "Les Enfants de Paris," would provide the chorus, an experienced conductor, Anthony Reiff, would lead the forces, and, according to the *Alta California*, the opera would be given "with a view of testing the taste of the public as an *avant courier* to the establishment of the French Opera in San Francisco."[7]

This short two-act comedy of Paer, an Italian composer born in Parma, was composed in 1821 for the Opéra-Comique and is sometimes staged in a single act; it has proved his most lasting success, playing regularly in Paris until the First World War and even thereafter on occasion revived. A spoof of *opera seria*, it tells of the music master Barnaba (a role for bass, though taken by Feret) who has written an opera, *Cleopatra*, which he endeavors to teach to his pretty cook, Gértrude. While he imitates the flute, the horn, and the drum, she is to sing the grand arias to the hatrack representing Marc Antony. The balance of the program was to consist of a French farce, some choral selections, and the Barcarolle and Prayer from Meyerbeer's *L'Étoile du nord*, sung by Feret.[8]

Though the evening apparently was a success, the group attempted nothing further, not even a repetition of *Le Maître de chapelle*, and the Ferets retreated into managing a music school they recently had started. Occasionally she appeared in concerts, usually singing a French opera aria or an excerpt from *Trovatore*, or in school programs with the pupils.[9]

The Feret school was the second in the city, for the year before Mons. and Mme Planel had opened one in their home on Stockton Street, where they offered "daily vocal and instrumental" classes for "five dollars monthly." Even though the French, despite several efforts, failed to establish a local French opera company, through their educational efforts, in which the Planels and Ferets were the leaders, they contributed greatly to the musical appreciation of the next generation of San Franciscans. And—perhaps a sign the French were ready to abandon their exclusiveness and assimilate in the creation of a general community—Mons. and Mme Planel, in their advertisements for their school, now referred to themselves as Mr. and Mrs.[10]

The Germans, too, in October made a characteristic contribution to the city's musical life, one that appears to have affected opera directly.

A group of them organized a new singing society, which, in honor of the patron saint of music, Cecilia, they christened the Caecilien-Verein. It was to meet once a week, on Friday evenings, and to be led by Rudolph Herold, who, since the departure of George Loder, had become the city's outstanding conductor. Significantly, nearly half the society's fifty members were women, and soon the Verein, or perhaps a section of it, was singing frequently in concerts, styling itself in the American idiom, as the Caecilien Glee Club. Most likely, too, some of its members, women as well as men, sang with the new German Chorus which that winter started to hire itself out to theatrical ventures.[11] With such developments, the difficulty of recruiting a chorus of female voices for opera gradually lessened—though after the local premiere of Verdi's *Macbeth*, in 1862, the critic for the *Bulletin* still complained of their absence (see review in Appendix E).

Also in October 1859, San Francisco's first celebrity soprano, Eliza Biscaccianti, returned from South America, and, according to the *Bulletin*, "with the aid of such local talent as can be procured, she proposes to give a series of concerts."[12]

The series, after a halting start because of the soprano's ill health, ran to five concerts, somewhat indifferently received. From the reviews in the *Bulletin* and the *Alta California* it seems clear that either Biscaccianti's voice had lost some of its quality or the public's experience of other singers, particularly those who sang Verdi, now led it to want more power, more color, more drama in the singing. Probably the reasons were mixed.

The *Bulletin* was the more forthright of the two papers. Of the fourth concert it reported:

> Musical Hall was very well filled last evening.... While the entertainment was on the whole rather enjoyable, we cannot refer to it in terms of unqualified approbation. Although Mme. Biscaccianti seems to have quite recovered from the indisposition which so seriously marred her efforts on the opening night, and notwithstanding she executes with much artistic skill, her voice is comparatively destitute of power and sympathy. We miss the full, clear, round tones of the true *prima donna*.... Mme. Biscaccianti's last contribution to the entertainment was the romanza, "D'amor sull'ali,"

from *Il Trovatore*. The selection was a little unfortunate, because it afforded the critical part of her audience opportunity to measure her powers by those of Mme. Bianchi. . . . Those who have heard both these ladies, sadly missed last evening the touching pathos with which Mme. Bianchi was accustomed to make this theme her own, betraying all listeners into forgetfulness of the singer in admiration for and sympathy with the heroine.[13]

Even in her own repertory, however—with "Home, Sweet Home," "The Last Rose of Summer," or "Ah, non giunge" from Bellini's *Sonnambula*—Biscaccianti seemed unable to stir her audiences in the old way. Apparently, to many ears the voice now sounded artificial and unsympathetic, the songs overdecorated, "disguised plagiarisms of our national music by some unknown Italian composer"; even "Ah, non giunge" aroused no calls for repetition. "She can always please her hearers," the *Bulletin* concluded, "but seldom excites them to enthusiasm." As her series progressed, she associated with her in the concerts more and more colleagues, and it became clear that she could no longer carry a program alone.[14]

After the fifth concert, on 18 November, at which she appeared with six assisting artists, she left for Sacramento, and when she returned, she was welcomed as a useful singer but without the powers of a "true *prima donna*." She sang in many joint concerts, usually in the smaller auditoriums, and frequently appeared in benefits for churches. It was a career starting on decline, and though she was able from time to time to arrest the downward slide, eventually, befuddled by drink and harassed by marital problems, she sank to singing in saloons and, ultimately, in 1896, died alone in Paris, in a home for impoverished artists.

Meanwhile, throughout the autumn Maguire, who had both the New Orleans English Opera Troupe and the Minstrels playing from time to time in his opera house, continued to prosper, though he was not without his personal troubles. In mid-October, when a creditor appeared to collect on a note, Maguire, angered by the man's behavior, spat in his face. Sued for assault and battery, Maguire was convicted and fined $100. The *Bulletin* reported, "He paid promptly."[15]

The combination of music, dance, and skits that his Minstrels of-

fered seemed never to lose its appeal for audiences, and the performers' talents unquestionably were very high. In November, with their
usual success, the company brought out a new opera burlesque, *The
Beauty and the Brigand,* based on Auber's perennial favorite *Fra Diavolo,*
which the English Opera Troupe repeatedly revived. Thus Maguire
was able to offer his audiences the opera as written (or at least in its
English version) and as parodied, almost back to back. Any little
idiosyncrasy or mishap that graced or marred the opera's performance
was sure to be burlesqued on the next night of the Minstrels.[16]

The English Opera Troupe, though it supposedly had given its
"farewell" performance on 3 October, after which one or two of its less
important singers had departed for the East, continued right on with its
repertory, usually proclaiming each performance as "positively the
last."[17] In mid-December, however, the troupe was still at its "good-
byes," and for a final three-night "season," in which its leading female
artists, Rosalie Durand and Georgia Hodson, were to make "their last
appearance here, positively," it announced performances of *Daughter of
the Regiment* with the first act of *Fra Diavolo* added, *Crown Diamonds,* and
The Bohemian Girl.[18] The second night, *Crown Diamonds,* was a gala
honoring the visit to San Francisco of a Russian man-of-war, and in the
house were the city's Russian consul and Admiral Popoff, with an escort
of twenty Russian naval officers, all in dress uniform. For the occasion
Maguire decorated the theatre with Russian and U.S. flags—the latter
now, because of Oregon's recent admission to the Union, with thirty-
three stars—and to follow the Russian national anthem he had the
orchestra play "Hail Columbia" and "Yankee Doodle."[19]

Soon after, on 20 December 1859, the *Bulletin* carried a report that
William S. Lyster, the troupe's "director," and his brother Frederick,
its leading baritone, were leaving that day for the East, with "instruc-
tions" from Maguire "to proceed to Europe and engage a number of
vocalists and instrumentalists." Thus reinforced, the troupe would
open a season of opera in the spring, adding several new works to the
repertory. Meanwhile, "others of the old troupe will remain in this
country."[20]

The chief of those remaining were Durand and Hodson, who, with

Maguire's backing, hired replacements locally for those who had left and opened a season in January in Sacramento. Their repertory was *The Child* [*sic*] of the Regiment, The Bohemian Girl, The Barber of Seville, and *Il trovatore*, this last in English, with Hodson as usual singing Manrico. After Sacramento, the singers moved on to Marysville; their success in these smaller cities must be taken in part as evidence of the people's longing for some sort of musical entertainment, for on many of the evenings the weather was harsh. From Sacramento the local critic reported, "The theatres, at this season, are so cold, that they cannot be visited without extreme danger to health and life."[21]

In San Francisco, meanwhile, the quality of opera, whether staged or in concert excerpts, continued to dissipate. In January, the high point of the concert season was a joint recital by Biscaccianti and Jenny Feret in Musical Hall, in which they were accompanied not by an orchestra but by two pianos. Biscaccianti, with the main part of the program, sang "Sombre forêt" from Rossini's *William Tell*, "O luce di quest'anima" from Donizetti's *Linda di Chamounix*, "D'amor sull'ali" from *Trovatore*, and, in a duet with Feret, "Quis est homo" from Rossini's *Stabat Mater*. Between the selections, four pianists at the two pianos played overtures and fantasies from operas by Herold, Bellini, and Rossini. As a novelty, Feret, one of the pianists, executed the Miserere from *Trovatore* on a harmonica. As encores, Mme Feret sang one of Azucena's arias from *Trovatore*, and Biscaccianti, two songs, "Kathleen Mavourneen" and "Comin' Through the Rye." Yet however good the singing, the lack of orchestra for the overtures and accompaniments, not to mention the harmonica for the Miserere, were musically backward steps.[22]

In the opera house, Maguire, too, moved in the wrong direction. That January, as a benefit night for the St. Francis Hook and Ladder Company No. 1, he revived *Rob Roy*, which he advertised as "the great operatic Scottish drama." But it would be described more truly as a play drawn from Walter Scott's novel and tricked out with some Scottish songs and dances.[23] Then in February for a week he offered *The Two Figaros*, which he called "an operatic comedy," though it, too, was more like a play. With a text by the English librettist James

Robinson Planché, it presented Cherubino, sixteen years older than in Mozart's opera and now an officer in the Dragoons, masquerading under the name of Figaro. The music, a mishmash of Mozart, Rossini, and Donizetti, presumably was based on the arrangements made for the work by Tom Cooke, an Irish tenor, violinist, and composer, who frequently assisted Planché in producing versions of operas for the London stage. The team's emphasis, however, typically fell on scenery and costumes; one of their most famous spectacles, notorious for leaving out almost all of the composer's music, was of Halévy's grand opera *La Juive*. Hence, despite the claims to opera, Maguire's *Rob Roy* and *The Two Figaros* at best were plays with incidental music and at worst, because they relied strongly on comic routines and shared the program with a farce, something closer to a variety show, a succession of slightly connected skits and "turns."[24]

Maguire's next production, *Pluto and Proserpine*, with music chiefly from *Trovatore*, was a spectacle in which, according to the *Bulletin*, "one scene alone in this piece cost, it is said, $2,500, and was taken from London to Australia, and brought thence." The star, Harriet Gordon, it reported, was "pleasing in a ballad" but not up to the "passages from Il Trovatore." The entertainment, which advertised itself as a "New and Original Mythological Extravaganza of the oo [*sic*] century" and promised "choice operatic airs, ballads, choruses, etc.," in both concept and performance was less true to the music it used than had been Bochsa's pastiche *Judith*, based on *Nabucco* and other of Verdi's early operas. Bochsa, at least, had stuck to one composer, created for his pastiche a story of similar atmosphere to that of the opera, and presented it with Anna Bishop, who could sing.[25]

Finally, in late February, Maguire brought back to the city the "Durand-Hodson" company and began to offer opera-lovers something better. At least the works presented, among them *The Bohemian Girl, Fra Diavolo, Daughter of the Regiment,* and *Sonnambula,* started with what the composers intended, though apparently all the operas were sung in English versions corrupted further by cuts and transpositions for the less talented singers replacing those who had gone East. The *Bulletin* in March commented that "the Durand-Hodson company of singers seem to have abated their original pretensions to the first rank of vocalists," though noting that "the orchestra and the German chorus is generally well up in its part." In Auber's *Fra Diavolo*, the critic concluded, the company "made a very satisfactory three hour entertainment."[26] But after a performance of Verdi's *Trovatore*, though he again complimented the German Chorus, the reviewer was caustic about the two female stars: "The ears of the general public are not very nice about fine musical sounds, when coming from pretty women." And from Boston, *Dwight's Journal* reported that its correspondent, "W.H.D.," had thought the performance so bad he had "left part way through the second act."[27]

There was better news coming, however. On 2 April, the *Bulletin* announced that the Messrs. Lyster, the leaders of the New Orleans English Opera Troupe who had gone East, and perhaps on to Europe, in their search for better singers, had been successful, and soon would return with a new prima donna and leading tenor, Lucy Escott and Henry Squires.

> [The singers] were immediately to leave London, and it is expected that they will be enabled to sail from New York for San Francisco on the steamer the 29th March. Mr. Squires is a tenor of excellent reputation. Miss Escott is likewise of high character in her profession. With their aid and the old members of the New Orleans troupe, assisted by an increased chorus and orchestra, it is expected that a new impetus will be given to operatic music in this city."[28]

In fact, Escott and Squires were hired in the United States, where they had been singing for some time. But no matter. Certainly a "new impetus" was needed, and as events would show, everyone was eager for it.

THIRTEEN

Success of the Maguire-Lyster Company, and Failure of *Rigoletto*

Throughout April 1860, the newspapers continued to hint at the plans of Maguire and the Lyster brothers to present the city with a revitalized opera company and repertory, and in mid-May William Lyster, the company's director, published a "Card" in the *Alta California*, announcing a season. He had just "returned from Europe," where he had succeeded in hiring Mme Lucy Escott, "formerly Prima Donna of the Teatro Nuovo, Naples, where she sang with the greatest success for two consecutive seasons; also of the Pergola Theatre, Florence, Royal Opera, Drury Lane, London, and the principal cities of Great Britain and Ireland" (Fig. 17).[1]

At this time the Teatro Nuovo was the second opera house in Naples, smaller and less important than the San Carlo yet creditable, and in London the Drury Lane similarly was subordinate to Convent Garden. The Pergola, conversely, was the chief house in Florence, but in a city notably less passionate about opera than Milan, Naples, Venice, or Rome. A contemporary operagoer, reading between the lines, might thus have judged Escott to be a reliable and rewarding artist, but as yet not outstanding. Somewhat surprisingly, though perhaps no one cared, amid the European flourishes Lyster omitted her native city, Springfield, Massachusetts.[2]

For the tenor roles there was "Mr. Henry Squires, whose career since his return from Europe has been one continued success, having sung in the Ullman and Strakosch Italian Opera Company with M'lle. Piccolomini, Mmes. Gazzaniga and Colson, at the Academies of Music in New York, Philadelphia and Boston" (Fig. 17). Squires, born in 1825 in Bennington, Vermont, had been billed in New York as early as 1852 as "the American tenor," a title that he, perhaps as much as any tenor of the time, deserved.³

Finally, there was John De Haga of unknown origin, a basso profundo "from La Scala, Milan, and other European opera houses, and lately Primo Basso of the Ferretti Opera Company, South America." The fact that the "other" European houses were not named, when combined with the recent tour in South America, would have led careful readers to temper their expectations. Many artists, after all, sang briefly at La Scala.

Besides the addition of these three, the company also would be strengthened by the return of Frederick Lyster, a baritone of proven competence, at least in English opera, and by the hiring of a chorus of "both ladies and gentlemen outnumbering by more than one-half any chorus hitherto organized in California." And another promise: "The Costumes and Decorations will be superb and strictly in historical keeping. The Scenery will be painted expressly for each opera, and every attention paid to the *mise en scène.*" Finally, though the operas to be given were not named, their number was set at "thirty-two . . . the greater number of which have never been given in the city." As events proved, Lyster was puffing.⁴

There was also much that he did not announce that later reports make clear. The company, in effect, had two wings, Italian and English, though the division was not rigid; and of the two the Italian was predominant, both vocally the stronger and performing more frequently. It was led by Escott and Squires, backed usually by De Haga and Stephen Leach, and for the smaller roles it employed former members of the Bianchi company. When a contralto or mezzo-soprano was needed, Georgia Hodson was used. Thus, when *Il trovatore* entered the repertory, this time in Italian, Hodson, who only four months

Fig. 17. Lucy Escott and Henry Squires in costume for *La favorita*. (La Trobe Collection, State Library of Victoria, Australia)

earlier had sung Manrico, now sang Azucena, surely a novelty in "switch" casting.

For the other wing, performing in English and offering English operas or English versions of others, such as *The Marriage of Figaro*,[5] the chief artists were Durand, Hodson, F. Lyster, and, a crucial addition, Squires for most of the tenor roles. Apparently, despite the weight of the schedule, from the start Squires had contracted to sing in both repertories.

All performances were to be in Maguire's Opera House, and for both the Italian and English operas Maguire provided an orchestra of twenty-five players, still small by Italian standards for a theatre seating 1,700, but large enough to fill the house with sound. The ultimate size of the chorus never is stated, but a report remarks that it consisted "chiefly of Germans," and inasmuch as the Caecilien-Verein could have furnished a mixed chorus of fifty voices, an ensemble of half that number seems not unlikely. As the season progressed, with the house usually sold out, it became clear that Maguire was prepared to give the stage every night of the week to opera, even at the cost of moving the Minstrels to another theatre; and gossip soon declared that he and Lyster had an agreement to split profits equally. Skeptics, no doubt, discounted the profits; in San Francisco opera habitually lost money.[6]

The season opened on 19 May 1860 with *Lucia di Lammermoor*, and Escott and Squires, to the delight of the audience, displayed better voices and artistry than any heard since the departure of the Bianchis.[7] After two repetitions of *Lucia*, Lyster staged his first novelty, the local premiere of William Wallace's *Maritana*, composed in 1845 and one of the best of the English romantic operas, though the critic for the *Alta California* soon grumbled: "Every judge of music knows how far superior [*Lucia*] is to the merely pretty succession of ballads which Wallace fitted to [*Maritana*] and called an opera. There is a gulf between them which admits of no comparison."[8]

His judgment presumably is fair, though with *Maritana* no longer performed it cannot be tested. The opera, however, held the stage in England for eighty years, and many of its songs became famously popular. The plot concerns a gypsy street-singer in Madrid, Maritana, who catches the eye of the King. He has her hastily married to an amusing, spendthrift nobleman, Don Cesar, whom he plans immediately to execute so that she may be established at court as an aristocratic widow and become his mistress. An armorer, once aided by Don Cesar, substitutes blanks for bullets in the guns of the firing squad, and after the execution Don Cesar jauntily rises and goes in search of his briefly met wife, whom he rather liked. At the start of the last act Maritana has been installed at court in a luxurious apartment where she awaits the King and, thinking of the husband she has lost, sings the opera's best-known song:

> Scenes that are brightest may charm awhile,
> Hearts which are lightest and eyes that smile;
> Yet o'er them, above us, though nature beam,
> With none to love us, how sad they seem!

The song is attractive, its structure simple, and its sentiment, though tritely expressed, pleasing; in these years, besides its life in the theatre and recital hall, it was a favorite in parlors and saloons.

In the remainder of the story, as in the operettas of the future, despite the many improbabilities all the plots and subplots turn out for the best. The villainous prime minister, Don José, is disgraced; the King discovers that he truly loves the Queen; and Maritana and a reformed Don Cesar, by the King's appointment now governor of Valencia, live happily ever after. Perhaps because it was the first new opera to enter the repertory Lyster gave it to Escott rather than Durand, and it had a solid success, playing for three successive nights and thereafter repeatedly revived.

Next came *La traviata*, with Escott, Squires, and Leach, and again, as in the Bianchi production, with costumes not of the early 1850s but of 1700. Apparently, despite a good performance, the opera continued to puzzle the audience, and its reception was tepid compared to the passion with which *Ernani* soon would be greeted—though the latter perhaps gained from excitement among the city's Italians over the success of Garibaldi's Sicilian campaign for Italian independence. With *Traviata*, however, even the critics still seemed uncertain of their response to it, losing their way in details rather than hewing to the heart of the opera and its performance. The reviewer for the *Bulletin,* for instance, though aware of the opera's drama, fumed over the women's chorus of gypsy maskers, "sung by only four weak voices" and "miserable." His colleague on the *Alta California,* after fussing inconclusively over the quality of Squire's voice, selected for admiration all the opera's most conventional arias, even as he observed that its orchestration, unconventional for the time, was "exquisite."[9] As yet there had been no flash of critical insight to separate the trivial from the important and bind these wavering opinions into a precise statement of Verdi's achievement.

With *Ernani,* however, the critics and audiences were at ease. On the first night, according to the *Alta California,* "the house was in an uproar of applause, and the stage was a flower garden, so numerous were the bouquets showered on it after each act. At the close of the first act a large wreath of red roses was thrown to Miss Lucy Escott. It was bound with ribband of the Italian national colors."[10]

The critic for the *Bulletin,* however, thought the performance sloppy and the enthusiasm artificial, and in his review he published what seems to be the first complaint in the city's history of an opera claque:

> The rendition last night, on the whole, was but an indifferent affair. The famous air and septette that closes the third act, *A Carlo Magno sia gloria e onor* ("To Charles the Great be glory and honor,") was perhaps never so ill done on our local operatic stage. There was confusion and uncertainty on the part of nearly all the singers that irresistibly provoked "odious comparisons" between the present company and the Barili-Thorne troupe in the same opera. The audience felt there was something wanting, and did not yield to the glorious enthusiasm that invariably on former occasions greeted this passage. However, thanks to the persistent efforts of some claqueurs with hands, heels and sticks, a respectable noise was raised. One fat, little bullet-headed, black haired fellow, with a gray shirt, in the parquette—a sort of character, apparently—was especially active in kicking up a din and annoying his neighbors. A number of persons were wonderfully officious in paying their personal compliments to Mme. Escott, by showering upon her innumerable fancy wreaths, flower baskets and expensive bouquets. The thing was unnatural and overdone.[11]

If the fat little man in the gray shirt was typical of the sort of fellow who supposedly filled the theatre's "pit," he soon would be driven to the back or side of the auditorium, or upstairs, for the gradual expansion of respectability from the gallery and boxes onto the parquet, or orchestra floor, was continuing. At the season's first performance of *Trovatore,* the critic for the *Alta California* noted that the opera played "to a completely full house—the dress circle containing a large number of ladies." Then, after a subsequent performance of *Trovatore,* he wrote: "Another crowded house and ladies in the parquette—the dress circle being unable to contain them all. Well," he continued, "the opera has taken San Francisco by storm, and there is no saying where it will all end."[12] Thus opera, and *Trovatore* in particular, hastened a change in the city's social customs.

It also served to display the better quality of voices in the Italian wing. Escott, by now, had proved herself a good dramatic soprano, with a full, agile voice that, linked with a talent for acting, made her the equal of Signora Bianchi and perhaps the superior. Squire's voice was small but perfectly placed, and though it lacked somewhat in power, he was able to do with it exactly as he wished, and with confident elegance. The audience apparently never doubted that it would meet his demands. As an actor he was less able than Escott, but sufficiently good for the Italian works; in the English, which had spoken dialogue, he could appear wooden.[13] Singing against these two in *Trovatore,* Hodson now seemed to both critics to be vocally inadequate. As the reviewer for the *Alta California* remarked, the role of Azucena, the Gypsy Mother, "should be taken by a contralto voice of considerable power, blended with forcible dramatic action"; but Hodson, he added, "fails in such a character."[14]

Her failure was indicative of a change in Italian opera that Verdi, chiefly, was bringing about. In the 1830s and 1840s, a soprano like Anna Bishop might have attempted almost any sort of opera, English or Italian, comic or tragic, with small or large orchestra. Opera then was in a period in which the differences of kind mattered relatively little, and even a large orchestra was small by later standards. But in these years operatic composers continually increased the number of players and instruments, and to sing over a full orchestra of the 1870s—Verdi's *Aida*, say, or Wagner's *Tristan* or *Meistersinger*—required more power than most sopranos of the previous generation could muster.

Similarly, because of the demands of contemporary composers the style of singing was changing, and in a way that sharpened the divisions between the varieties of opera and the artists who sang them. Emphasis on improvisation and coloratura, on displays of fleetness and high notes, was declining, even as composers asked for more force and color in a voice's higher range. Verdi, with emphatic underlining, once wrote of a soprano's performance in his *La forza del destino*, composed in 1862: "[The opera] could have gone a thousand times better if Jacovacci [the impresario] had been able to get it into his head that to achieve success *you need operas that suit the singers and also singers that suit the operas.* Of course, you don't have to be able to do coloratura to sing 'La Forza del Destino,' but you have to have a soul, and understand the *words* and express them."[15]

As composers began to want singers with "soul" to soar over a large orchestra, even as impresarios still sought those with agility and high notes for Rossini's fast passage work or with light, lyric charm for the operas of Auber and the English composers, the definition of "soprano" began to splinter into categories of specialization—roughly, dramatic soprano, coloratura, light or lyric, and *spinto*, the last a category for voices falling somewhere between lyric and dramatic.

Among tenors, too, the same divisions began to appear. The German romantic school, led by Wagner, demanded power and stamina, and in response there developed the *Heldentenor*, or heroic tenor. The heavier roles in the Italian repertory wanted a dramatic tenor, sometimes called *tenore robusto*, while for the lighter roles there was the lyric tenor, and, for the in-between, the *spinto*.

Meanwhile, the possibility of a single artist, like Bishop or Squires, being effective in all divisions became continually less. Indeed, some of today's critics see *Rigoletto*, *Trovatore*, and *Traviata* as the divide in Verdi's operas, the very last in which a coloratura or lyric soprano or a lyric tenor may manage, if skillful and vocally secure, to make a favorable impression.[16] After these works, and after this decade in

Italian opera generally, switching between categories becomes far more difficult and unusual. The soprano or tenor who can do justice to any of Verdi's operas composed after *Traviata* (1853), such as *Ballo in maschera* (1859), *Forza del destino* (1862), or *Aida* (1871), probably will have too much voice and too little charm for *Fra Diavolo* (1830) or *The Bohemian Girl* (1843). Hodson, who was "very acceptable" in the "sprightly roles" of her light repertory, was now judged out of place in a *Trovatore* sung in Italian with a good orchestra, chorus, and leading singers.[17] And that fact suggests how musically poor, by the emerging standards, the English versions of the Italian and French operas must have begun to seem.

It also, possibly, underlies the vehemence with which the critic of the *Alta California* condemned the season's second novelty, Balfe's *Rose of Castille*, another English romantic opera set in Spain. Lyster's production, in which he offered Rosalie Durand and Squires, was the opera's American premiere, only the second such in San Francisco's history and an event for which he doubtless expected praise. The reviewer, however, after remarking on the difficulties of staging any sort of opera in a city so far from the artistic centers of the East, and the need therefore to be charitable, continued:

> It was beyond doubt the worst apology for opera that we have seen for many months. Miss Durand certainly makes a very pretty appearance on the stage, but her singing is getting to be positively unbearable. That is our honest criticism on her performance of last evening. The truth must be told, that Miss Durand's powers are totally unfit for the greater part of the opera music which she attempts, and our most kindly endeavor to discover one redeemable feature results in a failure. Her efforts at executing any of the florid passages of opera music are nothing less than caricature and whoever does not laugh outright at them either knows nothing about music, or conceals his opinion for charity's sake.[18]

Though Durand in the previous weeks had sung acceptably as Susanna in *The Marriage of Figaro* and in Balfe's opera composed for Anna Thillon, *The Enchantress,* the critic bluntly suggested that she be replaced at once by either of the "two first-class operatic singers in San Francisco," Feret or Biscaccianti. Lyster did as told. After a second night of *Rose of*

Castille, playing "to a thin house" and "little applause,"[19] except for one more *Figaro* he banished Durand and opera in English for the remainder of the season. In her place he offered Biscaccianti singing in Italian, and during the season's final month she led four performances of *Sonnambula*, three of *Lucia di Lammermoor*, two of *I Puritani*, in the opera's local premiere, and one of *Ernani*, all apparently with moderate success.

Lyster's next new work, another local premiere, was *Rigoletto*; after the first performance on 1 July 1860 the critic for the *Alta California* wrote:

> Verdi's *Rigoletto* was given last evening to a crowded house, and, for an initial performance by a troupe which never essayed it previously, gave unmistakable evidence of proving ultimately a success. Verdi's compositions possess a power which none others can command. His melodies sway the feelings—they take possession of the sensibilities at once and hold permanently. *Rigoletto* is a succession of gems—two have been made familiar here by the efforts of the Bianchis: "La donna è mobile," and the duo "Addio, speranza ed anima," and the humble Savoyard [a term for an Italian organ-grinder, generally with a monkey to pass a cup for coins] has itinerated most of the others through the country, consequently the ensemble does not fall on the ear as strangely as many would suppose. The opera was written in three acts, but owing to the difficulties in stage effects rendered necessary in presenting double scenes at one time, it is given in four—the first and third being the Duke's palace, the second Gilda's residence, the fourth the inn of the assassin Sparafucile.

He concluded by supposing that the opera, "after one or two nights, will give the greatest satisfaction."[20]

The critic on the *Bulletin*, touching more directly on the music, reported:

> Rigoletto was produced last night to a crowded and noisy house. As performed, the opera made little impression on the audience till the last act when the remarkably fine rendition by Mr. Squires [the Duke] of the air La donna è mobile brought forth a general burst of enthusiasm. It is so great a pleasure to hear the charming voice of this gentleman . . . it was, therefore, to be regretted that one or two airs in this part, that occur in the second act (the third as represented) were omitted ["Parmi veder le lagrime" and its cabaletta, "Possente amor"]. There is much beautiful music in the opera. . . . The dance music in the first, and the elaborate storm music

of the last act, are among the leading features of the opera. The use of the inarticulate human voice in the representation of the storm is new and striking.[21]

In addition to this cut of the Duke's two arias, the first of which generally is thought to be a high point of the opera, the *Alta California* revealed that the opera's finale, a duet for Rigoletto and Gilda, also had been cut. The performance therefore may have ended with the Duke crossing the back of the stage singing snatches of "La donna è mobile," while Rigoletto shouts at the Duke's disappearing figure, "Maledizione! Olà . . . dimon . . . bandito!" He is aware that his plot to kill the Duke has failed but does not know, as does the audience, that his daughter, Gilda, has been murdered in the Duke's place. The final notes then would be the Duke's repeat of "di pensier," on a long-held, fading high B, a fine ironic ending. Or, perhaps, a few crashing chords were cobbled together to allow Rigoletto a cry of horror as he opens the sack and the curtain falls.

The reasons for the cuts, of course, are not stated, but presumably the first, of the Duke's double aria, was to spare Squires the most extended dramatic scene for tenor, which called for power that he lacked. The cut of the opera's final duet, though in these years very common (in England it continued to be made until well into the present century), is more mysterious. It does not seem to have been a result of censorship in any country, though many persons everywhere thought the opera, with its kidnapping, rape, and all but suicide, repulsive. Clara Louise Kellogg recorded that in 1861, for a tour to Boston, her company dropped the opera from its repertory: "Boston would not have *Rigoletto*. It was considered objectionable, particularly the ending." But she never states just what in the ending was considered so objectionable.[22]

In England, and possibly in France, there seems to have been an idea that musically the final duet, following the reappearance of the Duke, was an anticlimax.[23] Still, no American critic yet discovered makes that statement. Perhaps the reason for the cut was simply that sopranos objected to being stuffed in a sack. But if not the soprano, then who or what in the sack? At a performance in Barcelona where the duet was cut, the English baritone Charles Santley, a good Rigoletto of this period, in an act of dramatic fervor ripped open the sack only to discover a large black moustache. "I closed it again instantly, but the audience had already seen, and a general titter ensued."[24]

Whatever Lyster's reason for the cuts, this first production of the opera in San Francisco failed, though not so spectacularly as that of *Rose of Castille*. After three consecutive performances the company dropped the opera, and thereafter never revived it. Evidently the baritone Frederick Lyster, who sang the title role, was not good enough, for no one praises him, and the bass De Haga, who had earned a reputation for singing in a strangled tone and off pitch, spoiled the role of Sparafucile.[25] Like the previous year's *Attila*, *Rigoletto* in its lower male voices was badly cast, and the soprano and tenor arias and duets, however well sung, could not carry the opera. The composer, no doubt, would have said wearily, angrily, "To achieve success you need operas that suit the singers and also singers that suit the operas."

After *Rigoletto* Lyster and Maguire continued the season for another two and a half weeks, closing on 20 July with a performance of *Trovatore*. In all, they had presented opera on sixty-three consecutive nights, with Squires, who appeared in every opera but *The Marriage of Figaro*, singing leading tenor roles on fifty-nine of them, a feat that only a singer with flawless technique could achieve.[26] Two of the nights were galas presenting parts of operas. One offered the final act of *Rigoletto* and the first two of *Lucia di Lammermoor*; the other, the first act of *Traviata* and the "last two" of *Sonnambula*. During the sixty-one nights of individual operas, the Italian wing offered forty-six performances of nine: of Verdi, *Traviata*, *Ernani*, *Rigoletto*, and *Trovatore*; of Donizetti, *Lucia di Lammermoor* and *Lucrezia Borgia*; and of Bellini, *Norma*, *Sonnambula*, and *I Puritani*. Of these, Verdi's works were given twenty-one times; Donizetti's, fourteen; and Bellini's, eleven. The English wing in fifteen nights presented Wallace's *Maritana*, a local premiere, six times, Balfe's *The Enchantress* three, Mozart's *Marriage of Figaro* four, and Balfe's *Rose of Castille*, a U.S. premiere, twice. After the final *Trovatore* the company rested for a week and then departed for Sacramento and the interior.[27]

San Francisco had never previously enjoyed such a long, unbroken season of opera, and before it ended the critic on the *Bulletin* ascribed as one reason for it Maguire's low price scale, with a $1 top for the best seat. "In this city," the man remarked, "we are asked to pay no more to hear the classical productions of masters in music, than to witness an ordinary dramatic spectacle." As a result, "many persons make it a point of conscience to witness at least two representations of every opera produced," and "others never omit a single occasion."[28]

At the season's end the critic on the *Alta California* compared the city to its rivals in the East, purring happily: "When it is remembered that no city of one hundred thousand inhabitants supports an opera for more than a few weeks at a time, the taste and appreciation of the music patrons of this city will be fully appreciated." And indeed, a season of opera every night for nine weeks in a city and county of roughly 60,000 was astounding. Today's San Francisco Opera, for instance, with an annual season of thirteen weeks and the house dark at least one night a week, plays to a population in the city's metropolitan area of roughly 4,600,000—a season only half again as long but with a potential audience 777 times greater. The correspondent for *Dwight's Journal* touched on a fact even more startling, one that insured the company's prompt return after its tour of the inland cities: "Mr. Maguire, who already enjoys half profit of the engagement, has already made ten thousand dollars."[29]

FOURTEEN

The *Annus mirabilis:*
San Francisco
Mad for Opera

After its midsummer tour to Sacramento and the interior the Maguire-Lyster company returned to San Francisco and, on 28 August 1860 at Maguire's Opera House, opened its second season of Italian and English opera, twenty performances in twenty-one nights. This time the ratio of Italian to English performances decreased from roughly 3:1 to 2:1, partly because Eliza Biscaccianti was no longer on the roster. Why she was dropped is not clear, but presumably Lyster's reasons were mixed. Clearly, however well she had sung, in the same repertory as Lucy Escott she was the lesser draw at the box office; and probably, too, he wished to reactivate the English repertory, for which there was a large audience.

This time the Italian wing's new opera, though not a local premiere, was Donizetti's *La favorita,* which played five nights; and Donizetti, with an additional performance of *Lucia di Lammermoor* and two of *Lucrezia Borgia,* dominated the season. The other Italian composers represented were Bellini, with one performance of *Norma,* and Verdi, with two each of *Ernani* and *Trovatore* and one of *Traviata.* Verdi, however, had the first and last nights, opening the season with *Ernani,* and closing it, on 17 September, with *Trovatore.*[1]

The revival of *La traviata,* but not of *Rigoletto,* suggests that the

189

former, despite the burden of being costumed in the wrong period, had
begun to reveal its strength as an intimate drama. With so many
repetitions of operas, the critics for the most part had stopped reviewing them, but a remark in passing after a performance of *Traviata* hints
that the man on the *Alta California* now sensed that the opera, particularly in its tenor role, was quite different from *Ernani* or *Trovatore*. Of
Squires, he wrote:

> There is a natural grace and dignity about the acting, and a delicacy of tone
> in the singing, of this fine tenor, which we would not have him change for
> any attempt at *robusto*, or straining for effect. The peculiar tones of his voice
> have never yet been equalled here. In fact, he is *the* American tenor; none
> others at all approach him, and it is the refined elegance of his style which
> lends a charm to his exquisite voice.[2]

Elegance of style, delicacy of tone, are not the most important
qualities for singing the roles of Ernani or Manrico, both of which
thrive on vigorous "effect"—even if some strain is required to achieve
it. Indeed, to some degree a slight sense of strain fits the excitement of
the music in those operas, whether for tenor, soprano, baritone, or bass.
But that is less true, if true at all, of *Traviata*, a domestic drama in
which the passions are kept muted, inwardly felt rather than declared.
The opera seeks a different response from an audience than *Ernani* or
Trovatore, and for it to have a real success, as San Franciscans apparently were starting to discover, the audience must come to it with a
different expectation.

The first English opera of this second season, a single performance,
was a revival of *Maritana* with Escott, but the major production, not yet
staged by Lyster, was *The Bohemian Girl*, with Rosalie Durand making
her first appearance (except for one in *Figaro*) since the disaster of *Rose
of Castille*. Squires had the tenor role of Thaddeus, with Georgia Hodson, who used to sing that part, now shifting to the less demanding
contralto role of the Gypsy Queen. Durand, whose specialty was
charm, was thought generally to be at her best as Arline, the gypsy girl
who soon turns out to be—"I dreamt I dwelt in marble halls"—the
long-lost daughter of a haughty aristocrat. At the opera's end, sur-

mounting every obstacle, she weds the gypsy of her choice, Thaddeus, who himself, it is revealed, is a member of the nobility. As this revelation of aristocratic heritage is also the theme of *Martha*, where the simple farmer Lionel turns out to be the missing earl of Derby, and so a suitable husband for Lady Harriet, the two operas, both immensely popular in their day, expose the heavy streak of sentimentality in that part of the general audience that loved them.

The public treated Durand's appearance in *The Bohemian Girl* as her return to the stage. Before the curtain rose every seat in the house was filled, and "by the end of the first act," acknowledged the critic who only two months earlier had called for her permanent retirement, "every available foot of standing room was taken." She was, moreover, received with a perfect *furore* of applause.[3]

The new English opera of this second season was *Martha*—not heard in six years, not since the days of Anna Bishop—and with it, too, Durand had a success. She also repeated her Susanna in *Figaro*, with Hodson as Cherubino and Escott as the Countess, and in all she sang five of the season's twenty performances, a record that she and her public no doubt considered a vindication.

The season's final performance was a benefit for the company's prima donna, Escott, and the occasion, combined with the opera, *Trovatore*, packed the house. As the company, if possible, was even more popular, and profitable, than before, everyone was happy, and the critic for the *Herald* has left an account of how an impresario, an audience, and an artist of the day behaved in such circumstances.

> The operatic season which has never been surpassed, even in San Francisco, the greatest patron of the lyric art in the world, came to a close last evening with a benefit to Madame Escott, which proved an ovation that could not have been other than most gratifying to the artiste. At the end of the 1st act, Mr. William Lyster appeared with Madame Escott, and presenting her a splendid gold enamelled watch, ornamented with diamond springs and a superb chain, said to the following effect: "Madame Escott, I am commissioned by a number of your friends and admirers to present you with this beautiful and valuable gift, as a feeble expression of their admiration for you as an artiste and regard for you as a lady. I also avail myself of the occasion to tender you my heartfelt thanks for your

untiring exertions and great merit as prima donna of my company, and beg
to add my felicitations upon the unequivocal success which has attended
your efforts." Madame Escott, quite excited at the unlooked for compliment, returned her acknowledgements in pretty much the following terms:
"Mr. Lyster, I beg you to convey to the gentlemen, in whose behalf you
now act, my most heartfelt acknowledgements for their precious and
elegant gift and assure them that it will ever be regarded by me with
sentiments of profound appreciation and gratitude. Permit me also to
return you my cordial thanks for your undeviating kindness and gentlemanly conduct toward myself from the time of leaving New York to the
present moment." Then, turning to the audience, Madame Escott continued: "Ladies and Gentlemen, the memory of your many favors and
repeated expression of kindly feeling will ever be cherished by me with
truest gratitude. I thank you from the innermost recesses of my heart."[4]

The fact that the company's manager, Mr. Lyster, acting on behalf
of other gentlemen, made the presentation suggests how much audience behavior in the city already had changed. Six years earlier, in the
heyday of Biscaccianti or Hayes, the admiring gentlemen would have
made the presentation themselves by rushing down the aisles to hand
or hurl their bouquets and gifts at the soprano. The new mode, however, was no less manipulative. If Hayes had her agent, Bushnell, to
arrange such demonstrations, Escott had Lyster, and most likely he had
staged the event, just as it seems likely that he had hired the claque to
which a critic earlier had objected.

In any case, the next morning the *Alta California* crudely revealed
that the watch was worth "about $275" and had been "purchased at
Tucker's." And later that day the entire company left once again for
Sacramento, where it would perform during the Agricultural Fair,
returning in early October for yet another season in San Francisco.
Though no one reports any figures, Maguire and Lyster presumably
were continuing to profit handsomely from their venture; and as yet,
the city's fever for opera showed no sign of abating.[5]

The company's third season in Maguire's Opera House began on 21
October 1860 and ran through 29 November, forty performances on
consecutive evenings. It opened with a stunt that delighted and astonished the city's music-lovers: a festival of twelve successive nights of

opera without a repetition. The repertory, in order of presentation, was *Favorita, Lucia, Bohemian Girl, Traviata, Martha, Norma, Maritana, Ernani, Lucrezia Borgia, Trovatore, Sonnambula* (in Italian, but with Durand), and, lastly, the U.S. premiere of Wallace's *Lurline,* which had received its first performance only eight months earlier, at Covent Garden on 23 February. The opera was San Francisco's second such premiere in five months, and in this year no Eastern city had more. For the moment, at least, San Franciscans, with justice, could count themselves at the forefront of the art in the United States.[6]

The new opera, *Lurline,* was another successful example of the English romantic school, playing for a time in German-speaking countries and surviving in England into the next century. It produced a number of popular songs, of which the best known was "Sweet Spirit, Hear My Prayer." Based on the legend of the Lorelei, the story is of a water sprite, Lurline, who loves and saves the life of Count Rudolph, a charming but feckless nobleman with a castle on the Rhine. Today the opera is probably most famous for anticipating Wagner and, nine years before *Das Rheingold* was staged, presenting a scene at the bottom of the Rhine. In the Covent Garden production the scenic designer, claiming license for beauty's sake to be geologically incorrect, streaked the underwater world with reefs of pink, tropical coral.[7]

In San Francisco, too, even with Escott in the title role, the production's emphasis fell chiefly on the scenery.

> In the second act the principal feature is the introduction of a double scene, the spectator being supposed to be with Rudolph below the waters of the Rhine, looking towards the banks of that beautiful stream, down which are seen floating the boats of Rudolph's followers, lamenting the loss of their master. The illusion is felicitous. . . . The rising waters of the third act, at Lurline's invocation and the descent to the domains of the River King, are also excellently managed; the appearance of Rhineberg, on his crystal throne, illumined by the glare of many-colored fires, forms an appropriate close to this splendid piece of illusion.[8]

This critic, writing for the *Alta California,* has nothing at all to say of the music; evidently the scenery and costumes—"the dresses, too, are very appropriate besides being new in many instances"—were quite overwhelming. The man on the *Bulletin*, however, though admittedly "bewildered" by the "glitter and novelty," was not without criticism of both the settings and the music. Escott's water-sprite costume, which he assumed to be "traditionary," was a ballet skirt and, in his opinion, unbecoming and too short by several inches; and though he admired the opera's concerted finales, he found its arias, in their balladlike sweetness and simplicity, "occasionally cloying and tedious." Nevertheless, like *Maritana*, *Lurline* had a great success with the public, playing nine straight nights and revived later for a tenth.[9]

As the season approached its end, Lyster constantly stressed that the final performances truly would be the last, for he planned to sail in December with all his chief artists to Australia. For his part, Maguire began to advertise the next attraction in the opera house, the Martinetti-Ravel ballet in "the Grand Fairy and Comic Pantomime" *The Green Monster*, followed by a pas de deux, *La Vivandière*. In addition, the program would offer a group of aerial experts in "Evolutions on the Tight Rope." Ticket prices remained the same.

The first of the opera company's "farewell" benefits, on 20 November, was given for Durand, who appeared in Auber's *Fra Diavolo*, an opera with which she always had enjoyed success. Four nights later Squires had his turn, and the opera was *Trovatore*. Understandably, there was enthusiasm for the artist who had sung so often and contributed so much to everyone's enjoyment, and the critic for the *Alta California*, in announcing the benefit, celebrated the man as well as the singer, though he ended on a misconception that must have startled his Italian readers:

Had he [Squires] changed his name, with the affectation of some artists, from Squires, to a romantic, high-sounding Italian one, thousands would have taken him for a native of that sunny clime. . . . But Squires laughed at such suggestions, and preferred to retain his good old Yankee name. We do not believe that he has suffered at all in popularity by such a course. Verdi is said to be of English extraction, that his right name is Green, and that he "Italicized" for effect's sake. If so, he showed less good sense as a man than genius as a composer. "Il Trovatore" is Verdi's masterpiece, and "Manrico" in it is Squire's best part.[10]

Finally, for the season's last three nights Lyster offered the Italian wing in a series of gala programs. To lead off, Escott, as a demonstration of her position as prima donna, sang, for the first time in San Francisco, Amina in Bellini's *Sonnambula;* and the following night, her benefit, she and her colleagues appeared in the first act of *Traviata,* the second of *Lucrezia Borgia,* the Wedding scene and sextet from *Lucia di Lammermoor,* and the last act of *Favorita.* The final night, made up entirely of Verdi, presented the first act of *Ernani,* the last of *Rigoletto,* and the last of *Traviata.*[11]

In this final season, because of the long run of *Lurline,* the number of performances of operas in Italian and in English was equal, nineteen each. If the last two galas are included, however, the balance tips in favor of the Italian. Overall, in the three seasons in the city, Maguire and Lyster presented 123 nights of opera—of which four were gala programs of snippets—and Squires, "the universal tenor," apparently sang every night but seven. Excluding the galas, there were seventy-eight performances of Italian opera and forty-one of English.[12]

In May, at the start of his first season, Lyster had announced that he would present "thirty-two" operas, but in fact he produced nineteen, ten Italian and nine English, including in the latter his English versions of such operas as *Der Freischütz* and *The Marriage of Figaro.* He also had promised that "the greater" number of operas would be new to the city, and in that, too, he had exaggerated. But his record was not bad. In a period of seven months, besides reviving *Martha,* which had not been heard for six years, he presented five local premieres: *I Puritani, Rigoletto, Maritana, Rose of Castille,* and *Lurline,* of which the last two were U.S. premieres. Though he evidently had no lasting success with either *I Puritani* or *Rigoletto,* and had failed outright with *Rose of Castille,* he had triumphed with *Maritana* and *Lurline*—and probably any impresario in any age would consider two winners out of five a good proportion.

One composer seen slipping from the repertory during the Lyster and Bianchi seasons of 1859–60 is Rossini. His *Barber of Seville,* whether sung in Italian or English, continues as popular as ever; but with the departure of Anna Bishop in 1855, *Tancredi,* even in excerpts, had disappeared, and also *La gazza ladra.* The Bianchis one time announced

Semiramide, but did not produce it; and when the Durand-Hodson troupe merged back into the Lyster company, the English-language version of *Cinderella* was dropped. Rossini's sun was setting, its laughter and brightness giving way to the dark, romantic dramas of Donizetti and Verdi.

At the close of Lyster's season several of the local papers and journals offered summary accounts of the wonders of the opera year. One of the more interesting appeared in the *Alta California* under the title "Italian vs. English Opera." The writer, presumably the paper's regular critic, began with a discussion of money:

> The opera has become a regular institution among us. No other kind of public amusement has been so uniformly and extensively supported. The opera has never been very successful in the great cities of the Atlantic seaboard. In New York it generally results in managerial embarrassment, and the case, in all probability, is to be found in the fact that it is a species of amusement too expensive for the masses of the people. It is different with us. Wealth is more evenly distributed among our citizens, and there are but few who are compelled to deny themselves any kind of amusement they may prefer.[13]

Certainly, the economic depression that had gripped the city in the middle of the decade had lifted, and people again had money for entertainment. The structure of the population, however, continued to influence how the money was spent. Rounding the figures of the 1860 census to the nearest thousand, San Francisco County, which included the city and its immediate environs, had a total population of 57,000, of which men were 35,000 and women 22,000. Of the men, 21,000, or almost two-thirds, were between the ages of twenty and forty, with an additional 4,000 between forty and fifty. Though the number of men in proportion to women was declining, San Francisco was still a city predominantly of men, most of them single, most of them under forty. In the evening, if they had money, and most did, they sought entertainment—in the brothel, in the saloon, in the gambling hall, or in the theatre.[14]

The critic for the *Alta California*, however, soon abandoned his argument about wealth and population and went on to another. "The point to which we desire particularly to direct attention," he wrote, "is the preference which has on all occasions been manifested for the Italian over the English opera." Ignoring the demonstrated popularity of English opera, he dismissed brusquely any suggestion that the Italian was preferred for reasons of fashion or status; the truth lay elsewhere.

> English opera entirely destroys the illusion which contributes so essentially to the full enjoyment of the piece. It is all nonsense to try to make us believe that the Anglo Saxon warbles forth his sweetest notes when he is in a towering passion, makes known his love in song, or slays his enemy in a musical ecstasy. . . . Of course no one supposes for a moment that the Italians disport themselves under their native skies, in the highly artistic and entertaining manner set forth in opera, or that every Italian shepherd intones the admonitions that he may deem necessary to give his flock, speaks in song and prays in *basso profondo*, but they can come nearer to that perfection in melody than the Anglo Saxon; hence it is that we are content to give them a monopoly in the opera. In addition, the English language is not mellifluous enough for such performances.

After offering two English words, *splurge* and *cantankerous*, as examples of what no one could sing melodiously, though the language admittedly was "very fine" for business, science, or "to command a ship," he finished with the ringing assertion, "Italian opera always for us."[15]

Unhappily, he did not record for posterity his view of the musical qualities of the two schools. It would be interesting to know whether he, and that part of the audience for which he presumably spoke, found the English operas, with their simpler harmonies, orchestrations, and melodies, musically naive and, in their frequent resort to words alone for the climax of a story, musically disappointing.

In 1825, the German composer Carl Maria von Weber had pointed to this preference for words over music, particularly at the climax, as a crucial difference of approach. Invited to England to compose an English opera, *Oberon*, in conjunction with the librettist James Robinson Planché, he wrote to Planché: "The cut of an English opera is certainly very different from a German one. The English is more a drama with songs." And in another letter: "The intermixing of so many principal actors who do not sing—the omission of music in the most important moments—all of these deprive our *Oberon* of the title of an opera." An Italian composer equally would have deplored "the omission of music in the most important moments."[16] Imagine *Lucia di Lammermoor* if Donizetti, at the moment the tenor bursts into the wedding party to accuse the bride of breaking her vow to marry *him,* had resorted to spoken dialogue instead of composing the sextet "Chi me frena in tal momento?"

Yet in this decade in San Francisco, the experience of opera impresarios such as Sinclair, Bianchi, or Lyster seemed to indicate that a company must offer both kinds of opera if it was to prove profitable and survive. And the rule apparently still holds: if the audience for English opera and its successors, such as operetta or musical comedy, is not welcomed into the opera house and given a sizable share of the repertory, that audience will go elsewhere—Broadway, West End, or the circus. And with the loss of that audience's interest and support, opera aimed solely at the more musically inclined will be unable to sustain itself, will plunge into debt and need subsidy.

After the Maguire-Lyster seasons had finished, there was a short coda of Lyster without Maguire, the only period in 1860 when opera in the city was not produced by Maguire. Lyster had booked passage for the company on the 700-ton British clipper *Achilles,* and because its captain, H. F. Hart, did not plan to sail until the day after Christmas, there was time for a six-night season, 17 through 22 December, at the American Theatre.[17] With a capacity of 2,000 (300 seats larger than Maguire's house), the American changed slightly the balance between the singers, being an improvement for Escott, whose volume could bloom, but not so good for Squires.[18] On most nights Lyster provided something extra as a farewell gift to the audience which had been so kind; the operas, with their fillips, were *Ernani* and the first act of *Trovatore, La favorita, Lucia di Lammermoor* and the last act of *Rigoletto, Maritana* and the "Muleteer's Song" for tenor from *Rose of Castille, Lucrezia Borgia* and the brindisi from *Traviata,* and *The Bohemian Girl.*[19]

The three Maguire-Lyster seasons in San Francisco in 1860, if taken
alone, achieved an extraordinary number of performances for a small
city, a total of 123, and with the coda, 129. When to these are added the
sixteen performances earlier in the year by the Lyster company in its
reduced form, the Durand-Hodson troupe, the total becomes 145. Say
that on average 1,500 hundred seats were sold for each performance,
that would amount to 217,500 seats sold to a population of 60,000. If
today the Metropolitan Opera of New York, whose house seats 3,800,
were to sell proportionately the same number of seats to New York's
population of 8,000,000—3.63 seats per persons—to accommodate the
audience the Metropolitan would need to build twenty additional
houses of the same size and run all twenty-one every night of the year.
Or, to make the parallel more exact, if the Metropolitan company were
to give 145 performances in the year, the number achieved in San
Francisco in 1860, then to accommodate a proportionate audience it
would have to build and open for performance on 145 evenings an
additional fifty-two houses.

In the long history of music, there are several cities that at different
periods have gone mad for opera. In Europe in the mid–seventeenth
century, when opera was just beginning, it was Venice; and in the
United States, in the mid–nineteenth century, New Orleans. In the
years before the Civil War the continuity of New Orleans's passion
was quite unrivaled. In those years it was the only city of the United
States to sustain a resident company, and in the five years 1836/37–
1840/41, for example, it heard some 479 performances of opera. Yet
even New Orleans at its most frenzied, it seems, never matched the
intensity of San Francisco's opera-going in the final year of the Gold
Rush decade. In the United States, no other city, at any time, has had
a passion for opera to equal that of San Francisco in 1860.[20]

Epilogue

Most likely, depending on each reader's previous knowledge of San Francisco or Verdi, he or she will find in this history a different set of surprises. I, for one, had not expected the constant movement of singers, chiefly Italians, up and down the Pacific coast of North and South America—Santiago, Valparaíso, Lima, Mexico City, and then, in the early 1850s, San Francisco. Among those arriving directly from that circuit who contributed significantly to the development of opera in San Francisco were the two Pellegrinis, Leonardi, Cailly, and the two Bianchis.

Nor did I foresee the number of artists that Australia would lure from San Francisco in the late 1850s and early 1860s: Hayes, Bishop, Bochsa, Loder, the two Bianchis, the Frenchmen Laglaise and Coulon, and the Lyster company, including Escott, Squires, and Hodson. Taken all together, the impact of these artists on the musical life of Australia and New Zealand was tremendous.

In San Francisco I was startled by the large role played by the French. The Germans and the Italians, it seems to me, behaved much as they did in other cities; their contribution to the development of music throughout the country is well recognized. The French, however, while acknowledged to be the leaders in New Orleans and to have made influential tours in the first half of the century with the New Orleans opera companies, generally are thought to be less significant. But in San Francisco, during this first decade, the resident French were of equal, and often greater, importance than the Italians or Germans.

The French established the city's first resident opera company, were the first to present (of course, in French) *Lucie de Lammermoor* and *Le Barbier de Seville*; the first to stage a U.S. premiere, Grisar's *Gilles Ravisseur*; and the first to found a music school. Yet San Franciscans, in talking or writing of their city's operatic history, have little to say of the French.

I also was surprised by the strength of English opera throughout the decade. Usually its height is put in the years 1835–45, with a decline thereafter that was not reversed until the operettas of Gilbert and Sullivan in the 1870s. But in San Francisco in 1860, with the premieres of *Maritana, Rose of Castille,* and *Lurline,* the constant repetitions of *The Bohemian Girl,* and the occasional revivals of such operas as *The Enchantress* and *The Beggar's Opera,* English opera was more than a weak second to Italian and stronger than either French or German.

Unhappily for opera in general, in my opinion, when Gilbert and Sullivan began their revival of English opera, their works typically were produced in theatres rather than in opera houses: in London, at the Savoy, specially built for them; and in New York, throughout the 1880s, at the Fifth Avenue Theatre, not at the Academy of Music or at the Metropolitan. A large public that liked English opera was encouraged to go elsewhere than an opera house to hear it, and became used to the idea that it was something different from "serious" opera—call it, if you will, light opera, operetta, or musical comedy.

The English versions of operas, Henry Bishop's of the *Barber* or M.R. Lacy's of *Cinderella,* soon satisfied no one and by the turn of the century had disappeared. Opera in translation, a different species, continued an uneven life, but it, too, like the operettas or musical comedies, tended increasingly to be produced outside the major opera houses.

That widening split between "serious" and "light" opera, I believe, hurt both styles. The serious needs the audience that was lost, as well as the acting ability and charm of light opera's artists; and light opera, whether as operetta or musical comedy, needs in its orchestra pit and onstage the musical standards of the serious. When a Henry Squires sings in *The Bohemian Girl*, the opera gains quality. In the mid-twentieth century the Metropolitan Opera Company might have profited in more ways than one if it had held to the older tradition and offered its bass Ezio Pinza in *South Pacific* or its baritone Robert Weede in *The Most Happy Fellow*. And why not?

The departure for Australia of the Lyster troupe, which in one company and one house had so profitably combined English and Italian opera, signaled the end of an era in the cultural life of San Francisco. In referring to the troupe's seasons in the city, the critic for the *Alta California* had written proudly, "The opera has become a regular institution among us." But alas, it was not so. In all of 1861 the city had not a single performance of opera. The chief reason is obvious: in the East, in April, after months of suspense and agitation, the Civil War began, immediately damping interest in the arts in both the North and South and slowing for a time the flow of immigrants, including singers, into California.[1] When in 1862 opera reappeared in San Francisco, it started feebly with local artists, gaining vigor only when the Bianchis—coming from the West, not the East—returned from Australia.[2]

Another sign that the city's Gold Rush era was at an end came in 1861 with the completion of the transcontinental telegraph. The wire service greatly reduced the city's isolation, and the excitement of "steamer night," already lessened by the telegraph lines running up and down the Pacific Coast, faded into memory. The city, though still distant and different, became part of the United States.

The revival of opera in 1862 displays how far in eleven years San Francisco had advanced in musical resources and sophistication. This time there was no need to retrace the steps by which opera initially established itself in the city: first an aria or two sung in a recital of songs, then a recital of operatic excerpts, later still a concert of opera arias or scenes in costume, and finally a staged production. This time even the weak local troupe began with fully staged productions, though apparently with only a small chorus and orchestra and little in

the way of scenery. But with the return of the Bianchis, who absorbed
the best of the local troupe, the scale and standard of production
promptly resumed a level the critics and audiences now took as normal.[3]

Bianchi announced a roster of twelve singers and a conductor, and
on occasion added guest artists. The orchestra apparently numbered
close to thirty, still barely half of what a small house in a major Italian
city might supply, but enough to allow a string section of thirteen or
fourteen, the minimum needed for *La traviata,* two each of flutes, oboes,
clarinets, bassoons, French horns, and trumpets, and one percussionist.
Other instruments, such as trombones, were added as needed. The
total, however, was still small. In the years 1867–70, for example, the
New York Philharmonic Society, in order to play the new romantic
works of such composers as Berlioz or Wagner, enlarged its orchestra
pool from seventy-eight to over a hundred players.[4]

The chorus, twenty-four or more strong, now was always mixed,
though still at times shy on female voices; and the practice of occasionally recruiting additional singers from the German choral clubs continued, as it would elsewhere for many years. To use another example
from New York, the Metropolitan Opera, for the American premiere
of *Die Meistersinger* in 1886, enlarged its chorus of eighty-two by adding
sixty men from the Liederkranz and Arion societies.[5]

By way of comparison, consider a company starting in 1957—the
Santa Fe Opera—on what many persons then considered a frontier.
Based in a city of 30,000, but with three nearby cities bringing the
potential audience up to 300,000, the company for its first season
offered a repertory of six operas, twenty-seven performances in two
months, a theatre seating 450, a roster of thirteen singers for solo roles,
an orchestra of twenty-nine players and thirty-two instruments, five
conductors (in 1958 reduced to two), and a mixed chorus of eight. Only
two or three of the company were more than thirty-five years old, most
were under thirty, and about 70 percent of the audience never had
heard an opera.[6]

One practice, common for a time in San Francisco but never started
in Santa Fe, was the casting of women in roles composed for men. The

last occasion of it in San Francisco, at least in Verdi's operas, was Georgia Hodson's singing of Manrico in the two performances of *Trovatore* in March 1860. In England the custom held on longer, particularly for certain roles, such as Federico in *Mignon;* yet, because the practice plainly upset the composer's balance for concerted numbers, trios, sextets, and so forth, almost anyone whose interest was primarily musical was against it.[7]

In San Francisco, or anywhere on the frontier, to some extent the custom can be explained by the dearth of competent artists—surely the reason for Pellegrini and Bianchi casting *Ernani* and *Attila* with women in the baritone roles. But in these years in opera there was a strong tradition of such cross-casting—Anna Bishop, for one, liked to frolic in men's parts—and it pertained as well to the spoken theatre. San Francisco audiences in the 1850s witnessed at least four female Romeos, two Hamlets, an Oliver Twist, and a David Copperfield, as well as many child actors who took adult parts. One six-year-old girl, Anna Maria Quinn, played Hamlet.[8]

Another practice of these years that died more slowly was the introduction into an opera of an aria or ballad from some other opera, even if the work of a different composer—which, again, the musicians and those in the audience with an interest in music increasingly turned against. Clara Louise Kellogg, the American soprano, could state with regret that the public had no interest in an opera's artistic integrity and wanted only "to hear popular singers and familiar airs." But as her autobiography reveals, when she succeeded in giving a role some consistency, some depth of character, the audience usually responded. And although for another hundred years tradition would declare of certain operas, such as the *Barber of Seville,* that an aria or song by another composer might be inserted here or there, the trend was against the practice.[9]

Thus when the Bianchis, in May 1862, returned to San Francisco after two and a half years in Australia, they were able to reconstitute an opera company and open a season on terms taken for granted today: a small but adequate orchestra and chorus, an experienced conductor, a roster of singers that, on paper at least, suitably could fill the leading

roles, and a repertory that both artists and audiences would treat with
some respect for the composer's wishes. They even soon were able to
offer, in primitive form, a type of subscription: for the payment of ten
dollars in advance, the patron received twelve operas for the price of
ten.[10] By the end of the Gold Rush years, in short, opera production
in San Francisco had come to resemble its counterparts in most other
cities. Differences now were more ones of degree than of kind.

More than most cities, however, San Francisco continued to be
hospitable to opera. The Bianchis and Maguire, often in competition,
were lavish in their seasons, and after they retired two Germans
founded the Tivoli Theatre, which for almost thirty years (1880–1906)
put on a mixture of light and serious opera almost nightly. In that
period the Tivoli probably was the most active opera house in the
United States. Then, after a troubled period—beginning with the 1906
earthquake and extending through World War I—the present San
Francisco Opera was founded in 1923, and soon became one of the
country's best and most interesting companies. But those are stories for
another day.

Meanwhile, in the 1860s, in San Francisco and across the country,
audience behavior slowly improved; its habits can be followed most
easily in the more firmly established eastern institutions whose histories have been written. In New York in 1870, George Templeton
Strong became president of the Philharmonic Society and began a
campaign, through handbills, to curb the continual walking in and
out, talking, and giggling during performances. Spitting remained a
problem, also smoking; and at the turn of the century a new one
developed, outsized ladies' hats. On one occasion in the Manhattan
Opera House, the wife of a steel magnate refused to remove hers: it
was three feet across.[11]

The most effective leaders in the campaigns for better audience
behavior were the orchestra conductors and the house managers. The latter wanted to make the symphony hall or opera house
attractive to the fashionable and well behaved, and to families and
music-lovers; the conductors were determined to have the music

paramount. The managers had the power, which they sometimes ex-
ercised, to eject the rude and noisy; the conductors had the power of
ridicule. Once, in New York, when a man in the front row at a
concert continually talked and "snapped" explosive matches to light
his cigar, Theodore Thomas stopped the orchestra and said in a loud
voice, "Go on, sir! Don't mind us! We can all wait until you light
your cigar." And at a concert in Nashville, Victor Herbert admon-
ished some early leavers: "It will take ten minutes to play this piece.
You who are in a hurry perhaps had better leave now." Among those
who sheepishly resumed their seats was the governor of Tennessee.
But again, a price was paid for decorum: a part of the audience was
lost.[12]

Throughout the late nineteenth century, and into the early years of
the next, opera continued to be popular, aided by such stars as Caruso
and the development of such marvels as radio and the phonograph. But
gradually there was a falling off, and seemingly not just because of the
rise of competing forms of entertainment such as the movies. Some
scholars blame a deeper cultural shift that injured not only opera but
also, to some extent, the spoken theatre.

As Lawrence Levine, a historian of Shakespeare in nineteenth-
century America, has pointed out, the playwright lent himself to the
ethos of the day:

> When Cassius proclaimed that "The fault, dear Brutus, is not in our stars,
> / But in ourselves, that we are underlings" (*Julius Caesar,* I.ii), and when
> Helena asserted that "Our remedies oft in ourselves do lie, / Which we
> ascribe to heaven: the fated sky / Gives us free scope" (*All's Well That Ends
> Well,* I.i), they articulated a belief that was central to the pervasive success
> ethos of the nineteenth century and that confirmed the developing Ameri-
> can world view. Whatever Shakespeare's own designs, philosophy, and
> concept of humanity were, his plays had meaning to a nation that placed
> the individual at the center of the universe and personalized the large
> questions of the day.[13]

The same is even more true of opera, which seems in its essence to
celebrate the individual, not only in the stories that it mostly has found

suitable for musical telling, but in its performers as well. As W. H. Auden put it,

> The golden age of opera, from Mozart to Verdi, coincided with the golden age of liberal humanism, of unquestioning belief in freedom and progress. If good operas are rarer today, this may be because, not only have we learned that we are less free than nineteenth-century humanism imagined, but also have become less certain that freedom is an unequivocal blessing, that the free are necessarily the good. To say that operas are more difficult to write does not mean that they are impossible. That would only follow if we should cease to believe in free will and personality altogether. Every high C accurately struck demolishes the theory that we are the irresponsible puppets of fate or chance.[14]

In San Francisco, in the Gold Rush years, Verdi's operas spoke to men and women who put their trust in God and self-help, who believed that they carried their fates and souls in their own hands and were responsible for themselves, their actions, and, except for acts of God—earthquake, flood, shipwreck—for whatever happened to them. The burden of such responsibility proved too heavy for many, and there was much drunkenness and suicide. But the idea that perhaps their actions were predetermined by culture and that therefore they had no responsibility for them, or that society, and not the individual, was at fault for his or her failure, did not occur to them. Such ideas are difficult for music to express, in part because to some extent they deny the possibility of heroic action, or even of individuality, and persons drawn to these ideas as explanations of life no doubt find most opera very old-fashioned.

All that, however, was in the future. When the Bianchis returned to San Francisco in May 1862, they were, though they may not have known it, in the heyday of opera, with Verdi, at the moment, the dominant composer. In 1862 and 1863 they produced an extraordinary festival of his works (Fig. 18)—ten of the twenty-four existing operas, of which the most recent, *La forza del destino* (1862), probably was not yet available to them. In 1862 they presented *Nabucco* (5 performances), *Ernani* (6), *Attila* (2), *Macbeth* (4), *Rigoletto* (3), *Trovatore* (11), and *Traviata* (3); and in 1863, *Nabucco* (3), *Ernani* (7), *I due Foscari* (5), *Macbeth* (1), *I*

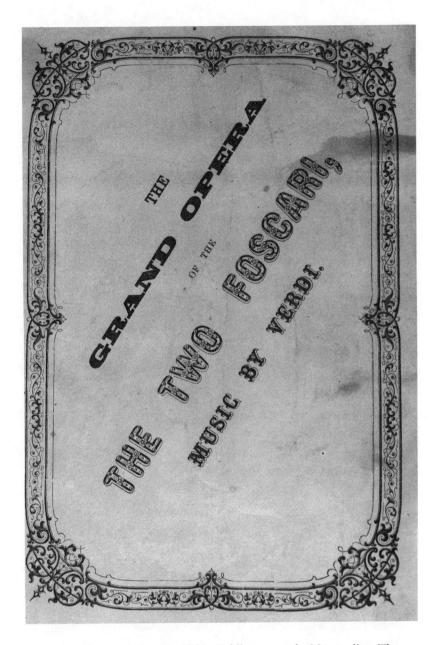

Fig. 18.   A libretto for the Bianchis' 1863 fall season at the Metropolitan Theatre, printed locally by Lewis, Book and Job Printer, and containing a synopsis of the opera and its text in English. There were performances on 23 and 26 October, 6 and 20 November, and 16 December. (Pierpont Morgan Library, New York; George W. Martin Collection)

masnadieri (8), *Luisa Miller* (3), *Rigoletto* (1), *Trovatore* (6), and *Traviata* (5). And two years later they added *I Lombardi* (3) and *Un ballo in maschera* (11).[15]

Plainly, for Verdi to attain such popularity, audiences must have responded to his music; but also, I think, they responded to his gloomy idealism. He could write, "In life there is only death. What else lasts?" Yet all his operas celebrate Auden's "liberal humanism"—a man or a woman, a free will and personality, taking action against odds for some noble purpose: liberty, honor, love, country, a nation's independence, and unity. In a time that did not have modern medicine, in a period of Civil War, men and women perhaps heard in Verdi's pessimism a reflection of their own melancholy and of the death they felt around them; and in his melodramas they thrilled to his call to make something fine of dying.

In these years the country was led by Abraham Lincoln, a man of the frontier and the most opera-loving president in our history. While in office he attended nineteen performances of opera, some without Mrs. Lincoln, who apparently cared for it less. At his first inauguration the band played selections from *Rigoletto*, and later, when the band was criticized for playing too much opera and too little martial or national music, Lincoln supported the bandmaster's choice of repertory. As part of the festivities of his second inauguration, he attended a specially mounted production of Flotow's *Martha*.[16]

In retrospect, perhaps the most poignant night of his operagoing occurred on 20 February 1861, when he was on his way to his first inauguration, traveling from Springfield, Illinois, via Albany and New York City, to Washington, D.C. Early in the trip he had received from Anna Bishop, who was singing at Niblo's Garden in New York, an invitation to a performance there of English opera; but instead, either he or his New York hosts decided that as president-elect he should go to the Academy of Music to hear Verdi's new opera, *Un ballo in maschera*.[17] Lincoln, who was both tired and aware that his presence in the Academy was disrupting the performance, left for his hotel after the second intermission; and so he did not see the final act, in which, at a ball set in an opera house, a head of state is assassinated. But the possibility of his own assassination had entered his mind, for the next day, during a speech in Philadelphia, he mentioned it. And four years later, on 14 April 1865, as he sat in a box at Ford's Theatre watching Laura Keene in *Our American Cousin,* he was shot by an assassin, and the next day died. In these years, between Verdi's operas and life, as opera-loving Americans experienced it, there was no gap of unreality. In Verdi's art *was* life, and truth.

Opera Premieres in San Francisco, 1851 Through 1860, with Theatre, Cast, and Number of Performances

In the following table an asterisk (*) indicates a U.S., and possibly Western Hemisphere, premiere. A question mark (?) indicates that either the initial or name of the person, or the role sung, is unknown. Or, if used with a name thus, [G. Loder?], it indicates that, although there is no statement, in either an advertisement, news item, or review, that Loder was the conductor for the performance, there is other, circumstantial reason for thinking so.

Appendix A

Opera	Composer	No. Perfs, 1851–1855	No. Perfs, 1859–1860	Total Perfs., 1851–1860	San Francisco Premiere	Theatre	Cast (Women; Men; Conductor) (Character's initial denotes role)
La sonnambula	Bellini	12	11	23	12 Feb. 1851	Adelphi	R. Mauri-Pellegrini (A), F. Abalos (L); I. Pellegrini (E), V. Acquasoni (R); [?]
Norma	Bellini	11	13	24	27 Feb. 1851	Adelphi	F. Abalos (N), M. Von Gulpen (A); I. Pellegrini (P), V. Acquasoni (O); [?]
Ernani	Verdi	7	15	22	8 Apr. 1851	Adelphi	R. Mauri-Pellegrini (E); I. Pellegrini (Er), M. Von Gulpen (mez-sop, C), V. Acquasoni (S); [?]

[No opera staged in 1852]

La Fille du régiment	Donizetti	11	8	19	18 Sept. 1853	Adelphi	H. Planel (M); [?] Laglaise (T), E. Coulon (S); T. Planel
La Favorite	Donizetti	10	10	20	25 Sept. 1853	Adelphi	H. Planel (L); [?] Laglaise (F), E. Coulon (A), A. Roncovieri (B); T. Planel
La Dame blanche	Boieldieu	3	0	3	16 Oct. 1853	Adelphi	H. Planel (A); [?] Laglaise (G), E. Coulon (Gv); [T. Planel ?]
Gilles Ravisseur*	Grisar	2	0	2	30 Oct. 1853	Adelphi	H. Planel; [?] Laglaise, [?] Richer, E. Coulon; [T. Planel?]
Il barbiere di Siviglia	Rossini	4	5	9	27 Nov. 1853	Adelphi	H. Planel (R); Richer (A), [?] Bonnet (F), E. Coulon (Dr. B); [T. Planel?]. In French

Appendix A (*continued*)

Opera	Composer	No. Perfs., 1851–1855	No. Perfs., 1859–1860	Total Perfs., 1851–1860	San Francisco Premiere	Theatre	Cast (*Women; Men; Conductor*) (*Character's initial denotes role*)
	1854					1854	
Crown Diamonds (Les Diamants de la couronne)	Auber	6	10	16	16 Jan. 1854	Metropolitan	A. Thillon (C); S. Leach (B), [?] Hudson (H); G. Loder
Black Domino (Le Domino noir)	Auber	2	0	2	30 Jan. 1854	Metropolitan	A. Thillon (A); S. Leach (M), [?] Hudson (GP); [G. Loder?]
The Enchantress	Balfe	9	3	12	6 Feb. 1854	Metropolitan	A. Thillon (St); S. Leach (R), [?] Hudson (S); [G. Loder?]
The Bohemian Girl	Balfe	8	15	23	13 Mar. 1854	Metropolitan	A. Thillon (A), J. Gould (GQ); J. Beutler (T), S. Leach (D); [G. Loder?]

Lucia di Lammermoor	Donizetti	4	13	17	16 Apr. 1854	Metropolitan	C. Cailly (L); [?] Maturin (E), [?] Laglaise (A), E. Coulon (En); [T. Planel?]. In French
*Le Maître de chapelle**	Paer	1	1	2	4 May 1854	Union	C. Cailly; E. Coulon, [?] Douchet; T. Planel. [In French?]
Dom Pasquale	Donizetti	3	2	5	11 May 1854	Metropolitan	A. Bishop (N); J. Beutler (E), J. Mengis (M), F.Leonardi(P); [?]
Cinderella	Rossini	4	4	8	19 May 1854	Metropolitan	A. Thillon (C), J. Gould (FQ); S. Leach (D), [?] Hudson (?), J. Mengis (?); [G. Loder?]. In English

Appendix A (continued)

Opera	Composer	No. Perfs., 1851–1855	No. Perfs., 1859–1860	Total Perfs., 1851–1860	San Francisco Premiere	Theatre	Cast (Women; Men; Conductor) (Character's initial denotes role)
Linda di Chamounix	Donizetti	3	0	3	18 June 1854	Metropolitan	A. Bishop (L), J. Gould (P); J. Beutler (A), J. Mengis (A); [?]. In English
Lucrezia Borgia	Donizetti	7	17	24	23 June 1854	Metropolitan	A. Bishop (L), J. Gould (M); J. Beutler (G), J. Mengis (A); G. Loder
Der Freischütz	Weber	8	2	10	19 July 1854	Metropolitan	A. Bishop (Ag), J. Gould (An); J. Beutler (M), J. Mengis (C); N. Bochsa. In English

Masaniello (*La Muette de Portici*)	Auber	0	6	6	17 Aug. 1854	Metropolitan	J. Gould (E), [?] Montplaisir (mute, F); [?] Phelps (M), S. Leach (P); [?]. In English
Juditb (pastiche, based on *Nabucco*)	Verdi	0	6	6	21 Sept. 1854	Metropolitan	A. Bishop (Jud); S. Leach (H), [?] Laglaise (Josh); N. Bochsa
Martha	Flotow	4	7	11	17 Oct. 1854	Metropolitan	A. Bishop (H), [?] Fiddes (N); [?] Laglaise (L), S. Leach (P); [N. Bochsa]. [In English ?]
Fra Diavolo	Auber	9	1	10	25 Nov. 1854	Metropolitan	[?] Fiddes (P), C. N. Sinclair (Z); A. Bishop (sop, D), [?] Laglaise (L), S. Leach (C); N. Bochsa. In English

Appendix A (*continued*)

Opera	Composer	No. Perfs., 1851–1855	No. Perfs., 1859–1860	Total Perfs., 1851–1860	San Francisco Premiere	Theatre	Cast (*Women; Men; Conductor*) (*Character's initial denotes role*)
Nabucco	Verdi	3	0	3	30 Nov. 1854	Metropolitan	M. Bedei (A), M. S. Voorhees (F); A. Lanzoni (N), F. Leonardi (Z), C. Scola (I); G. Loder
Maria di Rohan	Donizetti	2	0	2	6 Dec. 1854	Metropolitan	C. Barili-Thorn (M); M. S. Voorhees (sop, A), C. Scola (R), J. Mengis (E); [G. Loder?]
Robert le diable	Meyerbeer	6	0	6	12 Jan. 1855	Metropolitan	A. Bishop (A), J. Gould (I); [?] Collins (Ra), J. Mengis (R), S. Leach (B); N. Bochsa. In English

1855

1855

Opera	Composer			Date	Theater	Cast
L'elisir d'amore	Donizetti	4	0	8 Feb. 1855	Metropolitan	A. Bishop (A); C. Scola (N), A. Lanzoni (B), J. Mengis (D); [?]
Don Giovanni	Mozart	3	0	8 Mar. 1855	Metropolitan	A. Bishop (A), J. Gould (E), C. Barili-Thorn (Z); C. Scola (O), A. Lanzoni (G), J. Mengis (L), A. Ronconvieri (M); N. Bochsa
I due Foscari	Verdi	5	0	23 Mar. 1855	American	C. Barili-Thorn (L); C. Scola (J), A. Lanzoni (F); [G. Loder?]
I Lombardi alla prima crociata	Verdi	3	0	1 May 1855	Metropolitan	C. Barili-Thorn (G); A. Lanzoni (P), [?] Laglaise (A), C. Scola (O); G. Loder

Appendix A (*continued*)

Opera	Composer	No. Perfs., 1851–1855	No. Perfs., 1859–1860	Total Perfs., 1851–1860	San Francisco Premiere	Theatre	Cast (*Women; Men; Conductor*) (*Character's initial denotes role*)
La gazza ladra	Rossini	2	0	2	12 July 1855	Metropolitan	A. Bishop (N), M. Von Gulpen (P), [?] Beccherini (L); [?] Laglaise (G), J. Mengis (Mayor), A. Lanzoni (F); N. Bochsa. [In English ?]
Il trovatore	Verdi	[No opera staged in 1856, 1857, 1858]					
Il trovatore	Verdi	—	22	22	5 May 1859	Maguire's Op. Hs.	G. Bianchi (L), J. Feret (A); E. Bianchi (M), S. Leach (di L); [F. ?] Feret
The Beggar's Opera	Pepusch	—	3	3	26 July 1859	Maguire's Op. Hs.	R. Durand (P); G. Hodson (sop, Mc); A. Reiff

Jean de Paris	Boildieu	—	3	3	10 Aug. 1859	Maguire's Op. Hs.	R. Durand (Prn), A. King (R); G. Hodson (sop, V), F. Trevor (J); A. Reiff?]. [In English?]
La traviata	Verdi	—	12	12	13 Aug. 1859	American	G. Bianchi (V); E. Bianchi (A), S. Leach (G); R. Herold
Attila	Verdi	—	2	2	18 Aug. 1859	American	G. Bianchi (O); E. Bianchi (F), E. Kammerer (mez-sop, E) S. Leach (A); R. Herold
Le nozze di Figaro (in an arrangement by F. Lyster)	Mozart	—	7	7	3 Oct. 1859	American	R. Durand (S), G. Hodson (C), A. King (Cnts); F. Lyster (F), S. Leach (Cnt, [?] Boudinot (Bar), F. Trevor (Bas); [A. Reiff?]. [In English?]

Appendix A (*continued*)

Opera	Composer	No. Perfs, 1851–1855	No. Perfs, 1859–1860	Total Perfs, 1851–1860	San Francisco Premiere	Theatre	Cast (*Women; Men; Conductor*) (*Character's initial denotes role*)
	1860				1860		
Mariana	Wallace	—	9	9	22 May 1860	Maguire's Op. Hs.	L. Escott (M); H. Squires (Ce), S. Leach (J), G. Hodson (sop, L), J. De Haga (Ca); A. Reiff.
Rose of Castille	Balfe	—	2	2	18 June 1860	Maguire's Op. Hs.	R. Durand (R); H. Squires (M), F. Lyster (?), J. De Haga (?); [A. Reiff?]
Rigoletto	Verdi	—	3	3	1 July 1860	Maguire's Op. Hs.	L. Escott (G); H. Squires (D), F. Lyster (R), J. De Haga (S); A. Reiff.

| I puritani | Bellini | — | 2 | 18 July 1860 | Maguire's Op. Hs. | E. Biscaccianti (El), A. King (E); H. Squires (A), F. Lyster (W), J. De Haga (G), F. Trevor (B), A. Roncovieri (R); A. Reiff. |
| Lurline | Wallace | — | 10 | 1 Nov. 1860 | Maguire's Op. Hs. | L. Escott (L), G. Hodson (O); H. Squires (R), S. Leach (Rhine King), J. De Haga (Z); A. Reiff. |

[No opera staged in 1861]

Chief Theatres
for Opera
in San Francisco, 1851–60

Theatre	Dates	Persons and Events
Jenny Lind I (cap. 400?)	opened, 30 Oct. 1850; burned, 4 May 1851	Owner-manager, Tom Maguire; Von Gulpen sings first Verdi aria heard in city
Jenny Lind II (cap. 700?)	opened, 13 June 1851; burned, 22 June 1851	Owner-manager, Tom Maguire
Jenny Lind III (cap. 2,000)	opened, 4 Oct. 1851; sold to the city in August 1852 for a city hall	Owner-manager, Tom Maguire
Adelphi I (cap. 400?)	opened, 17 Oct. 1850; burned, 4 May 1851	Pellegrini season; first opera in city: *La sonnambula*, 12 Feb. 1851
Adelphi II (cap. 700?)	opened, 1 Aug. 1851	Planel French co. first season, Sept.–Nov. 1853
Metropolitan I (cap. 2,000)	opened, 24 Dec. 1853; burned, 15 August 1857	Owner-manager until June 1855, Catherine Sinclair; Thillon, Bishop, and Barili-Thorn seasons
Metropolitan II (cap. 2,000)	opened, 1 July 1861	
American I (cap. 2,000)	opened, 20 Oct. 1851; renovated, 15 May 1853	(Theatre, built on landfill, sank two inches on opening night)
American II (cap. 2,000)	opened, 4 Dec. 1854	Barili-Thorn stages *I due Foscari*, May 1855
American III (cap. 2,800)	renovated and enlarged, March 1859	Bianchi stages *Attila* and *Traviata*, Aug. 1859

Theatre	Dates	Persons and Events
San Francisco Hall (cap. 700?)	opened, 24 Dec. 1852	Owner-manager, Tom Maguire. Opened by a Biscaccianti concert
enlarged to become Maguire's Opera House (cap. 1,100)	reopened, 29 Nov. 1856	
Maguire's Opera House (cap. 1,700)	enlarged, reopened, 6 May 1858	Bianchis make concert debut, 23 Oct. 1858
Maguire's Opera House (cap. 1,700)	redecorated, April 1859	Bianchis stage *Trovatore*, 5 May 1859. In 1860, English Opera Troupe with Escott and Squires, Durand and Hodson; premiere of *Rigoletto*

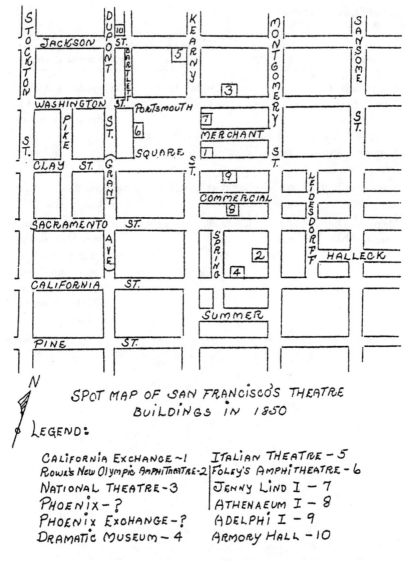

SPOT MAP OF SAN FRANCISCO'S THEATRE
BUILDINGS IN 1850

LEGEND:

CALIFORNIA EXCHANGE — 1
ROWE'S NEW OLYMPIC AMPHITHEATRE — 2
NATIONAL THEATRE — 3
PHOENIX — ?
PHOENIX EXCHANGE — ?
DRAMATIC MUSEUM — 4

ITALIAN THEATRE — 5
FOLEY'S AMPHITHEATRE — 6
JENNY LIND I — 7
ATHENAEUM I — 8
ADELPHI I — 9
ARMORY HALL — 10

These three maps are reprinted by permission of *San Francisco Theatre Research* from *Theatre Buildings,* vol. 15, part 1, WPA, San Francisco, 1940.

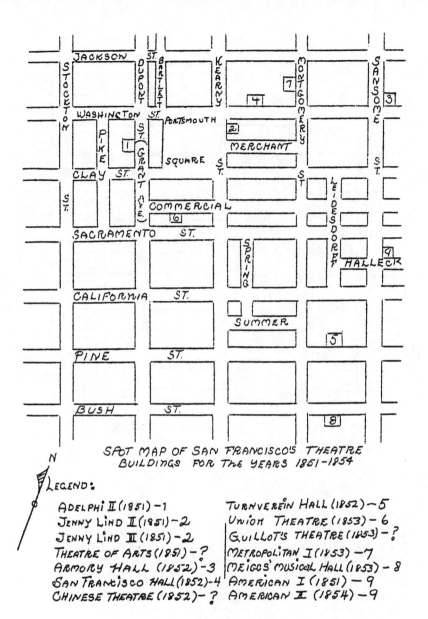

SPOT MAP OF SAN FRANCISCO'S THEATRE
BUILDINGS FOR THE YEARS 1851-1854

N

LEGEND:
ADELPHI II (1851) — 1
JENNY LIND II (1851) — 2
JENNY LIND III (1851) — 2
THEATRE OF ARTS (1851) — ?
ARMORY HALL (1852) — 3
SAN FRANCISCO HALL (1852) — 4
CHINESE THEATRE (1852) — ?

TURNVEREIN HALL (1852) — 5
UNION THEATRE (1853) — 6
GUILLOT'S THEATRE (1853) — ?
METROPOLITAN I (1853) — 7
MEIGGS' MUSICAL HALL (1853) — 8
AMERICAN I (1851) — 9
AMERICAN II (1854) — 9

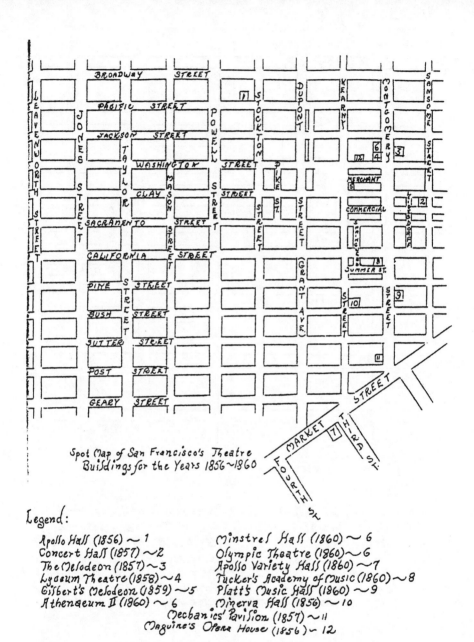

Spot Map of San Francisco's Theatre
Buildings for the Years 1856~1860

Legend:

Apollo Hall (1856) ~ 1
Concert Hall (1857) ~ 2
The Melodeon (1857) ~ 3
Lyceum Theatre (1858) ~ 4
Gilbert's Melodeon (1859) ~ 5
Athenaeum II (1860) ~ 6

Minstrel Hall (1860) ~ 6
Olympic Theatre (1860) ~ 6
Apollo Variety Hall (1860) ~ 7
Tucker's Academy of Music (1860) ~ 8
Platt's Music Hall (1860) ~ 9
Minerva Hall (1856) ~ 10

Mechanics' Pavilion (1857) ~ 11
Maguine's Opera House (1856) ~ 12

Transpositions and Tuning A
in San Francisco

The practice of transposition, the lowering or raising of an aria's key to make it easier to sing, raises an artistic question: Should not the artist sing the aria in the composer's key? Is it not unethical to change that key? No one, surely, would presume to alter Rembrandt's colors or the stance of Michelangelo's *David*.

The question soon proves more complicated than at first it may seem. Some persons hear in particular keys a unique quality, or "color," and for them a change in key will alter slightly the sound or quality of the aria. Further, some composers create patterns in the succession of keys used in an opera, and where this has been done, each aria will have a unique place in the scheme. Yet many composers have published a song for "high" voice in one key and the same song for "low" voice in another, which suggests that for some composers, at least, the key in which a song or aria may be sung is not of great importance. Indeed, composers, while often angry about cuts in their arias, for the most part have not objected to transpositions.

In San Francisco in these early years the history of transposition cannot be followed with any certainty, for so far as has been discovered, no critic or artist left an account of it. Yet the practice was prevalent, and evidence of it is all around, beginning with women singing the baritone roles in *Ernani* and *Attila* and Georgia Hodson, a contralto, singing the tenor part in *Trovatore*. Less obvious, but just as certain, Anna Bishop, who undertook to sing anything that caught her fancy, must often have adjusted the vocal lines to suit her voice, and so, too, must have Giovanna Bianchi, who described herself in the roster of the Bianchi company as "soprano and contralto."[1] One night she would sing the soprano role, Violetta, in *Traviata,* and another, the mezzo role, Azucena, in *Trovatore,* but never did she or any critic bother to recount the transpositions she must have made.

As an example of the practice, and no doubt typical of what went on in San Francisco, here is the conductor Luigi Arditi's translation of a letter he received in 1859 from the singer Pauline Viardot, a mezzo-soprano famous for her creation of the mezzo role of Fidès in Meyerbeer's *Le Prophète.* Viardot was preparing for a performance in Dublin of Verdi's *Macbeth,* in which she would sing Lady Macbeth, a soprano role, and she describes the adjustments she wants in the vocal line:[2]

CARO MAESTRO,— Here are the transpositions which I am making in the part of Lady Macbeth. The most difficult of all, which will necessitate certain changes in the instrumentation, will be that of the *Cavatina.* The recitative in D flat, the Andante, "Vieni, t'affretta" in B flat, and the Allegro "Or tutti sorgete" in D flat, consequently the whole scene must be a minor third lower. Not bad! All the rest of the act may be given as written. The *cabaletta* "Trionfai" is not sung.

In the banquet scene (Act II) there must be a transition from the concluding phrase of the chorus finishing with the words "Come," etc., in order to get into A flat, the key of the drinking song. The Allegro as written in F. For the second verse of the *Brindisi* it must be taken a whole tone lower, five beats before beginning the melody, by inserting A flat into the preceding chord of F; thus: — [she indicates the notation]. In this way we approach the key of A flat.

After the repeat of the *Brindisi,* a transition must be introduced at the seventh beat of the Allegro Agitato, where we again find ourselves in the key of F major. [She indicates the notation.] Or we might take the beat of Macbeth's "Va!" exercising [*sic*] the six previous beats.

The sleep-walking scene must be a tone lower; that is, the melody and recitative in E flat minor, and the Andante in B major. I fancy I see your orchestra making faces at the horrible aspect of the six double flats and five double sharps! Dear maestro, you must have the parts of these numbers copied because the orchestra we shall have only likes to transpose (transport) the public. . . .

PAULINE VIARDOT

Doubtless few singers were as knowledgeable as Viardot about their transpositions, but besides illustrating the practice, her letter also shows the relative position then between singer and conductor—and composer. If this kind of readjustment is what is needed to bring together a first-class singer and equally good opera, is it wrong?

Much of the need for transposition in the mid–nineteenth century was the result of fluctuations in pitch, disagreements from one city to the next as to what should be the fundamental pitch for performance. Before the opera begins, the orchestra tunes, settling on a note— tuning A (the A above middle C on a piano)—that sets the pitch. In some cities of Mozart's era this note sounded when a string vibrated at 422 cycles or oscillations per second. But gradually pitch, or the number of cycles per second (cps), rose, and by mid–nineteenth century British orchestras were tuning to an A of 453 cps, Viennese to an A of 456, and Americans to an A of 457, about three-quarters of a tone higher, effectively changing the key of every aria in an opera.

The chief culprit in this rise was the orchestra, whose members thought their instruments sounded more brilliant at the higher pitch. But the shift upward caused singers trouble, for an A of 440 cps is almost a half-tone higher than, say, Mozart's 422, an easily heard increase in pitch; the singer is thus forced to take Mozart's aria almost a half-tone higher than the composer intended. This shift upward, if continued over a long or difficult aria, may exhaust a singer, and if extended for an entire opera it can spell disaster, especially as during a performance, with singers and players becoming physically and emotionally heated, pitch in any case tends to rise. Eventually musicians agreed on a tuning A of 440 cps, but before then the transposition of arias downward was common, and even today is not infrequent.[3]

In San Francisco in the days of Lyster and Bianchi, what was the fundamental pitch? The only reference found to the question occurs, without citation, in a typescript published by the WPA Projects in June

1938. It tells of an incident involving the tenor Eugenio Bianchi, who favored the Paris Conservatory pitch of 435 cps.

> "At operas, between the acts," related August Wetterman who was conductor in this city since 1852, "Bianchi would come down to the music room with his tuning fork, the Paris Conservatory of Music pitch which had been founded upon the human voice. He hit the fork on his knee, then holding it to our ears, saying 'This is the right pitch. Gentlemen, you are all wrong. When I want to sing B flat you force me to sing B natural. This is outrageous. You must change your pitch or you will kill me.' And we stood the abuse," narrated Wetterman, "knowing he was right."[4]

Unfortunately, no other reference to Wetterman has been discovered, but there seems no reason to doubt the story. If Bianchi was complaining of a half-tone increase over 435, then the orchestra probably was tuning to, roughly, 455—very high, but not out of line with what was happening elsewhere.

Verdi's Operas:
World, Western Hemisphere,
United States, and San Francisco
Premieres, with Casts
for San Francisco

A question mark (?) indicates that either the initial or name of the person, or the role sung, is unknown. Or, if used with a name thus, [G. Loder?], it indicates that, although there is no statement, in either an advertisement, news item, or review, that Loder was the conductor for the performance, there is other, circumstantial reason for thinking so.

Opera World Premiere	Western Hemisphere Premiere	United States Premiere	San Francisco Premiere	San Francisco Premiere Cast (*Women; Men; Conductor*) (*Character's initial denotes role*)
Oberto, conte di San Bonifacio 17 Nov. 1893 Milan, Scala	17 Nov. 1939 Buenos Aires, Teatro Colón	18 Feb. 1978 New York, Amato Opera House		
Un giorno di regno (also known as *Il finto Stanislao*) 5 Sep. 1840 Milan, Scala	(in U.S.)	18 June 1960 New York, Town Hall	11 June 1980 Pocket Opera	M. Cope-Hart (M), H. Axelson (G); R. Tate (R), L. Venza (B), M. Klebe (T), W. Matthes (K); D. Pippin. In English
Nabucodonosor (*Nabucco*) 9 Mar. 1842 Milan, Scala	4 Dec. 1847 Havana, Teatro Tacón	4 Apr. 1848 New York, Astor Pl. Opera House	30 Nov. 1854 Metropolitan	M. Bedei (A), M. S. Voorhees (F); A. Lanzoni (N), F. Leonardi (Z), C. Scola (I); G. Loder
I Lombardi alla prima crociata (see *Jérusalem*) 11 Feb. 1843 Milan, Scala	1 Dec. 1846 Havana, Teatro Tacón	3 Mar. 1847 New York, Palmo's Opera House	1 May 1855 Metropolitan	C. Barili-Thorn (G); A. Lanzoni (P), C. Scola (O), [?] Laglaise (A); G. Loder

Opera					Cast
Ermani 9 Mar. 1844 Venice, Fenice	18 Nov. 1846 Havana, Teatro Tacón	15 Apr. 1847 New York, Park Theatre	8 Apr. 1851 Adelphi Theatre		R. Mauri-Pellegrini (El); I. Pellegrini (E), M. Von Gulpen [mez-sop] (C), V. Acquasoni (S); [?]
I due Foscari 3 Nov. 1844 Rome, Argentina	2 Jan. 1847 Havana, Teatro Tacón	10 May 1847 Boston, Howard-Atheneum	23 Mar. 1855 American Theatre		C. Barili-Thorn (L); A. Lanzoni (F), C. Scola (J); [G. Loder?]
Giovanna d'Arco 15 Feb. 1845 Milan, Scala	19 Aug. 1854 Buenos Aires, Argentino	1 Mar. 1966 New York, Carnegie Hall			
Alzira 12 Aug. 1845 Naples, San Carlo	20 Jan. 1850 Lima, Teatro Principal	17 Jan. 1968 New York, Carnegie Hall			
Attila 17 Mar. 1846 Venice, Fenice	23 Jan. 1848 Havana, Teatro Tacón	15 Apr. 1850 New York, Niblo's Garden	18 Aug. 1859 American Theatre		G. Bianchi (O); S. Leach (A), E. Kammerer [mez-sop] (E), E. Bianchi (F); [?]
Macbeth (see below) 14 Mar. 1847 Florence, Pergola	19 Dec. 1849 Havana, Teatro Tacón	24 Apr. 1850 New York, Niblo's Garden	18 Nov. 1862 Maguire's Opera House		G. Bianchi (L. M); J. Gregg (M), E. Grossi (B), E. Bianchi (Md); [?]

Appendix D

Opera World Premiere	Western Hemisphere Premiere	United States Premiere	San Francisco Premiere	San Francisco Premiere Cast (*Women; Men; Conductor*) (*Character's initial denotes role*)
I masnadieri 22 July 1847 London, Her Majesty's	7 Sep. 1849 Rio de Janeiro, Teatro de São Pedro	31 May 1860 New York, Winter Garden	29 May 1863 Metropolitan Theatre	G. Bianchi (A); E. Bianchi (C), A. Fellini (F), E. Brossi (M); R. Herold
Férusalem (*I Lombardi* revised, with ballet added) 26 Nov. 1847 Paris, Opéra	(in U.S.)	24 Jan. 1850 New Orleans, Théâtre d'Orléans		
Il corsaro 25 Oct. 1848 Trieste, Grande	1 Jan. 1852 Valparaíso, Teatro de la Victoria	12 Dec. 1961 Stony Brook, N.Y., Main Theatre		
La battaglia di Legnano 27 Jan. 1849 Rome, Argentina	7 Aug. 1853 Lima, Teatro Principal	28 Feb. 1976 New York, Cooper Union		

Opera				Cast
Luisa Miller 8 Dec. 1849 Naples, San Carlo	(in U.S.)	27 Oct. 1852 Philadelphia, Walnut St. Theatre	18 May 1863 Metropolitan Theatre	G. Bianchi (L), [?] Younker (F); E. Bianchi (R), A. Fellini (M), A. Roncovieri (W), E. Grossi (Wu); [?]
Stiffelio (see *Aroldo*) 16 Nov. 1850 Trieste, Grande	(in U.S.)	4 June 1976 Brooklyn, N.Y., Academy of Music		
Rigoletto 11 Mar. 1851 Venice, Fenice	(in U.S.)	19 Feb. 1855 New York, Academy of Music	1 July 1860 Maguire's Opera House	L. Escott (G), E. Kammerer-Schwegerie (M); H. Squires (D), F. Lyster (R), J. De Haga (S); A. Reiff
Il trovatore 19 Jan. 1853 Rome, Apollo	7 Sep. 1854 Rio de Janeiro, Teatro Fluminense	2 May 1855 New York, Academy of Music	5 May 1859 Maguire's Opera House	G. Bianchi (L), J. Feret (A); E. Bianchi (M), S. Leach (di L), A. Roncovieri (F); [?] Feret
La traviata 6 Mar. 1853 Venice, Fenice	15 Dec. 1855 Rio de Janeiro, Teatro Fluminense	3 Dec. 1856 New York, Academy of Music	13 Aug. 1859 American Theatre	G. Bianchi (V); E. Bianchi (A), S. Leach (G); [?]

Appendix D (continued)

Opera World Premiere	Western Hemisphere Premiere	United States Premiere	San Francisco Premiere	San Francisco Premiere Cast (*Women; Men; Conductor*) (*Character's initial denotes role*)
Les Vêpres siciliennes (*I vespri siciliani*) 13 June 1855 Paris, Opéra	16 Oct. 1857 Santiago, Chile, Teatro Municipal	7 Nov. 1859 New York, Academy of Music	12 Aug. 1871 Metropolitan	A. States (E); P. Cecchi (A), D. Orlandini (M), A. Susini (P); [?]. In Italian
Simon Boccanegra (see below) 12 Mar. 1857 Venice, Fenice	19 June 1862 Buenos Aires, Antiguo Colón	13 Mar. 1992 Sarasota, Florida, Opera		
Aroldo (*Stiffelio* revised with new last act) 16 Aug. 1857 Rimini, Nuovo	15 Nov. 1860 Buenos Aires, Antiguo Colón	4 May 1863 New York, Academy of Music		
Un ballo in maschera 17 Feb. 1859 Rome, Apollo	(in U.S.)	11 Feb. 1861 New York, Academy of Music	25 May 1863 Maguire's Opera House	O. Sconcia (A), [?] Fleury (O), A. Phillips (U); G. Sbriglia (R), D. Orlandini (Re); A. Reiff

		(in U.S.)	
La forza del destino (see below) 10 Nov. 1862 St. Petersburg, Imperial		24 Feb. 1865 New York, Academy of Music	
Macbeth (revised, with ballet added and new ending) 21 Apr. 1865 Paris, Lyrique	23 June 1939 Buenos Aires, Teatro Colón (revision likely used)	24 Oct. 1941 New York, 44th Street Theatre	27 Sept. 1955 War Mem. Opera House — I. Borkh (L. M); R. Weede (M), G. Tozzi (B), W. Fredericks (Md); F. Cleva
Don Carlos (see below) 11 Mar. 1867 Paris, Opéra	17 June 1873 Buenos Aires, Opera	12 Apr. 1877 New York, Academy of Music	5 Sep. 1986 War Mem. Opera House — P. Lorengar (E), S. Toczyska (Eb); N. Shicoff (C), A. Titus (R), R. Lloyd (F), J. Rouleau (I); J. Pritchard. In French
La forza del destino (scenes reordered; overture replaces prelude; new last scene) 27 Feb. 1869 Milan, Scala	14 Mar. 1869 Buenos Aires, Antiguo Colón	23 Mar. 1880 New York, Academy of Music	19 July 1881 Grand Opera House — A. Bianchi-Montaldo (L), G. Tiozzi (P); G. Roig (A), F. Lafontaine (C), G. Paoletti (G), A. Parolini (M); [A. Spadine?]

Appendix D (*continued*)

Opera World Premiere	Western Hemisphere Premiere	United States Premiere	San Francisco Premiere	San Francisco Premiere Cast (*Women; Men; Conductor*) (*Character's initial denotes role*)
Aida 24 Dec. 1871 Cairo, Opera	4 Oct. 1873 Buenos Aires, Antiguo Colón	26 Nov. 1873 New York, Academy of Music	17 Oct. 1877 Baldwin's Theatre	C. L. Kellogg (A), A. L. Cary (Am); J. Graff (R), G. Verdi [*sic*] (Ao); S. Behrens
Simon Boccanegra (revised; Council Scene new) 24 Mar. 1881 Milan, Scala	13 Aug. 1889 Buenos Aires, Opera	28 Jan. 1932 New York, Metropolitan	1 Nov. 1941 War Mem. Opera House	S. Roman (A); F. Jagel (G), L. Tibbett (S), E. Pinza (F); E. Leinsdorf
Don Carlo (cut from five to four acts; in Italian) 10 Jan. 1884 Milan, Scala	13 Nov. 1886 Mexico City, Nacional	23 Dec. 1920 New York, Metropolitan	16 Sept. 1958 War Mem. Opera House	L. Gencer (E), I. Dalis (Eb); P. M. Ferraro (C), F. Guarrera (R), G. Tozzi (F), G. Modesti (I); G. Sebastian. In Italian

Otello 5 Feb. 1887 Milan, Scala	18 Nov. 1887 Mexico City, Nacional	16 Apr. 1888 New York, Academy of Music	12 Feb. 1890 Grand Opera House	E. Albani (D); F. Tamagno (O), G. Del Puente (I); L. Arditi
Falstaff 9 Feb. 1893 Milan, Scala	8 July 1893 Buenos Aires, Opera	4 Feb. 1895 New York, Metropolitan	27 Sept. 1927 War Mem. Opera House	M. Donnelly (N), F. Peralta (A), E. Marlo (M), I. Bourskaya (Q); A. Tokaytan (Fe), L. Tibbett (Fo), A. Scotti (F); G. Merola

Reviews of San Francisco
Premieres and Early Performances
of *Macbeth, I masnadieri,*
and *Luisa Miller*

MACBETH

San Francisco premiere, 18 November 1862, at Maguire's Opera House, the Bianchi company. U.S. premiere, 24 April 1850, New York City.

Daily Alta California, 18 November 1862, 2:3. (Into this anticipatory report, published the morning of the premiere, the critic, who presumably had been attending the rehearsals and perhaps studying a vocal score, put many of his thoughts about the opera.)

Shakespeare's "Romeo and Juliet," "Midsummer Night's Dream," and "Macbeth," have afforded the composer themes for operas, almost as celebrated as their originals. This evening, Verdi's "Macbeth" will be produced by the Bianchi Opera Troupe, and we embrace this occasion to speak somewhat in detail of the composer's effort and its history. Verdi, in "Macbeth," has availed himself of the witches to create choruses of peculiar weird-like construction, to set unnatural appearances and disappearances to music, and, at the same time, to give a vivid musical picture of the various emotions of the principal characters—Macbeth, Macduff, Banquo, Lady Macbeth, etc. It may appear somewhat strange to hear the soliloquies of the timorous Thane rendered in music—to be entranced with the dulcet strains of Lady Macbeth, stimulating her craven lord to make good the predictions of the weird sisters, but the listener will soon become aware that the composer, with rare power, has been faithful to his task. The Witches' Choruses are remarkable for their power and effect. Lady Macbeth exhibits the true tragic muse in the dagger scene, the reading of the letter, and the somnambulic scene, while the *brindisi* at the banquet, is a gem of vocalization, contrasting, with great effect, the more serious part of her *role.* Macduff, Macbeth, Banquo, and the Physician are the principal male *roles.* "Macbeth" was first performed in America by Marti's Havana Troupe, at Castle Garden [incorrect, Niblo's Garden], New York— Bosio, Salvi [D. Coletti], Marini [Lorini], and Badiali in the cast. Strange to say, it has never been performed in England at all [not until 1860], or in the United States, save as instanced, and now, after a lapse of nearly fifteen years, it is brought forward on the Pacific coast. The composition, as an entirety, is strikingly grand, as the finale of the first act, on Duncan's death, will convince all. The principal part is that of Lady Macbeth, and as its representation conduced mainly to the establishment of the great fame of La Bosio, so we may opine it will place the crown of merit upon the well established reputation of Signora Bianchi, in our midst. It is a great rôle, and she will render it with full justice. The opera will be produced with an entire and enlarged chorus, new scenery and effect; the stage management having been entrusted to Mr. H. Courtaine, whose familiarity with Shakespeare and the Italian lyric drama are such as to assure a correct presentation of the opera. [complete]

Daily Alta California, 19 November 1862, 2:2:

"Macbeth" was produced to a crowded and elegantly fashionable audience last evening, and we are not asserting too much in saying that it passed off with greater satisfaction and gratification than any opera yet given on the Pacific. The music is grand—somewhat heavy at times; but nothing can be finer than the finale to the first and second acts. The lighter music of the banquet scene enlivened the whole opera. The Witches chorus and orchestration are very peculiar, and require rehearing to become familiar. Mr. John Gregg, as Macbeth, did admirably well. He was in good voice, and seemed to feel that the effort was requisite for him to maintain his position. He not alone sang well, but acted well. Signora Bianchi's Lady Macbeth is the greatest lyric effort ever witnessed in California. Her vocalization and energetic acting was all that could be desired. Signor Bianchi had little to do, but did that well; and Signor Grossi, as Banquo, was unusually effective. The opera was finely mounted, and given with greater precision for a fresh representation than ever before. "Macbeth" will be repeated to-morrow evening. [complete]

Daily Evening Bulletin, 19 November 1862, 3:4:

The production of Verdi's *Macbeth* last night was a notable event in the history of our lyric drama. So far as the stage management is concerned, the piece was mounted in excellent style. New scenery was painted for the occasion, and the chorus and supernumeraries were numerous and costumed in an imposing fashion. It will require repeated representations, however, before the public can fairly comprehend the spirit and beauty of the music, when given by the present Anglo-Italian company. The witch-music—which is a great feature of the opera—especially failed to satisfy expectation, from the imperfect rendering of a feeble female chorus. No doubt the management finds much difficulty in forming an efficient chorus of female voices for a single piece, as in this case, and—as we are perhaps obliged to accept the opera as it is, or dispense with it altogether—we can only lament that the case should be so. Notwithstanding the comparative failure of the witch-music, the opera as a whole was very well received by a crowded and sometimes enthusiastic audience. The stirring finale of the first act met with a storm of applause. Many other passages were very beautiful, and were well received. Among these may be mentioned the drinking song and chorus of the second act and in the fourth act the chorus of Scotch refugees, an air by Macduff (Signor Bianchi), a duet and chorus by Macduff, Malcolm (M. Charles,) and soldiers, and an air by Macbeth (Mr. Gregg). There was also a chorus of witches and a ballet by a sylph (Miss Howard) in the third act, that were very pleasing. The piece unhappily terminates in an abrupt Bowery-stage style, where there is a hacking and hewing of broadswords in the lowest of regular melodramatic mode. As "Lady Macbeth" Signora Bianchi looked and acted the royal murderess. *Macbeth* will be repeated to-morrow night. [complete]

Golden Era, 23 November 1862, 4:5:

We are content. Verdi's grand tragic opera of "Macbeth," emerged from its procrastinatory state of active preparation, last Tuesday evening, in magnificent style—complete in scenery, costumes, choral and orchestral adjuncts. More care has evidently been bestowed upon the production of this opera than upon any of its predecessors. It was a rare lyric treat, thoroughly enjoyed by a delighted audience. Signora Bianchi's Lady Macbeth was in look, person and action an identity; and her vocalism was superb. Her eminent fitness, physical and facial, for the *role* of the royal murderess, is patent to all who are familiar with her *personnelle* and the historic presentment of Macbeth's sanguinary and ambitious spouse. The drinking song in the second act, "Fill the Glasses with Choicest Wine," was given by the Signora with a dewy deliciousness of musical intonation. The "deranged" scene in the third act was sublimely wrought, so also was the murder scene, with the leering witches flitting athwart the fitfully flamed window of the castle; weird and unnoted witnesses of the bloody tragedy enacted within. Signor Bianchi was not very impressive as Macduff, nevertheless there is no occasion for special stricture. Mr. John Gregg's Macbeth was unexceptionable; he was in fine voice, spirited in action, and costumed to a nicety. Sig. Grossi's Banquo is deserving of equal credit. The witch scenes are produced with startling effect. As an entirety *Macbeth* is most engrossing. It is replete with action and interest, and has received that careful attention to detail that admits of the creeping in of no dissonant element to mar the satisfaction of the spectator. "Macbeth" was repeated on Thursday and Saturday evenings with undiminished potency. Minstrelsy with its circle of eccentric stars attracted lot of people upon the off nights. The tide of popular favor has set in strongly toward the Opera House; once more it is the favorite and fashionable resort. To-night, "Macbeth" is announced for the last time. [complete]

Daily Alta California, 24 November 1862, 2:3:

"Macbeth" was given last evening, it is said, for the last time, a determination which we hope the management will not persist in, as the production of a work unfamiliar to the troupe can never be said to be well rendered under half-a-dozen representations at least. [complete]

In all, *Macbeth* had four performances, on 18, 20, 22, and 23 November. It was revived the following year for a single performance, on 25 May 1863, and apparently not again until sometime in the next century.

I MASNADIERI

San Francisco premiere, 29 May 1863, at the Metropolitan Theatre, the Bianchi company. U.S. premiere, 31 May 1860, New York City.

Daily Alta California, 30 May 1863, 2:2:

The California public are familiar with Verdi's compositions, from his "Nabucco," "Trovatore," "Traviata," and "Luisa Miller." His compositions have been echoed and re-echoed through our hills, valleys and mountains, and no one is more popular. Last evening his opera of "I Masnadieri," founded on Schiller's play of "The Robbers," was presented for the first time in America [incorrect; see above]. We had a glimpse of the beauties of this work on the initial appearance of the Bianchis some years since at Maguire's Opera House, but after hearing the entire work we are somewhat surprised that it has never been presented previously. Few operatic works contain so much melody, or such a number of pleasing and captivating airs. Instead of finding the subject—a tragic one—treated in a ponderous or sombre style, "I Masnadieri" is a collection of vocal and instrumental gems rarely equalled in excellence. They ring upon the ear and captivate all listeners. It is not asserting too much to pronounce the performance last evening one of the most successful ever given in California. We doubt that an individual left the house but was fully impressed with the intrinsic excellence of the composition, and the admirable manner in which it was rendered. For ourselves, we are willing to brave the opposite of those familiar with "Il Trovatore" and accord the palm to "I Masnadieri." To our mind it evinces all the genius and talent of the composer, and possesses elements of popularity superior to any opera on the stage. It is strange that, notwithstanding the success of Verdi's later works, it has been reserved from his earlier productions to achieve sensations in America. A few weeks since his "Stiffelio" was produced in New York, under the title of "Aroldo," and made a great hit. In San Francisco "I Masnadieri" is given, and achieves the greatest success that has ever been accorded to an operatic work. The vocalization of Signor and Signora Bianchi, last evening, excelled all previous efforts and demonstrated them to be not alone reliable, but worthy artists, with but few equals in our memory. In point of vocal ability they can take rank among the first artistes in the world, and our public would prove recreant to all the vaunted musical taste of a cosmopolitan country, if they did not accord the highest lyrical honors to them. Signor Grossi, as the Count de Moor, deserves more than usual commendations. His rendition was a rare example of true dramatic and vocal force. Signor Fellini's Francesco was very commendably rendered. The chorus, who have an unusual amount of pleasing music, were conscientious and painstaking, whilst the orchestra was excellence itself. The successful production of this opera reflects great credit on Signor Bianchi, and the enterprise of Manager Tibbetts. It will be repeated tonight. [complete]

Daily Evening Bulletin, 30 May 1863, 3:4:

Verdi's grand opera of *I Masnadieri,* produced last night, was well received and the singers were at times enthusiastically applauded. With a great deal of *noise,* there are many beautiful airs and choruses in the piece. In the absence of a copy of the Italian libretto, (not to be had in the city, it appears,) we are unable to particularize the finer passages. The opera will be repeated tonight. [complete]

Golden Era, 16 August 1863, 5:2:

Signora Bianchi was positively superb as Amalia in *I Masnadieri,* given for the benefit of Mr. Schraubstadter [the tenor singing the small role of Arminio], on Friday evening. This one of Verdi's operas, (the libretto of which, based upon Schiller's German play of the "Robbers," is published in English by Mr. Lewis,) has never been produced elsewhere in America [incorrect; see above]. Signor Bianchi sang splendidly, and Signor Grossi's assumption of the *exigeant role* of the aged father evinced distinguished excellence. [complete]

In all, *I masnadieri* had eight performances, on 29 and 30 May, 1, 7, 11, and 15 June, 10 July, and 14 August. It was revived two years later for a single performance, on 23 August 1865, and apparently not again until sometime in the next century.

LUISA MILLER

San Francisco premiere, 18 May 1863, at the Metropolitan Theatre, the Bianchi company. U.S. premiere, 27 October 1852, Philadelphia.

Daily Evening Bulletin, 19 May 1863, 3:5:

Verdi's opera of Luisa Miller passed off very fairly last night, for a first performance. The second and third acts were considerably cut down from the printed libretto. The first act, (which contains some of the finest music, as given,) was enthusiastically received, especially the finale which led to a call of the leading singers before the curtain. Among the pieces that attracted most attention and applause in this act, were the opening chorus of peasants, the airs by "Luisa," (Signora Bianchi,) *Lo vidi, e'l primo palpito* and *T'amo d'amor ch'es-*

primere, the airs by "Miller" (Signor Fellini) *Sacra la scelta è d'un consorte,* and *Ah! fu giusto il mio sospetto!* and the finale. In the second act, the airs, *Tu puniscimi, o Signore,"* (Luisa,) and *Quando le sere,* ("Rudolpho"—Signor Bianchi) and in the third act several spirited duets between these characters, were among the most striking passages of the piece. Signora Bianchi is in excellent voice, and sang with great power and unusual sweetness. So, too, with Signor Fellini, in some portions of his part. The opera will be repeated tomorrow night. [complete]

Daily Alta California, 19 May 1863, 2:2:

Despite the rain and excitement attendant on the eve of an election, there was quite a large and fashionable audience on hand at the Metropolitan Theatre last evening to hear the initial performance of "Luisa Muller" [*sic*]. The representation proved a great success, for from principals to chorus, all seemed familiar with their relative roles. The music of "Luisa Muller" differs essentially from any other of Verdi's compositions, for delights in exquisite harmony are surrounded with all the sombre and sonorous tones of the German school. Still there is much to admire throughout. The concerted pieces possessed more melody than the solos; yet, at times, as in the case of the baritone, on whom falls the heaviest portion of the opera, many striking combinations are met with. For the initial representation of a work with which the majority of the performers are unfamiliar, we can accord it all the triumph of a success. Signora and Signor Bianchi were excellent; Signor Fellini never appeared to equal advantage, and Signor Grossi, Roncovieri, the chorus and orchestra were all that could be desired. [complete]

In all, *Luisa Miller* had three performances, on 18 and 20 May and 12 June, and apparently was not revived until sometime in the next century.

Performances of Verdi's Operas in San Francisco by Decade, 1851 Through 1899

1851–1860	
Ernani	22
Trovatore	22
Traviata	12
(Judith)*	(6)
Foscari	5
Nabucco	3
Lombardi	3
Rigoletto	3
Attila	2

*A pastiche, with music taken from Verdi's early operas, chiefly Nabucco.

1861–1870		1851–1870	
Trovatore	39	Trovatore	61
Traviata	34	Ernani	54
Ernani	32	Traviata	46
Ballo	20	Ballo	20
Nabucco	11	Nabucco	14
Rigoletto	10	Rigoletto	13
Masnadieri	9	Foscari	10
Attila	5	Masnadieri	9
Foscari	5	Attila	7
Macbeth	5	Lombardi	7
Lombardi	4	Macbeth	5
L. Miller	3	L. Miller	3

1871–1880		1851–1880	
Trovatore	39	Trovatore	100
Ernani	18	Ernani	72
Traviata	13	Traviata	59
Ballo	13	Ballo	33
Aida	12	Rigoletto	18
Rigoletto	5	Nabucco	14
Attila	2	Aida	12
Foscari	1	Foscari	11
Lombardi	1	Attila	9
Vespri	1	Masnadieri	9
		Lombardi	8
		Macbeth	5
		L. Miller	3
		Vespri	1

1881–1890		1851–1890	
Trovatore	117	Trovatore	217
Traviata	68	Ernani	131
Ballo	61	Traviata	127
Ernani	59	Ballo	94
Rigoletto	39	Rigoletto	57
Aida	34	Aida	46
Otello	2	Nabucco	14
Forza	1	Foscari	11
		Attila	9
		Masnadieri	9
		Lombardi	8
		Macbeth	5
		L. Miller	3
		Otello	2
		Vespri	1
		Forza	1

1891–1899		1851–1899	
Trovatore	65	Trovatore	282
Aida	40	Traviata	154
Rigoletto	29	Ernani	150
Traviata	27	Ballo	103
Ernani	19	Rigoletto	86
Otello	19	Aida	86
Ballo	9	Otello	21
Forza	1	Nabucco	14
		Foscari	11
		Attila	9
		Masnadieri	9
		Lombardi	8
		Macbeth	5
		L. Miller	3
		Forza	2
		Vespri	1

Notes

The following abbreviations have been used throughout for those newspapers most frequently cited:

DAC   Daily Alta California
SFDH   San Francisco Daily Herald
DEB   Daily Evening Bulletin
DEP   Daily Evening Picayune
DPN   Daily Pacific News

PROLOGUE

1. Evidence of a "circuit" can be found in Thomas G. Kaufman's *Verdi and His Major Contemporaries: A Selected Chronology of Performances with Casts* (New York: Garland, 1990). For example, Francesco Leonardi, an outstanding bass, who came to San Francisco in April 1854, sang in *Attila* in Lima in January 1850 and then again in Valparaíso in May 1850; in August 1850 he sang in *I Lombardi* in Valparaíso, and then in June 1852 in Santiago; and he sang *I masnadieri* in Valparaíso in November 1851, in Santiago in June 1852, and in Lima in May 1853. Similarly, Alessandro Lanzoni, a baritone, after singing in San Francisco in 1854–55, sang *Macbeth* in Lima in June 1856 and then again in Santiago in September 1857; and the same tenor and conductor, L. Cavedagni and A. Neumann, introduced *Alzira* to Lima in January 1850 and then to Valparaíso in November. Only rarely does a Pacific Coast artist appear in the records of Buenos Aires or Rio de Janeiro; the circuit was up and down the west coast of South America and Mexico.

2. On the number of French women in the city: Clarkson Crane, *Last Adven-*

257

ture: San Francisco in 1851; Translated from the Original Journal of Albert Bernard de Russailh by Clarkson Crane (San Francisco: Westgate Press/Grabhorn Press, 1931), p. 27. De Russailh arrived in San Francisco in March 1851 and died there of cholera in July 1852. He wrote a column for the *Daily True Standard*, one of the city's smaller papers, and edited its French section. He also had a hand in the drama productions mounted by a French troupe in the Adelphi Theatre. Most of the ten or twelve French women whom he counted in the city in 1851 were actresses or otherwise employed by this troupe. Of the women of all nations in the city he observed: "There are also some honest women in San Francisco, but not very many" (p. 30). For the headline "Large Arrival of Women": *DAC*, 21 August 1852, 2:4. For a report, "The French in San Francisco," see *DAC*, 13 May 1853, 1:7.

The 1850 federal census figures for San Francisco were lost in a fire, so another count was taken for the city in 1852; it lists the population as 34,876, of which 29,166 were white men and 5,154, white women; 16,144 were male foreign residents (i.e., not U.S. citizens) and 2,710, female. Frank Soulé, John H. Gihon, and James Nisbet, *The Annals of San Francisco* (New York: D. Appleton & Co., 1855), p. 485, in figures generally thought to exaggerate by at least 10 percent, estimated the city's population in early 1854 to be divided as follows: Americans (which includes all English-speaking immigrants, e.g. English, Irish, Scottish, etc.), 32,000; Germans, 5,500; French, 5,000; Hispano-Americans, 3,000; other whites and Negroes, 1,500; Chinese, 3,000. Of the total, 50,000, women were 8,000, and children, 3,000.

NOTE: The *Annals*, which cover up to the spring of 1854, have been republished as *The Annals of San Francisco, Together with the Continuation, Through 1855, Compiled by Dorothy H. Huggins* (Palo Alto, Calif.: Lewis Osborne, 1966). This edition, which offers an index to both parts, reprints the original *Annals* with its pagination unchanged, but starts the *Continuation* with a new page 1. When citing a page from the original *Annals* I give the book's title simply as *Annals;* when citing from the *Continuation*, as *Annals, Continuation*.

3. In general, Italian opera of the time called for more men than women in the chorus, and some of the popular operas did not require a women's chorus at all—e.g., Rossini's *Barbiere di Siviglia* and Donizetti's *Lucrezia Borgia*.

4. These figures, as well as most that follow, must be taken as approximate. They are based on my own count, gleaned from the contemporary journals and newspapers and checked against the statistics reported in the appendices to Works Progress Administration (WPA), *San Francisco Theatre Research*, ed. Lawrence Estavan, monograph 18 (in vol. 8): *The History of Opera in San Francisco, Part II* (San Francisco, 1938), and against the performances of Verdi's operas reported in Don L. Hixon, *Verdi in San Francisco, 1851–1899: A Preliminary Bibliography* (San Francisco: privately printed, 1980). The difficulty of counting performances when records are scarce is obvious, especially in a decade when operas frequently were produced in cut versions, in pastiches, or under varying titles. The general rule, observed by WPA, Hixon, and myself, has been to count only those performances in which

the opera was given as an entity, even if cut. Performances of selected acts or scenes are not counted.

5. Though the estimate is rough, it is not without a basis. See the discussion in the final paragraphs of Chapter 14.

6. Stephen J. Field, *Personal Reminiscences of Early Days in California* (1893; rpt. New York: Da Capo Press, 1968), pp. 6–7. See also the chapter "Society in California" in Bayard Taylor, *Eldorado, or Adventures in the Path of Empire, Comprising a Voyage to California, via Panama, Life in San Francisco and Monterey, Pictures of the Gold Region, and Experiences of Mexican Travel* (1850; rpt. New York: Alfred A. Knopf, 1949), pp. 233–36.

CHAPTER 1. TOWARD A THEATRE

1. See Kevin Starr, *Americans and the California Dream, 1850–1915* (New York: Oxford University Press, 1973), pp. 24, 31; George R. MacMinn, *The Theater of The Golden Era in California* (Caldwell, Idaho: Caxton Printers, 1941), pp. 24–25, 457–58.

2. Description of Yerba Buena: E. Gould Buffum, *The Gold Rush: An Account of Six Months in the California Diggings* (1850; rpt. London: Folio Society, 1959), p. 18. On Population: Jacob Piatt Dunn, *Massacres of the Mountains: A History of the Indian Wars of the Far West, 1815–1875* (1886; rpt. London: Eyre & Spottiswoode, 1963), pp. 116–19; and Starr, *Americans and the California Dream*, p. 49. For this period, see also Hubert Howe Bancroft, *Works*, vol. 34: *California Pastoral, 1760–1848* (San Francisco: The History Co., 1888).

3. Starr, *Americans and the California Dream*, p. 5.

4. Field, *Personal Reminiscences*, p. 2.

5. Starr, *Americans and the California Dream*, p. 51.

6. De Russailh, *Last Adventure*, pp. 11, 28–29. He says of the French women who worked in the saloons: "Nearly all these women at home were street-walkers of the cheapest sort." For a description of the music in the gambling halls of Sacramento, see J. S. Holliday, *The World Rushed In: The California Gold Rush Experience* (New York: Simon & Schuster, 1981), pp. 320–21.

7. T. A. Barry and B. A. Patten, *Men and Memories of San Francisco in the "Spring of '50"* (San Francisco: A. L. Bancroft & Co., 1873), pp. 45–46.

8. Taylor, *Eldorado*, pp. 206–8. See also Walter M. Leman, *Memories of an Old Actor* (San Francisco: A. Roman Co., 1886), pp. 231–34; and MacMinn, *Theater of the Golden Era*, pp. 28–34.

9. Taylor, *Eldorado*, p. 207.

10. Leman, *Memories*, p. 234; MacMinn, *Theater of the Golden Era*, pp. 38–39.

11. On Herz's arrival, see *DPN*, 27 March 1850, 2:1; *DAC*, 27 March, 2:2. On the first two recitals, *DAC*, 1 April 1850, 3:4; 2 April, 3:4; 3 April, 2:2; 6 April, 3:4; 8 April, 2:2. Despite the excitement of California, Herz, in his slight book of memoirs, seems to have found nothing to record about it. He is interesting, however, on the

size of the music publishing business in the United States, which flourished in part because the country did not participate in the international copyright treaties of the day. See Henri Herz, *My Travels in America*, trans. Henry Bertram Hill (Madison: University of Wisconsin Press, 1963) p. 56.

12. *DAC*, 8 April 1850, 2:2.

13. On the third recital, see *DAC*, 11 April 1850, 3:4; 12 April, 2:2.

14. On the farewell recital, see *DAC*, 27 April 1850, 3:5; review and reception, *DPN*, 29 April, 2:3.

15. On clothing, see Taylor, *Eldorado*, pp. 229, 231; on the mud, Henry Vere Huntley, *California: Its Gold and Its Inhabitants* (London: Thomas Cautley Newby, 1856), 1:2.

16. Samuel C. Upham, *Notes of a Voyage to California via Cape Horn, Together with Scenes in El Dorado, in the Years 1849–'50* (Philadelphia, 1878), pp. 291–92: "As tickets of admission were $4 each [to the recital], and no one was admitted without a 'biled shirt,' the audience was not large, but very *select*."

17. *DAC*, 27 April 1850, 3:5; *DPN*, 30 April, 2:2, 3:4.

18. *DPN*, 3 May 1850, 2:6.

CHAPTER 2. THE FIRST OPERA

1. The early history of the Parker House is summarized in Lois Foster Rodecape, "Tom Maguire, Napoleon of the Stage," *California Historical Society Quarterly* 20, no. 4 (December 1941): 292–94.

2. On seats for ladies, see advertisements in *DEP*, 6, 8, and 9 November 1850.

3. On opening night, see *DEP*, 26 October 1850, 3:3. John H. McCabe, "Theatrical Journals and Diary, 1849–1882 (ms., California State Library, Sacramento), 1:3, lists the performance and the artists.

4. On firemen, see *DEP*, 2 November 1850, 2:1. According to Huntley, *California* 2:228, "full uniform" for at least one company meant "red woolen frocks and blue trousers," and presumably there was some insignia.

5. *DAC*, 31 October 1850, 2:2, identifies the song and reported her voice to be "mellow, flexible, and satisfying," and her manner, "unaffected." The performance was advertised as her local debut (*DEP*, 26 October, 3:3), with previous appearances at the "San Carlo, Naples, and New York Theatres."

6. *DEP*, 5 November 1850, 2:2 (review).

7. On the apparent repeat of aria, see advertisement in *DEP*, 5 November 1850, 3:2.

8. Description of Korsinsky–Von Gulpen: *DAC*, 16 December 1850, 2:3. For her career in New York as Korsinsky, see references in Vera Brodsky Lawrence, *Strong on Music: The New York Scene in the Days of George Templeton Strong, 1836–1875*, vol. 1: *Resonances, 1836–1850* (New York: Oxford University Press, 1988). In November 1847, she sang in a short season of opera in Philadelphia with Anna Bishop; see

W.G. Armstrong, *A Record of the Opera in Philadelphia* (1884; rpt. New York: AMS Press, 1976), p. 57.

9. On the program, see *DAC*, 15, 16 December 1850, 3:4; a news item appears on 16 December, 2:3; and a review on 17 December, 2:1. See also McCabe, "Journals," 1:4.

10. On the concert miscellany, see *DAC*, 23 December 1850, 2:3. It seems likely that the "Grand Aria" was "Dagli immortali" because that was one of the opera's most popular arias, a "double aria" with a cantabile and cabaletta and therefore "Grand," and, being for baritone, it would lie well for trombone. Abalos had appeared as an assisting artist at Herz's third recital, 11 April 1850. According to a review (*DAC*, 12 April, 2:2), her first selection, unidentified, she sang poorly; her second, "a very stupid little Spanish air," she had to repeat twice.

11. On the Adelphi's French programs, see Leman, *Memories*, p. 234; "General Remarks," *Pioneer Magazine*, December 1854, p. 372; and theatre's advertisements. See also de Russailh, *Last Adventure*, pp. 18, 23–24 and passim. On the saloon piano, see *DEP*, 9 November 1850, 2:1, reviewing a play: "If they *must* have music down stairs, let it be *between the acts.*"

12. On the program (in final advertisement), see *DAC*, 29 January 1851, 3:2; also McCabe, "Journals," 1:5. The review in *DAC*, 30 January, 2:3, states only that the recital was "exceedingly well attended."

13. *DEP*, 11 January 1851, 2:5 (advertisement); *DAC*, 12 January, 2:4 (news item), and 13 January, 2:2 (review); and ad for subsequent concert, stressing instrumental music, in *DEP*, 29 January, 2:5.

Concerning Planel's first name: Neither his name nor initials ever appear in a news-story, review, or advertisement; he is always "Mons." or "Mr. Planel." But one time he wrote a letter on musical matters to the the editor of the *Alta California* and signed it "L. T. Planel" (*DAC*, 9 May 1855, 2:4); and in the *San Francisco Directory* for 1861 and for 1867 he is listed as "Theo. Planel" and "Theophile L. Planel," respectively. A death notice in the San Francisco *Daily Morning Call*, 6 February 1889, 7:2, reports: "Louis T. Planel Sr., a well-known musician, who resided in California from 1851 to 1874, died in Paris January 5th, aged 84 years. Deceased leaves a son of the same name, also a talented musician, who resides in Paris."

14. On the *Tennessee*, see *DEP*, 8, 9 January 1851, 2:5; *DAC*, 9 January, 3:1. The singers were not named in news-stories of the passengers, and so their arrival seems wholly unexpected; *DAC*, 12 January, 2:3, states they arrived on the *Tennessee*.

15. *DAC*, 10 January 1851, 3:2 (announcement); see also news item, *DAC*, 10 January, 2:3, on the troupe's intent to give concerts—with the news item no doubt a reward for the costly advertisement. The announcement was repeated on 11 and 12 January. Pellegrini asserted the same claims to distinction before concerts in Sacramento; see news item in *Sacramento Union*, 1 April 1851, 2:3.

16. See the reviews in *DEP*, 25 January 1851, 2:2; and *DAC*, 26 January, 2:3.

McCabe, "Journals," 1:5, dates the concert on 14 January, apparently a slip of the pen for 24, which is confirmed by the newspaper advertisements and reviews. McCabe comments that the event was an "Italian operatic concert," and adds: "1st in city."

17. A news item in *DAC*, 28 January 1851, 2:3, besides hinting at the program, states that Pellegrini's company is "recently organized in this city." See also McCabe, "Journals," 1:5.

18. An early announcement of season, in the review of Pellegrini's first concert, appears in *DAC*, 26 January 1851, 2:3; see also the advertisements in *DEP*, 11, 12 February, 2:4; and *DAC*, 12 February, 2:2, which gives the cast. Regarding the first violinist conducting: The impresario Max Maretzek has a hilarious account of one at work—see his *Crotchets and Quavers, or Revelations of an Opera Manager in America* (1855; rpt. New York: Da Capo Press, 1966), pp. 15–17.

19. On the *Sonnambula* premiere, see *DAC*, 13 February 1851, 2:3. See also McCabe, "Journals," 1:5; "1st time in state full Italian opera."

20. On the repeat performances on 15, 18, and 25 February, see advertisements in *DAC* and *DEP*; also McCabe, "Journals," 1:5. McCabe omitted the first repeat, but both newspapers advertised it, and *DEP*, 17 February, 2:2, reviewed it.

21. A review appears in *DAC*, 28 February 1851, 2:3; on the repeat performance on 3 March, see McCabe, "Journals," 1:6.

22. This is the orchestra of the Germania Concert Society for a series of twelve concerts in the summer of 1855 (see advertisement, *SFDH*, 1 July 1855, 1:1); presumably four years earlier the orchestras were even smaller. Cf. *DAC*, 29 July 1854, 2:5 (advertisement), when for the premiere of *Der Freischütz* an orchestra of "upwards of thirty" was announced with fanfare: it was to be formed by uniting "the Verandah Concert Society" with "the Opera Band of the Metropolitan" theatre; see also *DAC*, 6 August 1855, 3:6. See *DAC*, 23 March 1852, 3:4, for a complaint about an orchestra's small size; and *Pioneer Magazine*, February 1854, pp. 114–16, for a summary of prevailing deficiencies in music-making. On the rarity of tympani, see *SFDH*, 3 September 1855, 2:2.

23. The orchestras were sufficiently small that announcements often listed the names of players, most of whom were German. For a report, "The Germans in San Francisco," see *DAC*, 16 May 1853, 2:3: they number "about 5,000," and "most of the dealers in cigars, musicians, and brewers are German"; also, "The Union Band is composed entirely of Germans." According to Soulé, Gihon, and Nisbet, *Annals*, pp. 445–47, the Germans in 1854 numbered 5,000 to 6,000. The French "monopolized many professions of a semi-artistic character. They are the chief shoeblacks and hairdressers, cooks, wine importers and professional gamblers." They also were "partial to public amusements, and often have a theatre open, when plays, vaudevilles and operas in their own language are performed" (ibid., p. 461).

24. See announcement for *Der Freischütz, DAC*, 29 July 1854, 2:5. On the Turn Gesangverein, see Soulé, Gihon, and Nisbet, *Annals*, p. 460.

25. On the Adelphi, see *DEP*, 18 October 1850, 2:3.

On the press, see *DAC*, 13 May 1853, 2:2: "It is not always possible for members of the press to be on the spot when the doors open, but unless they contrive to be, whenever there is a rush, they have no chance of securing a place from which the play can be appreciated. It would be well for the managers to think of this." The last sentence, considering the venality of the typical U.S. newspaper of the day, possibly was intended as a threat of bad notices. On the low estate of music criticism in New York, see Lawrence, *Strong on Music* 1:xii, 19. The critics in San Francisco, perhaps because writing anonymously, seem to have been more balanced and honest than those in New York, but the spate of news items about Pellegrini in the *Alta California* no doubt was stimulated by his advertisements in the paper. The press received its seats free; see the advertisement for the Metropolitan Theatre, *SFDH*, 10, 11 July 1855, 1:3: "The usual theatrical free list will be suspended, except the Press." For retaliation by the New York City press in 1870, when advertising and the number of free tickets were reduced, see Howard Shanet, *Philharmonic: A History of New York's Orchestra* (Garden City, N.Y.: Doubleday, 1975), pp. 151–52.

Concerning the venality of the press in San Francisco, or in the United States generally, it is, of course, hard to prove bribery by cash payment. But for what it is worth, there is this curious episode. In September 1855 the English singer Anna Bishop ended a visit to the United States with a stay of eighteen months in San Francisco. Her next stop was Melbourne, Australia, and upon arriving there one of her first actions was to send a letter to the editor of the *Melbourne Punch* enclosing a roll of bank notes. The paper's critic, James Smith, later described his own and his editor's response: "Mr. Sinnett and myself waited upon her at the Prince of Wales [Theatre] the next morning, to hand them back, and to inform her that, whatever might be the practice in America, the Melbourne press was honest and incorruptible" (Harold Love, *The Golden Age of Australian Opera: W. S. Lyster and His Companies, 1861–1880* [Sydney: Currency Press, 1981], p. 27).

Lest anyone think that the sins of the American press are all in the past, consider: In 1987 the San Francisco *Chronicle* fired a critic for reviewing a ballet performance that, because of a last-minute schedule change, had not taken place; and the critic's review had been harsh.

26. On hats, see *DAC*, 10 August 1853, 2:2, reviewing a concert: "Pretty faces upturned toward the singers' places, half buried in hat trimmings or shaded by opera hoods and other fashionable head-fixings." See the illustration of the audience in the Metropolitan Theatre, San Francisco, on 7 June 1854 (Fig. 10). Also see Lawrence, *Strong on Music* 1:68 n. 10.

27. Lawrence, *Strong on Music* 1:68n.10; and note the actors in the illustration cited above.

28. On segregated seating, see *DAC*, 21 February 1851, 3:3: "The gallery has been fitted up in elegant style expressly for respectable colored people." The *Golden Era*,

9 April 1854, 2:5, reported, "There are now residing in San Francisco near 1500 colored persons who own property to the amount of $1,000,000.00. Generally speaking, they are civil and industrious."

Concerning the Adelphi Theatre, de Russailh (*Last Adventure*, p. 24) describes the theatre, but because of the imprecision of such terms as *boxes, parterre, parquet,* and *pit* it is not clear whether the house had two or three galleries or balconies. It seems, however, that the lowest of these, except perhaps for either end, had rows of seats and was not separated into boxes. When the theatre was rebuilt after the May 1851 fire, according to de Russailh, it was slightly enlarged, "with the whole balcony divided into boxes."

29. For earnings at the mines, see Buffum, *Gold Rush,* pp. 64, 75–76, 86–88, 94–95. San Francisco prices are taken mostly from de Russailh, *Last Adventure,* pp. 11, 29. In 1849, according to Buffum (pp. 143–44), a bed and breakfast in the city cost $3.50, an unskilled laborer could earn $8 a day, and a carpenter or plumber up to $20. Taylor (*Eldorado*, p. 208) states that early in 1850 at the Eagle Theatre, Sacramento, a bass soloist received $96 for a single song, and a member of the orchestra, $16 for the evening.

30. On dress, see Huntley, *California* 2:224–28: "The audience on these occasions present a motley display of dress; many well-dressed ladies and gentlemen occupy positions close to the workman in his red or blue woolen frock in which he works—certainly it is generally a new one. The dollar decides the right of seat without regulating the dress of the person occupying it." MacMinn (*Theater of the Golden Era,* p. 30) quotes a theatregoer of 1854 who regrets the passing of the more colorful days of 1849, "when we wore habiliments to our fancy, sported high-tops, blue shirts, and most rascally sombreros."

31. On elegant French, see Soulé, Gihon, and Nisbet, *Annals,* pp. 461–65. On raucous Irish, *DAC,* 1 December 1852, 2:3.

32. *Wide West,* 11 February 1855, 2:7.

33. *DEB,* 26 August 1862, 3:5: "It may be interesting to those who do not attend 'the opera' to know that 'apples and peaches' are now regularly cried for sale among the fine ladies of the dress circle. Oranges and peanuts are as yet confined to the reserved seats in the parquette." MacMinn (*Theater of the Golden Era,* p. 100) quotes the *San Francisco Chronicle* of January 1854 in a description of how a "walnut-cracking holiday audience" was silenced by Matilda Heron's performance of Shakespeare's Juliet.

34. *DEP,* 25 January 1851, 2:2.

35. On spitting, see *DAC,* 3 February 1851, 2:4.

36. On *Norma* and *Sonnambula* repeated, see newspapers; and McCabe, "Journals," 1:6. On the omission of Verdi's name, see *DAC,* 28 March 1851, 3:2; on its inclusion, *DEP,* 27 March, 3:5.

37. Charles Santley, *Student and Singer: The Reminiscences of Charles Santley* (London: Edward Arnold, 1892), pp. 31–33. For some remarks on the categories of

singers, see Julian Budden, *The Operas of Verdi* (London: Cassell, 1973–78; New York: Oxford University Press, 1981), 1:22, 33–35, 421, 449, 484.

38. *DAC,* 29 March 1851, 2:3. Because this notice followed the scheduled date of performance, it suggests that Von Gulpen's decampment was very sudden.

39. *DAC,* 7 April 1851, 3:2; and *DEP,* 7 April, 3:1. See also *DAC,* 8 April, 2:4, 3:2; *DEP,* 8 April, 3:3; McCabe, "Journals," 1:6.

40. McCabe, "Journals," 1:6: "closing night 1st Italian Opera season." Hixon (*Verdi,* p. v) is uncertain whether the performance took place because "subsequent mention or review not encountered." McCabe's note is that subsequent mention.

41. *Sacramento Union,* 1 April 1851, 2:3 (news item) and 3:2 (advertisement).

42. *Sacramento Union,* 19 April 1851, 2:1 (news item) and 3:2 (advertisement); 26 April, 3:2 (advertisement).

43. I could find no record of the Pellegrinis, either before or after their visit to San Francisco, in either the local newspapers and journals or in Kaufman, *Verdi and His Major Contemporaries.* I should note, however, that Kaufman gives as the premiere of *Ernani* in San Francisco a performance on 14 November 1854, which I count to be the second performance (see n. 40). Similarly, I could find no further report anywhere of Angelo Francia, James Weitz, or V. Acquasoni. Mathilde Korsinsky–Von Gulpen and Francisca Abalos continued to live in San Francisco and, on occasion, to sing. Von Gulpen, for example, on 15 April 1855 sang two songs at a concert presented by the New Germania Concert Society in the Turn-Verein Hall, and in midsummer took a minor role in a production of *La gazza ladra* (see advertisement of the Metropolitan Theatre, *SFDH,* 10 July 1855, 1:3). Abalos in 1853 gave a concert with two of her children that was reviewed in *DAC,* 14 November 1853, 2:3: "The concert at Schappert's Saloon was crowded last evening. Madame Abalos was in excellent voice, and gave her favorite Spanish ballads with her usual ability. The dance by Miss Sophia was rapturously applauded. Miss Caroline Abalos, a younger daughter, appeared and gave an old-fashioned, whole-souled hoe-down, with a refreshing and consoling heartiness."

CHAPTER 3. THE CELEBRITY SOPRANOS

1. Regarding audience behavior, Huntley, *California* 2:224–28, describes the audience and reports, "In many of these [bouquets] there was a fifty-dollar gold piece. One person in this manner presented a valuable diamond brooch." See also Lawrence W. Levine, *Highbrow/Lowbrow: The Emergence of Cultural Hierarchy in America* (Cambridge, Mass.: Harvard University Press, 1988), pp. 25–29, 186–197; and references in Lawrence, *Strong on Music,* vol. 1, passim; and MacMinn, *Theater of the Golden Era,* passim.

2. On whistling and yelling, see de Russailh, *Last Adventure,* p. 21. On the Foreign Miners Tax, Holliday, *The World Rushed In,* pp. 400–401; Josiah Royce, *California, From the Conquest in 1846 to the Second Vigilance Committee in San Francisco*

(Boston: Houghton, Mifflin, 1899), pp. 358–68; and Hubert Howe Bancroft, *History of California*, vol. 6: *1848–1859* (Santa Barbara: Wallace Hebberd, 1970), pp. 402–8. On French exclusiveness, de Russailh, *Last Adventure*, p. 78; on the American love of violence, ibid., pp. 15, 18. On the French, see Soulé, Gihon, and Nisbet, *Annals*, pp. 461–65.

3. De Russailh, *Last Adventure*, p. 22.

4. *DAC*, 19 February 1852, 2:2.

5. The count is taken from the figures of the *Placer Times and Transcript*, cited in MacMinn, *Theater of the Golden Era*, p. 387. For a tribute in the *Stockton Journal* to Biscaccianti, "the first to venture with her store of melodies to this far-off and neglected land," see *DAC*, 1 December 1852, 2:3. For a brief account of her life and career (with some inaccuracies), see Oscar Thompson, *The American Singer: A Hundred Years of Success in Opera* (New York: Dial Press, 1937), pp. 38–40; and also WPA, *San Francisco Theatre Research*, monograph 17 (in vol. 7): *History of Opera in San Francisco, Part I* (San Francisco, 1938), pp. 19–30.

6. The American Theatre, a house of brick and wood on Sansome between California and Sacramento streets, was built on landfill of sand over soft mud, and on opening night, 20 October 1851, when the house for the first time was full, it sank nearly two inches, fortunately uniformly. Thereafter it remained stable. See Soulé, Gihon, and Nisbet, *Annals*, p. 354.

7. Reviews in *DAC* of her first series of ten recitals appeared on 23 March 1852, 3:4; 25 March, 2:3; 27 March, 2:2; 30 March, 2:2; 1 April, 2:3; 2 April, 2:3; 3 April, 2:3; 6 April, 2:2; 8 April, 2:3; 10 April, 2:4; 13 April, 2:3. In every instance the recital was the previous evening. See also McCabe, "Journals," 1:13–15. An advertisement for her first recital, a "Grand Concert" with George Loder conducting the orchestra, appears in *SFDH*, 20 March 1852, 3:1.

8. *DAC*, 23 March 1852, 3:4: "*The Last Rose of Summer* was executed with a brilliancy and beauty which has seldom, if ever, been surpassed. There are those who do not like anything resembling ornament in an old ballad; but if any such were present last night, they were utterly silenced in the loud and vociferous encore which followed that song." See also letter from "O. Fogy" against embellishments, *Wide West*, 30 July 1854, 2:2.

9. This summary and the figures that underlie it are my estimate, based on announcements and reviews, of songs and arias rescheduled or repeated.

Regarding "Old Folks At Home": Although today this song perhaps more than any other is associated with Foster, because of the terms on which he sold it to E. P. Christy, of Christy's Minstrels, until 1879 Christy's name appeared on the music as the composer. Biscaccianti, however, was a friend of Foster and presumably knew the truth. The *DAC*, however, apparently did not, for it consistently referred to the song as "the Ethiopian melody"—i.e., a minstrel song—and never used Foster's name. In her tenth concert, according to *DAC*, 22 April 1852, 2:2, Biscaccianti sang "brilliant variations" on the song.

10. *DAC*, 23 March 1852, 2:4. See also "Musical Intelligence: California,"

Dwight's Journal 1 (8 May 1852): 39; and 2 (23 October 1852): 23. For a similar reaction to one of her last concerts, see *Golden Era*, 9 January 1853, 2:7; and to her "farewell," *DAC*, 12 January 1853, 2:2.

11. McCabe, "Journals," 1:14; *DAC*, 30 March 1852, 3:6 (advertisement); *DAC*, 31 March, 2:3 (review).

12. The first Jenny Lind Theatre, which opened with Von Gulpen singing in the intermission, burned on 4 May 1851. The second, again on the second floor of the rebuilt Parker House, burned on 22 June 1851, before its scaffolding had been taken down. The third opened on 4 October 1851.

13. McCabe, "Journals," 1:19; and *DAC*, 28 July 1852, 2:3.

14. McCabe, "Journals," 1:18: "Grand Oratorio for benefit of Grace Church," 26 July 1852. On the bar in the church, see Huntley, *California* 2:60–61; on general levity in church, ibid., 1:165–66; and on spitting, *DAC*, 3 February 1851, 2:4.

15. *SFDH*, 1 December 1852, 2:3. See also "Musical Intelligence: San Francisco," *Dwight's Journal* 2 (22 January 1853): 126, citing a report of 16 November 1852 in an unidentified paper. Dwight's "16 November," however, is misleading. That is the date of the letter to the paper, not the date of publication.

Alessandro Biscaccianti's letter (see Fig. 5) to Mr. Gregory Yale, 10 December 1852, is in the Bancroft Library, University of California, Berkeley. Yale, who had arrived in San Francisco with Stephen J. Field on 28 December 1849, became one of California's most distinguished lawyers; see Field, *Personal Reminiscences*, pp. 4–5.

16. Despite McCabe, "Journals," 1:23, which states that Biscaccianti left on 1 February 1853, two other notices announcing her departure, with the ship and date of sailing listed, seem conclusive: *DAC*, 6 January, 2:4; and 9 January, 2:3. She sang her farewell recital on 10 January; see *DAC*, 12 January 1853, 2:2 (review). For a report from Lima, see *DAC*, 7 August 1853, 2:3.

17. For her arrival on the *Oregon*, see *DAC*, 21 November 1852, 2:1; for information on her mother, Huntley, *California* 2:219–20. Mengis's name may be found in a letter he wrote to *DAC*, 18 May 1853, 2:2; the fact that he came from Europe is in *DAC*, 13 November 1852, 2:4. On his being a German Swiss, given the constant "Herr" and also because to introduce himself to the city he sang in the first recital a "Swiss Song" titled "The Happy Switzer" composed by one Mengis, presumably himself, see *DAC*, 28 November, 3:7 (advertisement); and he sang it again later: see *DAC*, 9 September 1854, 3:4. He was good at patter songs; see the review of their initial concert, *DAC*, 1 December 1852, 2:3.

18. On Barnum's agent preceding her and the terms of her contract, see *DAC*, 21 October 1852, 1:2. See also *DAC*, 13 November 1852, 2:3, 2:4, and "Musical Intelligence: San Francisco," *Dwight's Journal* 2 (22 January 1853): 126. It is possible that sometime during her San Francisco visit she broke with Barnum (see *DAC*, 16 May 1853, 2:2), though she continued to be managed by his agent, Bushnell (see Chapter 5, n. 9).

19. On the fire companies, see Huntley, *California* 1:275–76, 2:228; on balls,

Soulé, Gihon, and Nisbet, *Annals,* p. 355. On outings, see *DAC,* 8 June 1852, 2:4; with festivities and cost, *DAC,* 9 February 1859, 1:1; 10 February, 2:3; 14 February, 2:2; on benefits, *DAC,* 22 April 1852, 2:2; 15 May, 2:3; on the fire companies' rivalry, *DAC,* 5 December 1852, 2:2. For a celebration over a new hook and ladder truck, see *SFDH* (steamer ed.), 16 November 1854, 5:5.

20. On the auction, see two news items, both *DAC,* 4 December 1852, 2:1; and Huntley, *California* 2:224–28. Word of the auction reached Boston and was reported as "a Barnum *furore*" in *Dwight's Journal* (see n. 18 above) see also Huntley, *California* 2:253–56. WPA, *Opera, Part I,* p. 33, states that the final bid was $1,150.

21. On hats thrown, see *DAC,* 1 December 1852, 2:3. Huntley, *California* 2:224–28, states that one Irishman cried out: "By the powers! darlint, here's my hat for yer, and it's all I have got to give ye!"

22. *DAC,* 1 December 1852, 2:3.

23. On numbered seating, see *DAC,* 28 November 1852, 3:7 (advertisement); 1 December, 2:3 (review).

24. In addition to *DAC,* 1 December 1852, 2:3; and 16 May 1853, 2:2; see *Pioneer Magazine,* February 1854, comparing Anna Bishop and Hayes; and *Golden Era,* 19 December 1852, 2:7; 30 April 1854, 2:4; and 21 May 1854, 2:4.

25. *DAC,* 28 December 1852, 2:2; also 1 April 1852, 2:3; 24 December 1852, 2:2; and 9 January 1853, 2:3: "The Adelphi is thronged every night without regard to wind or weather." On the mud, see Huntley, *California* 1:2.

26. Even such an uncommon event as Biscaccianti's debut was "looked forward to in our musical and fashionable circles" merely "for more than a week," *DAC,* 23 March 1852, 3:4. An advertisement (*SFDH,* 10 July 1855, 1:3) for a production of *La gazza ladra* states that tickets for the Thursday performance would begin sale on Tuesday.

27. Von Gulpen and her assisting artist at her second Grand Concert, on 29 January 1851, had sung a duet from *Elisir d'amore* (probably "Quanto amore" from Act II) in costume, but that was quite different from presenting an entire program in which costumes were changed appropriately for each selection.

28. The first concert-in-costume was on 23 December 1852; the last, on 1 February 1853; see McCabe, "Journals," 1:21. On the bare stage and lavish costumes, see *SFDH,* 24 December 1852, 2:1; *DAC,* 28 December, 2:2.

29. Mengis received consistently favorable notices; see the description of his voice in *DAC,* 1 December 1852, 2:3; and, for a testimonial to his popularity with audiences, *DAC* 18 May 1853, 2:2. After its review of Hayes's farewell performance, the *DAC* (16 May 1853, 2:2) added a separate "farewell review" for him: ". . . This popular singer will depart today. . . . He has acquired . . . a true popularity, though it . . . [was not granted] a complimentary benefit (as we would have thought good taste might have dictated) . . . He has been more than half the attraction at Miss Hayes' concerts." Presumably, the person of "poor" taste, in the critic's view, was

Hayes, though the veto of a benefit for Mengis may have been urged by her agent, Bushnell, who seems to have been thought uncharitable by some; see *DAC*, 20 May 1853, 2:4.

30. *DAC*, 14 May 1853, 3:7.

31. *DAC*, 16 May 1853, 2:2; "Passenger List for *John L. Stephens*," *DAC*, 17 May 2:5; and McCabe, "Journals," 1:25. *DAC* (7 August 1853, 2:3) reported that Biscaccianti was having a success in Lima and that Hayes, who had arrived there on 17 June, after a short stop without performing went on to Valparaíso.

32. For the *Masnadieri* performances, see Kaufman, *Verdi and His Major Contemporaries*, pp. 354, 356. Kaufman also records (p. 259) that Hayes sang in Milan at the La Scala premiere (21 February 1846) of Federico Ricci's *Estella* and at Venice in the La Fenice premiere (13 March 1847) of Ricci's *Griselda*. Presumably by the time she reached San Francisco she no longer was at her best. According to her entry in *The New Grove Dictionary of Music and Musicians*, ed. Stanley Sadie (London: Macmillan, 1980), 8:414, she made her operatic debut at Marseilles, on 10 May 1845, singing Elvira in Bellini's *I puritani*. For a brief account of her, see WPA, *Opera, Part I*, pp. 30–39.

CHAPTER 4. MORE OF *ERNANI*; AND THE FIRST RESIDENT COMPANY

1. *DAC*, 26 July 1853, 2:3; 27 July, 2:3.

2. For reviews of the seven concerts, see *DAC*, 27 July 1853, 2:3; 30 July, 2:3; 3 August, 2:4; 10 August, 2:2; 17 August, 2:3; 20 August, 2:3; 24 August, 2:3. In every case the concert was the preceding evening. In addition, the Troupe appeared as part of a "Grand Vocal and Instrumental Concert," conducted by Rudolph Herold, on 13 August.

3. In the course of Eliza Biscaccianti's first ten recitals Loder, besides conducting the orchestra, played the piano and flute; he also composed for her a "Greeting to California."

4. *DAC*, 8 June 1852, 2:4.

5. MacMinn (*Theater of the Golden Era*, pp. 395–97) states that it was founded in the summer of 1852. "Musical Intelligence: California," *Dwight's Journal* 2 (13 November 1852): 47 and (22 January 1853): 126, also refers to it.

6. For Loder's career in New York, see references in Shanet, *Philharmonic*; and Lawrence, *Strong on Music*, vol. 1. On the N.Y. Philharmonic's conductors and repertory, see Shanet, *Philharmonic*, pp. 109, 293.

7. Lawrence, *Strong on Music* 1:589. According to Lawrence (p. 135), Loder's opera parodies in New York "closely adhered to the originals." In 1855 he would join the San Francisco Minstrels as the conductor and arranger of their opera burlesques; see *DAC*, 19 July 1855, 2:5.

8. *DAC*, 27 July 1853, 2:3. Verdi began to exhibit his rhythmic skill as early as

the finales of his third opera, *Nabucco* (1842); on this point, see Budden, *Operas of Verdi* 1:35.

9. *SFDH*, 30 July 1853, 2:3.

10. In its review *DAC* (20 August 1853, 2:3) does not mention the selection. The Trio, with a new Latin text and title, "Jesu Dei Vivi," by the turn of the century had become very popular with choirs in Roman Catholic churches; see George Martin, *Aspects of Verdi* (New York: Dodd, Mead, 1988), pp. 224–25.

11. *Pioneer Magazine*, December 1854, p. 373.

12. On the Concord coaches, see *DAC*, 3 March 1855, 1:3 (advertisement); and John W. Caughey, with Norris Hundley, Jr., *California: History of a Remarkable State*, 4th ed. (Englewood Cliffs, N.J.: Prentice-Hall, [1940] 1982), pp. 202–3.

13. *DAC*, 4 February 1854, 2:4: "It being 'steamer night,' the house was not so crowded as it would have been under other circumstances." See also *Wide West*, 4 February 1855, 2:4; and *DAC*, 2 May 1855, 2:4, reviewing *I Lombardi*. For a description of the crowd's behavior on the pier during a mail steamer's arrival, see Huntley, *California* 1:277–78. The eyewitness account is Amelia Neville, *The Fantastic City: Memoirs of the Social and Romantic Life of Old San Francisco*, ed. and rev. Virginia Brastow (Boston: Houghton Mifflin, 1932), pp. 92–93.

14. *SFDH*, 4 March 1855, 2:7 (advertisement).

15. Rudolph Herold played a piano fantasy at Hayes's first recital, *DAC*, 1 December 1852, 2:3; as this apparently is the first mention of him in the city, it seems likely that he came with her as an accompanist. *DAC* (21 October 1852, 1:2) reports that she was bringing Mengis "and other artists," and eleven years later *DAC* (17 August 1863, 2:2) states: "Mr. Herold came to this State, we believe, with Catherine Hayes, and he has resided here ever since."

16. On the Hauser concert, see *DAC*, 12 November 1859, 3:7 (program); and 13 November, 2:4 (review). The assisting artists were the Pacific Musical Troupe and a guitarist.

17. For a review of *La Favorite*, see *DAC*, 26 September 1853, 2:3; of *Gilles Ravisseur*, presented twice, *DAC*, 31 October, 2:4; 7 November, 2:5.

18. On the Adelphi, see *Golden Era*, 20 February 1853, 2:7. On the theatre as a focus of the French community, see *Pioneer Magazine*, December 1854, p. 372. The benefit for the Société de Bienfaisance was held there; see *DAC*, 14 November 1853, 2:3; and de Russailh, *Last Adventure*, pp. 18, 23–24.

19. On *Barber*, see *DAC*, 28 November 1853, 2:5; on *Gilles Ravisseur*, *DAC*, 7 November, 2:5; and *SFDH*, 31 October, 2:2.

CHAPTER 5. ANNA BISHOP
AND *JUDITH* (*NABUCCO*)

1. *Morning Post*, 9 October 1846; quoted in the entry for Bishop in the *New Grove Dictionary* 2:741. This entry and the one on Bochsa (pp. 831–32) are good short

biographies of the two artists. For a brief account of Bishop in California, including her second visit, in 1865, see WPA, *Opera, Part I,* pp. 40–48. On the qualities of her voice in 1847, see W. G. Armstrong, *A Record of Opera in Philadelphia* (1884; rpt. New York: AMS Press, 1976), p. 58.

2. *DAC,* 5 February 1854, 3:7. There was no newspaper comment on the numbered seating, perhaps because of protests about the prices charged, which for the subsequent recitals were reduced; see *DAC,* 6 February, 2:2; 10 February, 2:2.

3. *DAC,* 15 February 1854, 2:4.

4. The seven recitals took place on 7, 10, 14, 16, 18, 21, and 25 February. There are announcements and sometimes reviews in both *DAC* and *SFDH;* the initial announcement appeared in *DAC,* 7 February 1854, 3:7. At her second recital, besides Scottish songs, she sang the prison scene from Donizetti's *Anna Bolena* (in English), a selection from his *Linda di Chamounix* (in costume and in English), and ended with a Mexican song, "La Catalumba," for which she dressed as a Mexican boy. See *DAC,* 11 February, 2:2 (review). The review in *SFDH,* 11 February, 2:1, closed with this censure: "It would be well to omit the nonsense contained in the pamphlets disposed of at the door as a key to these concerts. It is impossible to read the silly anecdotes related in this key, and enter fully into the spirit of the very fine music of these concerts." The announcement of the *Tancredi* scene in "warrior costume" appeared in *DAC,* 17 February 1854, 3:7. Besides those operas already mentioned Bishop sang arias or scenes from Bellini's *Sonnambula* and *Norma,* Donizetti's *Roberto Devereux* (costumed as Queen Elizabeth), and *Lucia di Lammermoor.* She repeated the scene from *Tancredi* on 1 March and had a great success, a critic declaring it to be "the great feature of the evening, and we hope soon to see the whole opera" (*DAC,* 2 March, 2:5).

5. Hayes arrived on 3 April aboard the steamer *John L. Stevens,* accompanied by her mother, her agent, W. A. Bushnell, and Herr Mengis; *DAC,* 3 April 1854, 2:2. On *Norma,* see McCabe, "Journals," 1:37; *DAC,* 26 April 1854, 2:4 (review). Also *DAC,* 16 May 1853, 2:2: "Though the reputation which was kindled for Miss Hayes, on her arrival here . . . was greater than her merits as an artist would justify, it did not detract from her success." For her previous failure in recital with Norma's aria "Casta diva," see *DAC,* 1 December 1852, 2:3: "It was not sung with the expression that seemed required, and . . . the staccato in which it was rendered detracted from the merit of the execution."

6. An announcement of Bishop's *Norma* appeared in *DAC,* 30 April 1854, 3:7. A news item (*DAC,* 1 May 1854, 2:3) recommended a comparison of Hayes and Bishop in the role.

7. Announcements and reviews for the eight-day "season" appeared regularly in both *DAC* and *SFDH.*

8. *Pioneer Magazine,* February 1854, pp. 114–19, has a discussion of the relative merits of Bishop, Hayes, and Anna Thillon; see also *Golden Era,* 21 May 1854, 2:4. Even before Bishop's arrival the *Golden Era* had been steadily and often satirically

critical of Hayes: see, e.g., 19 December 1852, 2:3; 13 February 1853, 2:2; 27 February, 2:3; and 20 March, 2:4.

9. On Hayes's final concert and departure for Australia, see news item, program, and review, *DAC*, 7 July 1854, 2:4; 7 July, 3:4; and 8 July, 2:5; on the gold brooch, 8 July, 2:3. In 1857, in Rome, she married the agent, W. A. Bushnell, who had represented her so ably in San Francisco.

10. McCabe ("Journals," 1:37) records the *Norma* as the first appearance of Leonardi. For his roles in South America, where he sang both Attila (bass) and Ezio (baritone) in *Attila*, see Kaufman, *Verdi and His Major Contemporaries*, pp. 329, 333. "Best basso": *Pioneer Magazine*, December 1854, p. 374.

11. Leonardi's career in Peru and Chile can be followed to some extent in Kaufman, *Verdi and His Major Contemporaries*. The four concerts were given on 24, 26, 30 May, and 3 June 1854. On "Dagli immortali," see *DAC*, 24 May, 3:4 (program); the review, 25 May, 2:5, merely names Leonardi. On "Profezia," on 3 June, see *DAC*, 3 June, 2:5 (program; there was no *DAC* review); and *SFDH*, 4 June, 2:2, without comment on the music.

12. *DAC*, 7 July 1854, 3:4 (program; no review).

13. An advertisement for Atwill's new location describing the store appears in *DAC*, 1 December 1852, 1:4. On librettos for sale, e.g. for *Trovatore*, see *DAC*, 6, 7 May 1859, 1:9. On leaving addresses, see, e.g., *DAC*, 20 November 1852, 3:7 (for George Loder and Mr. Planel); and 21 June 1854, 2:5; 3 July, 3:4 (S. W. Leach). As to finding new music: It is possible, of course, that the enterprising artist was not Smith or Coulon but George Loder, who frequently seems to be conducting when new works by Verdi are introduced. But the argument then would run: for the same reasons he found it easier to persuade the men than the women to try the new pieces. For a notice of new music received, including "selections from the most recent operas," see *DEB*, 11 February 1860, 3:4.

14. On Bishop's selections being available for purchase at Atwill's store, see the advertisement for her recital in *DAC*, 12 February 1854, 3:7. For lists of arrangements offered by Verdi's Italian publishers, see Luke Jensen, *Giuseppe Verdi and Giovanni Ricordi with Notes on Francesco Lucca, from "Oberto" to "La traviata"* (New York: Garland, 1989). For lists of arrangements offered by American publishers and in print in 1870, see *Complete Catalogue of Sheet Music and Musical Works, 1870* (rpt. New York: Da Capo Press, 1973). For *I Lombardi* and *Ernani*, for example, Jensen's totals are 243 and 344, and the *Catalogue*'s, 58 and 113.

A Bostonian visiting the city in April 1856 reported in *Dwight's Journal* 9 (3 May 1856): 37 that "Mr. Atwill, formerly of New York, tells me he sells much first class music." A problem for musicians in the city, according to this person, was the lack of good pianos. For a description of Atwill's New York store in 1842, see Lawrence, *Strong on Music* 1:176–77. On Atwill, see Soulé, Gihon, and Nisbet, *Annals*, pp. 781–83.

15. Cailly arrived on the steamer *John L. Stevens* on 3 April, accompanied by

"Mons. Cailly," whose first name remains unknown, and an unspecified number of children; see *DAC* 3 April 1854, 2:2. During her San Francisco season, however, the manager of the Union Theatre was Jules Cailly and possibly her husband. According to *DAC* (4 April 1854, 2:2), she had embarked at Lima and was "of the National Academy of Music in Paris, and prima donna of the Theatre Royale in Brussels." In Lima, in 1853, she had sung at least two operas with Leonardi, one of them Verdi's *I masnadieri*; see Kaufman, *Verdi and His Major Contemporaries*, p. 357. "The very good French operatic company": *DAC*, 4 April 1854, 2:2.

16. *Wide West*, 23 April 1854, 2:3, reviews the opening night, 16 April, of *Lucie di Lammermoor*. For an announcement of the season at the Union Theatre, see *DAC*, 13 May, 2:5. *Golden Era*, 21 May, 2:4, comments on *Le Barbier* and announces *Norma*. *DAC*, 21 May, 2:5 (news item), states that *Norma* will be sung in French.

17. On the *Lucia* "challenge scene," see *Wide West*, 4 March 1855, 2:3, which refers to another performance of it, when it was sung as an excerpt by E. Coulon and [?] Laglaise in Planel's first season after the third performance of *La Fille du régiment* (see *DAC*, 2 October 1853, 3:7). Evidently in these years, at least among the French, it was an admired part of the opera. On *Crown Diamonds*, see *DAC*, 28 May, 3:7 (advertisement), which promises a female chorus and suggests that the opera will be sung in French.

18. See *DAC*, 3 May 1854, 3:7 see (advertisement), for the benefit next day; there was no review.

In Italian scores of *I Lombardi* there is no Polecca or Polonaise, but in Verdi's revision of it for Paris, which he entitled *Jérusalem*, the aria "Non fu sogno" became "Qu'elle ivresse," was moved from Act IV to Act II, and in French scores and sheet music was titled "Polonaise." *Jérusalem* was performed in Paris in 1847, in Brussels in 1848, and reached New Orleans on 24 January 1850. Since Cailly and most, possibly all, of her associates in this San Francisco season were of French origin or descent, it seems likely that they knew the aria through its French editions; indeed, she probably sang both the Polonaise and the aria from *Ernani* in French. The variations "expressly composed for her" possibly were the work of M. Planel, who the following year prepared the orchestral parts for a production of *I Lombardi* in San Francisco by an Italian troupe. See his letter to the editor, *DAC*, 9 May 1855, 2:4.

After this season Cailly apparently never again sang in San Francisco, but no report has yet been found of her leaving the city. Kaufman (*Verdi and His Major Contemporaries*, p. 358) records her in a performance of *I masnadieri* in Montevideo in 1859, so she did continue her career.

19. According to McCabe ("Journals," 1:32), on 31 December 1853 Thillon arrived in the city with her husband, Charles, and accompanied by a tenor, S. W. Leach (see Chapter 10, n. 20). For an article anticipating her season, mentioning Loder and the chorus, see *DAC*, 15 January 1854, 2:2. See McCabe, "Journals," 1:33, for opening night at the Metropolitan, *Crown Diamonds*, 16 January 1854; for open-

ings of other operas, see pp. 33–35. Reviews of *Bohemian Girl: SFDH*, 14, 16 March 1854, 2:1; of *Cinderella: Golden Era*, 21 May 1854, 2:4.

20. See *Wide West*, 16 April 1854, 2:3, for the review of Thillon's *La Fille du régiment*. According to WPA, *Opera, Part I*, p. 50, Thillon, after a short and unsuccessful tour of the mining towns, left San Francisco on 1 June. Before then, in the final weeks of May, she premiered *Cinderella* and revived *The Bohemian Girl* (see advertisements in *DAC*, 19–28 May). Her final appearance was on 28 May; *DAC*, 29 May, 2:3, reviews her performance and comments on her health and difficulties with the California climate. According to *DAC*, 30 May, 2:1, she would depart with a profit from her five-month visit of $30,000, but the paper deplored the system of "stars" and urged more support for local singers and companies.

21. On English versions of arias and operas, with cuts and interpolations, see Charles Hamm, *Yesterdays: Popular Song in America* (New York: W. W. Norton, 1970), pp. 62–88; also Lawrence, *Strong on Music* 1:15, 132, 164, 267, 335, 589.

22. On cuts in *The Enchantress*, see *Wide West*, 28 January 1855, 2:3; on *Cinderella*, *DAC*, 26 May 1854, 2:5. The *Pioneer* article is in the February 1854 issue, pp. 114–19. When Bishop later produced *Bohemian Girl*, with heavy cuts and alterations, she had a failure; see *DAC*, 4 February 1855, 2:4. Bishop had another failure with an altered version of *Fra Diavolo* on 25 November 1854. According to *DAC*, 26 November 1854, 2:5, the opera was "more singularly and unfortunately cast than any opera we ever witnessed before. Madame Bishop herself appeared as Fra Diavolo [tenor]—all well enough as a novelty, but very inappropriate and unnatural."

23. This brief season, 18–25 June 1854, can be followed in the advertisements and reviews starting with *DAC*, 18 June, 3:4.

24. On *Der Freischütz*, see news item announcing first performance "tonight," *DAC*, 19 July 1854, 2:4; and advertisement naming the farce, ibid., 3:3. The review in *DAC*, 20 July, 2:4, reported a good performance except for a mishap in the Incantation scene: "The effect, however, was not at all heightened by the entrance of a supernumerary with a blue bucket and exceedingly rusty tin dipper to extinguish the fire in the magic circle which, through lack of precaution on the part of the property man, burnt rather too freely." On the chorus and orchestra, see *DAC*, 28, 29 July, 2:5; 30 July, 4:5; on the orchestra of thirty-two, *SFDH*, 31 July; a review can be found in *Golden Era*, 23 July, 2:6.

25. Concert Society orchestra of thirty: *DAC*, 1 September 1854, 3:4.

26. In Bishop's third recital after her arrival in San Francisco, she sang a "Bouquet Musical" employing eight languages; see *DAC*, 16 February 1854, 3:7. Leman (*Memories*, p. 235) states she could sing in twenty. Whatever the number, it was sufficient to be remarkable. The sensation of her 1848 season in New York was a skit, *La sfogato*, in which, "with a series of swift costume changes, she impersonated a singer at a manager's audition pretending to be six other singers of various nationalities, respectively performing in their native tongues (and costumes): French, German, Italian, English, Russian, and 'Tartarian' " (Law-

rence, *Strong on Music* 1:527). For *La sfogato* in Philadelphia in 1848, see Armstrong, *Record of the Opera in Philadelphia*, pp. 61–62. In a San Francisco recital she sang scenes from *Lucia di Lammermoor, Linda di Chamounix, Der Freischütz*, and *Lucrezia Borgia* respectively in French, English, German, and Italian; see *SFDH*, 18 September 1854, 2:2 (review). On Von Gulpen replacing Gould, see *DAC*, 29 July 1854, 2:5 (advertisement). The review (*DAC*, 31 July, 2:5) states the language now to be German.

27. For a review of *La Muette*, see *SFDH*, 22 August 1854, 2:1; an enthusiastic review of the second performance appears in *DAC*, 19 August, 2:3.

28. For more opera than New York, see *DAC*, 13 May 1854, 2:5; and *Golden Era*, 9 April 1854, 2:5: "California at present can boast of being the center of theatrical attraction of the whole Union." The critic's complaint is from *Pioneer Magazine*, January 1855, p. 51.

29. For a brief account of Bishop's theatrical intrigues in Naples, see F. Schlitzer, "Verdi's *Alzira* at Naples," *Music and Letters* 35 (1954): 125.

30. An advertisement for *Judith, DAC*, 22 September 1854, 3:3, gives the cast, which was drawn from the pool of singers in the city, chiefly Thillon's tenor S. W. Leach (see Chap. 10, n. 20), secondary singers from the French troupe, and local dancers. The advertisement incorrectly announces that the performance on 22 September would be the first; the review the next day, *DAC*, 23 September, 2:3, reveals it was the second. For review of first performance, see *DAC*, 22 September 1854, 2:2.

31. See the pertinent appendices in Jensen, *Verdi and Ricordi*. See also *New York Herald*, 20 August 1850, 5:6 (announcement); and the review of 21 August, 4:2: "This piece, which is a very appropriate combination of the best musical gems of Verdi has been admirably and well arranged by Mr. Bochsa ... who also composed the marches and recitatives for this grand operatic spectacle." Also *New York Morning Express*, 21 August, 2:4; 23 August, 2:4; and 27 August, 2:3 (reviews).

32. *Pioneer Magazine*, January 1855, p. 55.

33. On the "brindisi" from *Macbeth*, see *DAC*, 22 September 1854, 2:2; at the second performance of *Judith* her singing of it was extravagantly praised by *DAC*, 23 September, 2:3. For her later performance of it in recital, see *SFDH*, 23 September 1855, 2:2.

Concerning *Macbeth*: In the United States and England the opera was given very seldom, presumably because it was thought to compare unfavorably with Shakespeare's play. George Templeton Strong saw it in New York on 26 April 1850 and recorded in his diary: "*Macbeth*, almost scene-for-scene with the tragedy, and absurd enough is the attempt to marry Northern legend to modern Italian music, even were the legend not canonized and beatified by Shakespeare, and the music not that of Verdi. The music is Verdiesque. Screaming unisons everywhere, and all the melodies of that peculiar style the parallel whereof is rope-dancing; first a swing and flourish, hanging on by the hands, then a somerset, and then another swing to an erect position on the rope, a few shines cut there, and then down again. The unfortunate man is incapable of real melody—his airs are such as a man born deaf would compose by calculation of the distances of musical notes and the intervals between them. His *supernatural* music in this opera is especially comical. Like very many of his brethren of this day, the deluded author has no means whatever of expressing *feeling* in music except by coarse daubing of *color.* Passion is typified and portrayed by a musical phrase instrumented with the brass; softer emotion by the same phrase written for the oboes and flutes; terror by ditto through the medium of the brasses judiciously heightened with the big drums and the ophicleide; and so of every other subject of musical expression" (*The Diary of George Templeton Strong,* ed. Allan Nevins and Milton Halsey Thomas [New York: Macmillan, 1952], 2:13–14). The opera had its San Francisco premiere on 18 November 1862, and was repeated on 20, 22, and 23 November, and on 25 May 1863. For reviews, see Appendix E.

34. On the enlarged orchestra, see *DAC,* 21 September 1854, 2:2. Performance dates for *Judith* were 21, 22, 23, and 24 September, and 16 October (unannounced, but see *DAC,* 17 October, 2:4); the second act was combined with *Martha* on 25 October. For the final performance on 27 November, see *DAC,* 28 November 1854, 2:2. See also McCabe, "Journals," 1:44–46.

35. *Pioneer Magazine,* December 1854, p. 373. *DAC,* 17 October 1854, 2:4, reviewing the final performance, stated: "We have previously spoken of the excellent manner in which this opera is managed and performed."

CHAPTER 6. *ERNANI, NABUCCO, I LOMBARDI,* AND *I DUE FOSCARI*

1. *DAC,* 12 November 1854, 3:5 (announcement); and *SFDH,* 13 November, 3:1. The troupe arrived on the steamer *S.S. Cortes* on 31 October 1854; see Soulé, Gihon, and Nisbet, *Annals, Continuation,* p. 21. Though the announcement says "from Italy," the troupe's prima donna, Clotilda Barili-Thorn, had been singing as recently as August 1853 in Lima, in performances of Verdi's *La battaglia di Legnano;* and previously, in May 1850, she had sung *Ernani* in Mexico City; for both, see Kaufman, *Verdi and His Major Contemporaries,* pp. 367, 300. For descriptions of Barili-Thorn in her opening season in New York, 1847, see Lawrence, *Strong on Music* 1:427–29.

2. *DAC,* 7 December 1854, 3:4; *SFDH,* 9 December, 2:1.

3. *Pioneer Magazine,* January 1855, p. 56.

4. On its being the "first complete company," see *Pioneer Magazine,* December 1854, p. 373. The following month (January 1855, p. 54), however, it was merely "more complete" than its predecessors.

5. Lawrence, *Strong on Music* 1:434, quoting the *New York Herald;* also pp. 434–35, 445.

6. *DAC*, 12 November 1854, 3:5; *SFDH*, 13 November, 3:1.

7. *Pioneer Magazine*, December 1854, p. 372, incorrectly lists as arriving in San Francisco with the troupe two men who had been singing in the city for some time, Leonardi and Alfred Pierre Roncovieri. The last, a Frenchman resident in San Francisco, was hired by almost every troupe as a comprimario; see WPA, *Opera, Part I*, pp. 14–16.

8. On the frequent "hoarseness," see *Pioneer Magazine*, January 1855, p. 55; and *Wide West*, 4 February 1855, 2:4. For Barili-Thorn's "severe cold" on opening night, see *Pioneer Magazine*, December 1854, p. 374; for her return to the stage after long indisposition, *SFDH*, 17 February 1855, 2:2; 19 February, 2:1; and for her weakness at the end of her stay, *DAC*, 14 June 1855, 2:3.

9. *Wide West*, 19 November 1854, 2:4. See also *DAC*, 15 November, 2:4 (review); and, regarding the "largely augmented" chorus, *SFDH* (steamer ed.), 16 November, 1:1.

10. *Pioneer Magazine*, December 1854, p. 373.

11. On the lack of a women's chorus, see *DAC*, 17 November 1854, 2:5; on Scola's poor stage presence, ibid. and *Pioneer Magazine*, December 1854, p. 373; on his failure to improve in the role, *DAC*, 14 June 1855, 2:3; and for a comparison of him to Eugenio Bianchi, *DAC*, 20 May 1859, 2:4.

12. *Golden Era*, 19 November 1854, 2:5.

13. *SFDH*, 15 November 1854, 2:2.

14. *DAC*, 17 November 1854, 2:5.

15. Abramo Basevi, *Studio sulle opere di Giuseppe Verdi* (Florence: Tipografia Tofani, 1859), p. 159.

16. Lawrence, *Strong on Music* 1:520; "Italian Opera," *Dwight's Journal* 5, (26 August 1854): 165.

17. See, e.g., his letter of 22 May 1844 to Francesco Maria Piave: "There is no contrast in idea to set off the adagio" (in *I copialettere di Giuseppe Verdi*, ed. Gaetano Cesari and Alessandro Luzio [Milan, 1913], p. 426). Verdi was not unique in his pursuit of variety. Berlioz, ten years older and whose music Verdi would hear in Paris, once declared, "Variety wisely ordered is the soul of music." And in an opera Berlioz, like Wagner, sought a unity of dramatic purpose to which all the parts contributed—scenery, stage direction, voices, and orchestra. This idea of an organic unity based in variety was part of the general concept of artists in the romantic age and owed a great deal to their readings of Shakespeare. See D. Kern Holoman, *Berlioz* (Cambridge, Mass.: Harvard University Press, 1989), p. 361.

18. Verdi, Letter of 22 April 1853 to Antonio Somma; quoted in Franz Werfel and Paul Stefan, eds., *Verdi: The Man in His Letters*, trans. Edward O. Downes (1942; rpt. New York: Vienna House, 1973), pp. 174–76.

19. On Walt Whitman's "haughty attitudes" and "fiery breath," see *New York Dissected by Walt Whitman: A Sheaf of Recently Discovered Newspaper Articles by the Author of "Leaves of Grass,"* ed. Emory Holloway and Ralph Adimari (New York:

Rufus Rockwell Wilson, 1936), p. 22. The article quoted here was published first in *Life Illustrated,* 10 November 1855, and recounts for the reader a typical night at the opera—which is playing *Ernani.* Whitman describes the house, the audience, the orchestra "of nearly forty performers," and "the stormy music of Giuseppe Verdi." The poem quoted has similar images of *Norma, Lucia di Lammermoor, I Puritani, La Favorite,* and *Sonnambula.* Another "night at the opera" that uses *Ernani* as its example, this time in Philadelphia, is "Scrici," *Physiology of the Opera* (1852; rpt. New York: Institute for Studies in American Music, Brooklyn College, 1981). (Note: *DAC,* 22 January 1855, 2:4, makes clear that on the previous night, despite the announcement of the complete opera, only two acts of *Ernani* were sung. This requires a correction to Hixon's listing of full performances of the opera.)

20. *Pioneer Magazine,* January 1855, p. 55.

21. *DAC,* 30 November 1854, 2:5 (news item with synopsis of opera); ibid., 3:5 (advertisement with cast). For reviews, see *DAC,* 1 December, 2:5; and *SFDH,* 1 December, 2:1. The conductor is named in the review of *SFDH,* 5 December, 2:1.

22. Enthusiastic reviews of *Nabucco* appear in *DAC,* 3 December 1854, 2:5; 5 December, 2:5; *SFDH,* 3 December, 2:1; 5 December, 2:1; and *Pioneer Magazine,* January 1855, p. 55; also in *SFDH* (steamer ed.), 9 December, 3:3: "It was indeed an entertainment which would have deserved success in any city of the United States."

For those parts of *Nabucco* that impressed a critic at a revival, when the opera's title was *Nino* and the story slightly changed, see *DEB,* 26 May 1862, 3:5: "The music, though occasionally of a noisy character, is often beautiful, and some of it very striking. . . . Among the many fine things that are in the opera may be mentioned the quintet and chorus of the 2nd act, when the impious Nino calls on the people to worship him; the air in the 3rd act where he entreats Abigail to spare the life of Fenena; the grand though simple chorus of the captive Babylonians in the same act; the lament of Fenena when led to martyrdom; and the glorious hymn to Isis (or originally, to the God of Israel) that closes the work. The funeral march in the 4th act, and the short triumphal march on the first appearance of Nino are fine. . . . There is a pleasing introduction, which from its length may almost be called an overture, that contains morsels of the melodies that afterwards occur in the piece." From this description, it seems the production omitted the death of Abigaille, Verdi's final scene.

23. *Pioneer Magazine,* January 1855, p. 54. This first season of the Barili-Thorn troupe ran from 14 November through 18 December 1854.

24. On the Sacramento visit, see *DAC,* 10 January 1855, 2:2. The *Ernani* performances on 19 and 21 January are reported in *SFDH,* 25 January 1855, 2:6 (announcement); and *DAC,* 27 January, 2:7. Francesco Leonardi's last performance in the city of an opera was as Dr. Bartolo in *Il barbiere di Siviglia,* on 14 December 1854; he then sang in a concert that closed the troupe's season on 18 December, and thereafter I found no trace of him, of when he left the city or where he went.

25. *Wide West*, 28 January 1855, 2:3. Regarding the impresario: The announcement of the first Barili-Thorn season in *DAC*, 12 November 1854, 3:5, states that the troupe's director, Luigi Bazari, "has entered into an arrangement with Mrs. Sinclair to produce in the Metropolitan Theatre, for fifteen nights, the following operas. . . ." And a news item, *DAC*, 12 December, states that a performance that night will be a benefit for "Bazzini, the impresario." Thereafter his name, however spelled, does not appear again except once as "Bazani" in a public statement by Mrs. Sinclair (*DAC*, 9 May 1855, 2:4). Soulé, Gihon, and Nisbet, *Annals, Continuation*, p. 21 (31 October 1854), states that among the passengers aboard the *S.S. Cortes*, which docked that day, was Barili-Thorn "and others of the Italian troupe engaged by Mrs. Sinclair."

Mrs. Sinclair (1817–91), born Catherine Norton Sinclair, was an actress. In 1837 she married the great American tragedian Edwin Forrest (1806–72), and in 1850, in one of the sensational divorces of the era, they parted. She resumed her maiden name but kept her matron's title. The Margaret Sinclair Voorhees who sang Fenena in *Nabucco* was her sister; see *Pioneer Magazine*, December 1854, p. 375.

26. *Wide West*, 28 January 1855, 2:3.

27. *SFDH*, 28 January 1855, 2:1. On another joint program, see *DAC*, 17 February 1855, 3:1; and *SFDH*, 17 February, 1:3: *L'elisir* (Bishop, Scola, Lanzoni, Mengis), finale of *Anna Bolena* (Bishop), ballet and churchyard scene from *Robert le diable* (Mlle Thierry, ballerina).

28. *Wide West*, 11 February 1855, 2:7 (review).

29. *DAC*, 3 March 1855, 3:3; *SFDH*, 10 March, 1:4 (advertisements).

30. The audience dancing onstage during a performance surely was rare, and although there is no report of music added for the occasion, certainly some must have been required. At the Boston premiere of Verdi's *Un ballo in maschera*, the audience was invited onto the stage for the masked ball of the final scene, and according to the advertisement, music from the "Grand Bal Masque of Gustavus III" (doubtless from Auber's opera) was added. See George Martin, "La prima rappresentazione di *Un ballo in maschera* a Boston, 15 marzo 1861," *Atti del Primo Congresso Internazionale di Studi Verdiani* (Parma: Istituto di Studi Verdiani, 1969), pp. 378–82.

31. For a review of *Don Giovanni*, see *DAC*, 9 March 1855, 2:3; on the "sold out" house, *SFDH*, 10 March, 2:1. On the economic depression, see *DAC*, 20 January 1855, 3:1; also in New York City, *DAC*, 10 January, 2:2; and on continuing hard times, *SFDH* (steamer ed.), 4 April 1856, 5:4.

32. *DAC*, 7–9 January 1855, 3:5.

33. *DAC*, 12 January 1855, 3:5.

34. Frederick H. Martens, *A Thousand and One Nights of Opera* (New York: D. Appleton and Co., 1926), p. 152. At the time this was published, the diction already was long out of date—often the case with opera synopses.

35. *DAC*, 13 January 1855, 2:4.

36. *DAC,* 17 January 1855, 2:5.

37. On the revised production, see *DAC,* 4 February 1855, 2:5 (news item) and 3:1 (advertisement). A review appears in *Wide West,* 11 February, 2:7. For an incorrect prediction that the French community would turn out "en masse" for the opera in French, see *Wide West,* 4 February, 2:4. This review states, as others do not, that the opera first was sung in English.

38. *DAC,* 14 February 1855, 2:3.

39. Lawrence, *Strong on Music* 1:432, 438–39, quoting the *Albion,* 6 March 1847, p. 120.

40. *SFDH,* 1 May 1855, 2:1 (news item) and 3:1 (advertisement).

41. *DAC,* 2 May 1855, 2:4 (review). On costumes and carriage hire as the start of the quarrel, see Sinclair's statement, *DAC,* 9 May, 2:4. For a suggestion that this first performance of *I Lombardi* was underwritten by interested patrons, see *DAC,* 30 April, 2:3.

42. *SFDH,* 4 May 1855, 2:2; *DAC,* 4 May, 3:3.

43. *SFDH,* 6 May 1855, 2:1.

44. Barili-Thorn's letter appears in *DAC,* 7 May 1855, 2:4, as does Mrs. Sinclair's. An editorial, "The Operatic Quarrel," is in ibid., 2:3.

45. For Sinclair's figures, see *DAC,* 9 May 1855, 2:4, which includes an interesting table of the theatre's staff; for Planel's letter, ibid.

46. *DAC,* 21 May 1855, 2:4; and see *SFDH,* 20 May, 2:1, which lauds "a chorus we have never heard surpassed in power and effect" singing to a house that was "good" but not "crowded." Presumably Rudolph Herold, who was the company's musical director at the Union Theatre, conducted; see *DAC* 26 May, 3:7 (advertisement).

47. Gino Monaldi, *Verdi, 1839–1898,* 2d ed. (Turin: Bocca, 1926), p. 60.

48. I found no advertisement or review of the *Foscari* premiere, but the performance is announced in a news item, *DAC,* 23 March 1855, 2:4, and it is confirmed in a news item for the second performance, on 25 March, in *SFDH,* 25 March, 2:2. An advertisement for the second performance (*SFDH,* 25 March, 1:5) gives the cast. (Note: These first two performances do not appear in Hixon's listing.) For the third and fourth performances, see *DAC,* 26 May, 3:7 (advertisement); 1 June, 2:4 (news item) and 2:5 (advertisement); and *SFDH,* 1 June, 1:4 (advertisement) and 2:1 (news item).

49. *DAC,* 16 June 1855 (steamer ed.), 1:5: On Saturday 9 June Sinclair "took a farewell benefit, concluding her long and arduous service as theatrical manager." She acted Lady Teazle in Sheridan's *School for Scandal* and a scene from Shakespeare's *Henry VIII* in which she played Catherine of Aragon. In her farewell speech she remarked on her financial losses, saying that "within the past few months I have, in common with almost every member of this community, suffered from the disastrous state of affairs."

50. See the review in *DAC*, 14 June 1855, 2:3, with adverse comments on Scola's acting.

51. *DAC*, 18 June 1855, 2:4 (review). For a critic in London who similarly retained "forever" a memory of the Doge's "agony" in the final scene, see Henry F. Chorley, *Thirty Years' Musical Recollections* (New York: Alfred A. Knopf, 1926), p. 211. Presumably Loder conducted on the sixteenth; he had been announced for *Maria di Rohan* in *DAC*, 16 June, 2:7.

52. Regarding Lanzoni's liking for Verdi: On leaving San Francisco, he sang in the premiere productions of Verdi's *Macbeth*, *Trovatore*, and *Traviata* in Lima, 1856–57, and *Macbeth* in Santiago, 1857; see Kaufman, *Verdi and His Major Contemporaries*, pp. 346, 411, 425, 342. The review is in *DAC*, 18 June 1855, 2:3.

53. *DAC*, 1 March 1855, 3:3; 2 March, 3:3 (programs); *Wide West*, 4 March, 2:3 (review). Carlotta Patti made her debut as a vocalist, singing Schubert's *Serenade* in English, between the acts of the second performance of *I due Foscari*; see *SFDH*, 1 June 1855, 1:4; and *DAC*, 1 June, 2:5 (advertisement).

54. *SFDH*, 9 July 1855, 2:2; *DAC*, 9 July, 2:5 (programs); *DAC*, 10 July, 2:2 (review without comment); on Loder at the piano, see the review of *SFDH*, 11 July, 2:1.

55. *SFDH*, 6 August 1855, 2:1; *DAC*, 11 November, 3:6 (reviews).

56. *DAC*, 9 July 1855, 3:6 (program); *SFDH*, 12 July, 2:1 (review).

57. On the three-month tour, see *DAC*, 15 June 1855, 2:4; 12 July, 2:4; and 16 July (steamer ed.), 1:2. On *Gazza ladra*, see *SFDH*, 11 July 1855, 1:3; *DAC*, 12 July, 2:4.

58. On the *Norma* travesty, see *DAC*, 16 July 1855, 3:6; *SFDH*, 20 July, 2:1 (review). On Bochsa's illness, *DAC*, 16 July, 2:3.

59. *DAC*, 27 July 1855, 3:6 (advertisement); *DAC*, 31 July, 2:3 (review). On Bochsa's illness and the postponement of the performance, see *DAC*, 1 August, 2:1.

60. *DAC*, 8 August 1855, 2:4.

61. *DAC*, 7 July 1855, 2:4.

62. On singers' dispersal, see *DAC*, 27 August 1855, 2:5. For "Ernani, involami," see *SFDH*, 31 August 1855, 3:1; 3 September, 2:2 (review).

63. For the "Brindisi" program, see *DAC*, 22 September 1855, 2:5; and *SFDH*, 23 September, 2:2. On Comassi, see *SFDH*, 28 October, 1:3 (program).

64. On the repetition of "Ernani, involami," see the programs in *DAC*, 24 September 1855, 2:6; and 25 September, 3:6; for the recital on the twenty-fifth, see *SFDH*, 26 September, 2:4 (review).

65. The program appeared in *DAC*, 27 September 1855, 2:5. News item on loss of Bishop: *SFDH*, 28 September, 2:1; also *DAC*, 28 September, 2:5. She was scheduled to sail for Australia on the *Kit Carson* on 30 September; see *DAC*, 24 September, 2:2.

66. *SFDH*, 20 November 1855, 2:2 (news item).

67. *SFDH*, 3 September 1855, 2:2.

CHAPTER 7. ECONOMIC DECLINE,
IL TROVATORE IN EXCERPTS,
AND THE VIGILANTES OF 1856

1. Stewart Edward White, *The Forty-Niners* (New Haven, Conn.: Yale University Press, 1918), pp. 172–73.

2. See, e.g., Roger W. Lotchin, *San Francisco, 1846–1856: From Hamlet to City* (Lincoln: University of Nebraska Press, 1974), pp. 245–50; Walton Bean, *California: An Interpretive History* (New York: McGraw Hill, 1968), pp. 143–48; Hubert Howe Bancroft, *History of California,* vol. 6: *1848–1859,* pp. 747–53; and White, *The Forty-Niners,* pp. 174–265.

3. Soulé, Gihon, and Nisbet, *Annals,* pp. 354–55, analyzes the ships' origins and types. By far the greatest number were American, then British, French, and German. Some of the ships for a time were used as warehouses.

4. Buffum, *The Gold Rush,* p. 124; Caughey, *California,* pp. 132–34, 157–60.

5. On gambling, see *DEB,* 4 December 1856, 2:2; on its being not yet stamped out in San Francisco, *DEB,* 12 October 1859, 2:1, or in Yuba County (Marysville), *DEB,* 1 December 1859, 1:1; on a perceived decrease, see *DEB,* 3 January 1860, 3:3: "Whatever gambling is done is behind barred doors and in secret chambers." On drinking, see Soulé, Gihon, and Nisbet, *Annals,* pp. 645–46; also Starr, *Americans and the California Dream,* p. 55. For smoking and spitting, see Huntley, *California* 1:37.

6. On brawling and "noisy and obscene language in the Opera House," see *DEB,* 28 October 1859, 3:1; the "slungshot" in the Union Theatre is mentioned in *DEB,* 16 November 1859, 3:4. The "crowder" is in *DAC,* 20 November 1856, 2:1; it is not certain, though likely, that a court case reported two days later refers to this man; if so, he was fined $180 for unprovoked assault; see *DAC,* 22 November, 2:4. The polling-booth argument is described in *Golden Era,* 26 August 1855, 2:5. On lynching, see Buffum, *The Gold Rush,* pp. 99–102; on homicides and suicides, de Russailh, *Last Adventure,* pp. 10, 61; and Starr, *Americans and the California Dream,* pp. 57, 128–29. The figures are from the *Encyclopedia Britannica* (Chicago: University of Chicago Press, 1946), 19:944, "San Francisco," citing Bancroft, *History of California.*

7. On the Bateman case, see Soulé, Gihon, and Nisbet, *Annals, Continuation,* p. 4; and *DAC,* 7 July 1854, 2:5. Testimony in the case was published in *DAC,* 30 August 1854, 2:5; 1 September, 2:4–5.

8. On the increase in dueling, see Soulé, Gihon, and Nisbet, *Annals,* p. 550. See Field, *Personal Reminiscences,* p. 102, on the public support for it and a judicial method by which it might be curbed; and in general, with numerous examples, Bancroft, *Works,* vol. 35: *California inter pocula* (San Francisco: The History Company, 1888), pp. 734–84. For the fist fight, see *DAC,* 18 May 1854, 2:1.

9. See Bancroft, *California inter pocula,* p. 759; *DAC,* 22 May 1854, 2:2; and 23 May, 2:1.

10. Soulé, Gihon, and Nisbet, *Annals,* p. 485. A state census of 1852 lists the population of the city as 34,876, of which 29,166 were white men and 5,154 white women; 16,144 were male foreign residents (i.e., not U.S. citizens) and 2,710, female.

11. De Russailh, *Last Adventure,* pp. 10, 61.

12. *Golden Era* and *Wide West* both quoted by MacMinn, *Theater of the Golden Era,* p. 145. On Mrs. Sinclair's departure, see *DAC,* 28 April 1856, 2:1 (news item); Loder's was after mid-April, for he conducted a weeklong Ladies' Festival in the city through 19 April; see *DAC,* 15 April 1856, 3:8 (advertisement), and 18 April, 2:3 (news item). (Note: The article on George Loder in *The New Grove Dictionary* has him leaving for Australia with Anna Bishop in September 1855, but as is evident, he remained in San Francisco an additional seven months.)

13. On gas, see Soulé, Gihon, and Nisbet, *Annals,* p. 517. For Milan, see Santley, *Student and Singer,* p. 53.

14. *DAC,* 3 November 1855, 2:4, mentions Garbato, "who seems to have appeared in California without the usual attendants of newspaper puffing and exaggerated placards." The advertisements for her programs are notable for their lack of stress on costumes. One (*SFDH,* 23 November 1855, 1:3), stating that a final number, the Spanish song "La pepa," will be sung "in the National Spanish Dress," is almost unique.

15. *DAC,* 10 November 1855, 2:4.

16. *DAC,* 1 November 1855, 3:6, and *SFDH,* 1 November, 1:4, 2:1.

17. "Italian Opera," *Dwight's Journal* 5 (26 August 1854): 165. Cf. Chorley, *Thirty Years' Musical Recollections,* p. 165, in which he describes the soprano, Rita Borio, who introduced *Ernani* to London: "A lady not in the least afraid of the violent use to which the latest Italian maestro forces his heroines, but able to scream in time, and to shout with breath enough to carry through the most animated and vehement movement."

18. For two critics disagreeing on the extent to which singing Verdi could damage a voice, see Henry Edward Krehbiel, *Chapters of Opera, Being Historical and Critical Observations and Records Concerning the Lyric Drama in New York from Its Earliest Days Down to the Present Time* (New York: Henry Holt, 1908), p. 40.

19. "Italian Opera," *Dwight's Journal* 5 (2 September 1854): 175.

20. Ibid., 26 August 1854, p. 165.

21. *SFDH,* 23 November 1855, 2:2; also, *DAC,* 31 October, 2:4.

22. *SFDH,* 4 November 1855, 2:1, *DAC,* 5 November, 2:6.

23. On the Anvil Chorus, see *SFDH,* 23 November 1855, 1:3.

24. *DEB,* 21 November 1855, 2:1.

25. *DEB,* 8 December 1855, 2:2. New York also had problems with women of ill-repute in the audience. According to Lawrence, *Strong on Music* 1:175, citing the *Herald,* 18 June 1842, the management of the Concert Hall promised police protection so that respectable persons could attend without fear of molestation; see also pp. 12, 130, 164.

26. *DEB*, 17 January 1856, 2:2. On King and his character, see Lotchin, *San Francisco*, pp. 250–59.

27. *SFDH*, 20 February 1856, 1:6, 2:1.

28. *DAC*, 5 January 1856, 1:1; 15 February, 2:5; 24 March, 2:6 (program in news item); and 25 March, 3:1 (review).

29. This period of San Francisco's history is much discussed. Besides the analyses of older historians such as Bancroft and Royce, more contemporary treatments include Lotchin, *San Francisco*, pp. 245–75; Bean, *California*, pp. 126–31; Caughey, *California*, pp. 162–67; and Starr, *Americans and the California Dream*, pp. 94–95.

30. On the vigilantes, see *DAC*, 26 May 1856, 2:1; also *Memoirs of General William T. Sherman, by Himself* (Bloomington: Indiana University Press, 1957), p. 181.

31. *DAC*, 28 April 1856, 2:1.

32. On Sinclair and Loder, see n. 12; for the Metropolitan artists leaving, see *DAC*, 7 April 1856, 2:5; 23 April, 2:1. The Frenchmen, E. Coulon and [?] Laglaise, apparently left sometime in 1856, for in April 1857 they were singing together in *Ernani* in Sydney; see Kaufman, *Verdi and His Major Contemporaries*, p. 293.

33. On Mrs. Chapman, see MacMinn, *Theater of the Golden Era*, p. 149; on Booth, see *Wide West*, 1 June 1856, 2:6.

34. *Wide West*, 1 June 1856, 2:6.

35. "Musical Correspondence, San Francisco, Cal.," *Dwight's Journal* 9 (3 May 1856): 37: "The vocal part of the performance [a concert given by the Germania Society] was decidedly poor. There is at present only one good female singer here—Signora Garbato, whom I have not yet heard." Concerning her departure: advertisements in *DAC*, 9, 10 October 1856, 1:9, announce a "Farewell Concert" on 10 October at the Musical Hall; a "Fireman's March," composed by Signor Garbato and dedicated to the San Francisco Fire Department, "will be produced for the first time, by a full orchestra." No reviews have been found.

CHAPTER 8. MAGUIRE, HIS OPERA HOUSE, AND THE BIANCHIS

1. The best description of the new house is in *DEB*, 28 November 1856, 3:2; see also *DAC*, 27 November, 2:3 (news item) and 2:4 (advertisement); and 28, 29 November, 1:9. The minstrels enlarged to fifteen; see *DEB*, 28 November, 3:2.

2. For a full account of Maguire and his career, see Rodecape, "Tom Maguire, Napoleon of the Stage," *California Historical Society Quarterly (CHSQ)* 20, no. 4 (December 1941), 21, nos. 1, 2, and 3 (March, June, and September 1942). The four parts of this long study amount to a small book, and the author cites her sources. Maguire's remark is quoted in a news story in the *Daily Morning Call*, 7 November 1880. Rodecape places it at the end of her biography, as an epitaph. Maguire's birthdate is unknown, but he died in New York City, in poverty, on 20 January

1896. On 10 May 1894, his friends in New York had held a "Monster Benefit" for him in the Metropolitan Opera House, but after the proceeds ran out he apparently was dependent on the charity of the Actor's Fund. Nonetheless, until a few weeks before death, a friend reported, Maguire "was around and about as usual with a cheery smile and friendly grip." See also, WPA, *San Francisco Theatre Research,* ed. Lawrence Estavan, monograph 3 (in vol. 2): "Tom Maguire" (San Francisco, 1938), pp. 1–69. Of the twelve theatres he built, eight were in San Francisco, two in Sacramento, one in Virginia City, and one in Marysville.

3. David Belasco (1853–1931) became Maguire's secretary in 1876. Belasco, later an author and producer of plays, had a large role in developing a style of realism in the staging and performance of plays in American theatre, and also, incidentally, by his productions of the underlying plays inspired Puccini to compose *Madama Butterfly* and *La fanciulla del West.* See Rodecape, "Maguire," *CHSQ* 21, no. 3, pp. 253–57; and Stanley Kauffmann, "Two Vulgar Geniuses: Augustin Daly and David Belasco," *Yale Review* 75, no. 4 (Summer 1987): 496–513. On Maguire's background and courage, see WPA, "Tom Maguire," pp. 2–3, quoting a letter by James O'Meara to the *Bulletin,* 25 January 1896.

4. On Collins and the repertory, see *DAC,* 16 July 1855, 3:6; on Loder, *DAC,* 19 July, 2:5.

5. On the funeral march, see *DAC,* 23 May 1856, 2:2; on the gold watch, *DEB,* 18 September, 3:2; otherwise see Rodecape, "Maguire," *CHSQ* 20, no. 4, p. 307.

6. *DEB,* 28 November 1856, 3:2; see also *DAC,* 27 November, 2:3.

7. Alonzo Delano, *Pen Knife Sketches; or Chips of the Old Block* (1853; rpt. San Francisco: Grabhorn Press, 1934), p. 38. Neither the original edition (published in Sacramento at the *Union* office) nor the reprint names the journal in which the piece first appeared.

8. *DAC,* 26 February 1859, 2:2.

9. *Pioneer Magazine,* January 1855, p. 52.

10. Regarding the curtain with advertisements: The exact date is unclear because the incident is told in a recollection in *DEB,* 24 November 1862, 3:4: "seven or eight years ago." On the classical scene, see MacMinn, *Theatre of the Golden Era,* p. 53.

11. *DEB,* 28 November 1856, 3:2. The painter of the drop curtain was Charles Rogers.

12. See Starr, *Americans and the California Dream,* pp. 365–79, on the Italian quality of northern California.

13. On Maguire touting his curtain, see Rodecape, "Maguire," *CHSQ* 20, no. 4, p. 308.

14. *Golden Era,* 5 July 1857, 4:5, carries the item in a column entitled "Desultory Theatricals."

15. Constance Rourke, *Troupers of the Gold Coast, or the Rise of Lotta Crabtree* (New York: Harcourt Brace, 1928), pp. 140–41; also David Dempsey, *The Triumphs*

and Trials of Lotta Crabtree (New York: William Morrow, 1968), pp. 120–21. "Lotta" ultimately became very popular in San Francisco, and in 1875 she gave the city an ornate drinking fountain, placed on Market Street, near Kearny. It has survived San Francisco's many disasters and is the last vestige of the city's first theatre district.

16. *DEB,* 5 May 1858, 1:6 (advertisement) and 3:2 (news item). Regarding ventilators: Bad air in theatres was equally a problem in New York: "As for theatregoers, they seem to take foul air for granted: many ladies and gentlemen accept headache as a necessary concomitant of public entertainment, and fainting in public places is quite common. There are several places on Broadway, it is said, where the poisonous exhalations of the audience are dense enough to dim the lights in the upper parts of the house" (Shanet, *Philharmonic,* p. 7).

17. On "The Snug," see Rodecape, "Maguire," *CHSQ* 21, no. 1, p. 45.

18. A news item on the coming season at Maguire's New Opera House, *DAC,* 11 October 1858, 2:3, reports no opera. The current attraction was a minstrel version of *Uncle Tom's Cabin,* which was to be followed by an English comedian who had been playing in Australia.

19. On the arrival of the Bianchis, see "Passengers" and "Shipping Intelligence," *DAC,* 16 October 1858, 2:6; also McCabe, "Journal," 1:94. On the *John L. Stephens,* see *DAC,* 17 October, 1:3. According to information in the Bianchi folder in the San Francisco Performing Arts Library and Museum, Eugenio Bianchi was born about 1823 in Lucca, and his wife, about 1827 in Padua. They met and married, she for the second time, in Mexico. On the premiere of *Macbeth* in Mexico City, see Kaufman, *Verdi and His Major Contemporaries,* p. 346.

20. Bianchis "unheralded": *DAC,* 18 July 1859, 2:3; "Finest tenor": *DAC,* 23 October 1858, 2:3. Other descriptions, on their return to San Francisco after a two-year absence, appear in *DEB,* 20 May 1862, 3:5; also see the summary appraisal of them in *DAC,* 8 September 1859, 2:3. An article on the death of Signora Bianchi (*San Francisco Morning Call,* 23 February 1895, 4:1) quotes an unidentified newspaper report of her in 1859: Her "style is epic. She hits the great points and leaves you to feel the rest. Her gestures are voluminous."

21. *DAC,* 24 October 1858, 2:3 (review of first concert). Lorenzo Salvi came to the United States in 1851 to join Jenny Lind on her tour of the country. In 1839 he had sung in the world premiere of Verdi's first opera, *Oberto,* and on the tour he frequently sang a romanza from it, "Ciel che feci"; see W. Porter Ware and Thaddeus C. Lockard, Jr. *P. T. Barnum Presents Jenny Lind: The American Tour of the Swedish Nightingale* (Baton Rouge: Louisiana State University Press, 1980), pp. 88, 102, 118.

22. On the contract, see *DAC,* 30 October 1858, 2:4 (news item); on the costumes etc., see the advertisement in ibid.

23. *DAC,* 25 October 1858, 2:3. On prices, see *DAC,* 30 October, 2:4.

24. *DAC,* 22 October 1858, 2:3, lists the program of the opening concert, which

had no chorus, as comprising: (Part I) Overture to *Zanetta,* Auber, orchestra; "Ah si, ben mio," *Trovatore,* Eugenio Bianchi; "Anch'io dischiuso," *Nabucco,* Giovanna Bianchi; flute solo on themes from *Fille du régiment,* C. Koppitz; unidentified song, S. W. Leach [bass-baritone]; Grand Duo from *I masnadieri,* E. B. and G. B.; (Part II) Overture to *La Pait du diable,* Adam, orchestra; Romanza, *I due Foscari,* G. B.; Grand Aria, *Ernani,* E. B.; "Approach to Spring" polka, with imitations of cuckoo, nightingale, cricket, orchestra; Trio, *I Lombardi,* E. B., G. B., and Leach.

25. An announcement of costumes, enlarged orchestra, and chorus appears in *DAC,* 31 October 1858, 1:9. The program was not stated but apparently was repeated at the fourth concert, see *DAC,* 4 November 1858, 1:9.

26. *DAC,* 11 November 1:9. (review of sixth concert).

27. For the program of the eighth concert, see *DAC,* 18 November 1858, 2:4; of Donizetti, Giovanna Bianchi sang an aria from *Don Pasquale,* she and Eugenio Bianchi then sang a duet from *Linda di Chamounix;* and together with the bass-baritone and chorus they closed part one with Bellini's "finale of *La sonnambula*" (presumably the finale to Act I).

28. For the program of the tenth concert, see *DAC,* 25 November 1858, 2:4; of the fourteenth, *DAC,* 8 December, 2:4.

29. Duet from *Attila,* tenth concert; Acts III and IV of *Ernani,* ninth and tenth concerts. For the programs of the final two concerts, see *DAC,* 16 December 1858, 2:5; and 19 December, 2:3.

30. Advertisements in *DAC* show concerts on 23, 24, and 31 October; 4, 7, 11, 14, 18, 21, 26, and 28 November; and 2, 5, 9, 16, and 19 December. McCabe ("Journals," 1:94) agrees, except that, apparently by mistake, in place of 9 December he lists 12 December. "Vastly popular": *DAC,* 24 November 1858, 2:3; largest crowd: 5 November 1858, 2:4; see also 7 November, 2:4.

31. On Maguire's control of Sacramento theatres, see Rodecape, "Maguire," *CHSQ* 21, no. 1, pp. 43–44. On the Bianchis' tour beginning in Sacramento, see *DAC,* 27 December 1858, 2:4; on the Forrest Theatre, *DAC,* 7 January 1859, 1:6; and on their sojourn in Marysville, *DAC,* 19 January, 1:8.

CHAPTER 9. *IL TROVATORE* PREMIERED; *ERNANI* REVIVED

1. On repainting, see Rodecape, "Maguire," *CHSQ* 21, no. 1, p. 46, citing *DAC,* 16 April 1859; and *SFDH,* 20 April.

2. *DAC* 3, 4 May 1859, 2:3 (news items); 5, 6, 7 May, 1:9 (advertisements).

3. James Nisbet (1816–65) was born in Glasgow, Scotland, came to San Francisco in November 1852, and was hired by James King of William in 1856 to work as an editor on the *Evening Bulletin.* Previously he had worked on the *Chronicle* and assisted Frank Soulé and John Gihon to write *The Annals of San Francisco.* Nisbet was known as a literary man and before coming to California had published a

novel. He drowned in a shipwreck off the Pacific Coast; the eulogies in *DEB* (3 August 1865, 2:1) and *DAC* (4 August, 1:1), while mentioning his literary interests, do not suggest that he wrote music reviews for the *Bulletin*. Nevertheless, he is a likely candidate for author. For an account of him, see Soulé, Gihon, and Nisbet, *Annals, Continuation*, pp. xxi–xxv.

4. *DAC*, 6 May 1859, 2:3.

5. Verdi, Letter to Salvatore Cammarano, 9 April 1851, *I copialettere*, pp. 118–21; there is a translation in Werfel and Stefan (eds.), *Verdi: The Man in His Letters*, pp. 164–67.

6. *DAC*, 9 May 1859, 2:3. The most notable operatic expression of homesickness in the mining camps occurs in Act I of Puccini's *La fanciulla del West* in Jake Wallace's song followed by Larkens's outburst. The opera was based on David Belasco's play *Girl of the Golden West* (1905); Belasco was born in San Francisco in 1853 and for many years pursued his theatrical career in the city. See Chapter 8, n. 3.

7. *DAC*, 11 May 1859, 2:3.

8. *DAC*, 12 May 1859, 2:3.

9. *DEB*, 6 May 1859, 3:3 (from which come all subsequent quotes of the critic in question); for the same point, at another performance of *Trovatore*, see *DEB*, 20 May 1862, 3:5; and at an Italian Benevolent Society benefit, see *DAC*, 2 September, 2:3.

10. Camillo Bellaigue, *Verdi: Biografia critica* (Milan: Treves, 1913), p. 53.

11. See Budden, *Operas of Verdi* 2:95n; and Imogen Holst, *Tune* (London: Faber & Faber, 1962), p. 150. The critic wrote in the *Bulletin*: "Our space prevents comment on the many beauties in this opera. . . . The prison scene, where Leonora seeks to persuade Manrico to fly, which he refuses, while she is dying before him of poison, and Zingara [the gypsy Azucena] dreams on her restless couch of her mountain home and the olden joys that will never, never again return, is very striking—both in the music and the dramatic action of the characters:

> Ai nostri monti ritorneremo,
> L'antica pace ivi godremo
> Tu suonerai sul tuo liuto,
> In sonno placido io dormirò.

Thus the old gypsy dreams, and sings gently in her slumber, while life and death are struggling before her, and the lovers in a few minutes will be dead before her eyes." And then the critic quotes the four lines again, this time in English. In all, he devotes a sizable part of the review to this scene and, within it, to this aria of nostalgia for home.

12. On the baritone's illness, see *DAC*, 19 May 1859, 1:9; reviews of the Act III finale may be found in *DAC*, 20 May, 2:4; and *DEB*, 20 May, 3:2; a review of the

second performance appears in *DAC*, 21 May, 2:3; and on the cancellation of the final performance, see *DEB*, 21 May, 3:2.

13. *DAC*, 21 May 1859, 2:3.

14. *DEB*, 20 May 1859, 3:2.

15. On the Bianchis wanting more rehearsal time, see *DAC*, 26 May 1859, 2:3. The lawsuit is mentioned in *DEB*, 27 June, 3:2; 28 June, 3:1; also *SFDH*, 28 June, 2:2: "The music alleged to have been stolen comprises bound parts of the operas Lucrezia Borgia, Linda di Chamounix, La Sonnambula and others, of the value altogether of $400. . . . The music remains in the meantime in the hands of the Signor, with the consent of Mr. Maguire, so that the want of it may not interfere with his present engagement, he is agreeing as soon as possible to place it in the hands of an officer of the court until such time as the suit is decided."

16. A news item on Troupe's arrival appears in *DAC*, 25 May 1859, 2:3; see also 26 May, 1:9 (advertisement); and 28 May, 2:3 (review). The "ungentlemanly" behavior is mentioned in *DAC*, 31 May, 2:4. The Troupe apparently consisted of Rosalie Durand and Ada King, sopranos; Georgia Hudson, contralto; Frank Trevor, tenor singing only secondary roles; Frederick Lyster, baritone; Anthony Reiff, Jr., conductor; and William S. Lyster, manager. The last was the baritone's elder brother by five years. The best account of the Troupe's origin appears in Love, *Golden Age of Australian Opera*, pp. 8–9, 12, 18.

17. *DAC*, 31 May 1859, 2:4.

18. On the Feret quarrel, see *DAC*, 15 June 1859, 2:3; on the Bianchis as their own producers, *DAC*, 24 June, 2:3. It seems likely that the Ferdinand Feret listed in the city directories for 1860 through 1864 as a music teacher, usually at his residence but also, in 1862, at Union College, was the husband of Jenny and conductor for the Bianchis.

19. On the eighteen-voice chorus, see *DAC*, 24 June 1859, 2:3; and 28 June, 2:3. For the chorus "composed of Frenchmen and Italians," see *DEB*, 28 June, 3:2.

20. *DAC*, 13 July 1859, 2:5.

21. The English Troupe left for Sacramento on 27 June; see *DAC*, 27 June 1859, 2:3.

22. *DAC*, 20 July 1859, 2:4.

23. Ibid. (review). For some performances by the Troupe in 1858 in Charleston, S.C., Chicago, and Memphis, see Kaufman, *Verdi and His Major Contemporaries*, pp. 413–14; also Love, *Golden Age of Australian Opera*, pp. 8–9, 12, 18.

24. *DAC*, 23 July 1859, 2:3: it was advertised as "the original of the *Trovatore*" and was to be followed by "an amusing dance, in supposed imitation of the Chinese."

25. I base the assertion on the statistics reported in the appendices to WPA, *Opera, Part II*, checked in part by the performances of Verdi's operas listed in Hixon, *Verdi*, and by my own count for the early years. The WPA figures may not be wholly accurate, but even if we take them as loose approximations, the primacy of *Il trovatore* is beyond question.

CHAPTER 10. THE BIANCHIS PRODUCE
LA TRAVIATA AND *ATTILA*

1. *DAC,* 22 July 1859, 1:9 (benefit advertisement); 23 July, 2:3 (review). On the Troupe's repertory and departure for "the interior," see *DAC,* 15 August 1859, 2:3.

2. *DAC,* 14 July 1859, 1:9 (advertisement); also 28 July, 2:3; 1 August, 2:4, 6 August, 2:4 (news items).

3. For a description of English opera, including a German's irate account of this version of *Figaro,* see Eric Walter White, *A History of English Opera* (London: Faber & Faber, 1983), pp. 251–55.

4. For the report on the "forward state," see *DAC,* 6 August 1859, 2:4. For the opera "founded on a plot similar to Camille," see *DAC,* 11 August, 2:3.

5. MacMinn, *Theater of the Golden Era,* pp. 293–308, gives an account of various productions of *Camille.* The possibility of the play and opera being banned is not fanciful. Throughout the decade there was a constant battle over Sunday performances between "Sabbatarians" and theatre- and music-lovers, chiefly the French, German, and Italian immigrants, with victory periodically shifting sides; see ibid., pp. 270–76. As a general rule, the *Alta California* would not publish any theatrical news, not even a review, in Sunday editions. Even in the supposedly more sophisticated East there was opposition to the opera *Traviata;* in 1861, in Brooklyn, New York, a campaign against it delayed its local premiere for a year; see Clara Louise Kellogg, *Memoirs of an American Prima Donna* (New York: G. P. Putnam's Sons, 1913), p. 69..

6. *DAC,* 12 August 1859, 2:4.

7. *DAC,* 16, 18, 19 August 1859, 1:9.

8. *DEB,* 15 August 1859, 3:3.

9. A review of the premiere may be found in *DAC,* 15 August 1859, 2:3; of the second performance, in the issue of 16 August, 2:3; a news item concerning the third performance appears in the issue of 17 August, 2:3.

10. The Teatro la Fenice, Venice, which at this time seated possibly about 1,400, hired for its 1850–51 season sixty-seven players, though the number used on any night probably was slightly less. First violins numbered fourteen, and second violins, ten; see *Rigoletto,* vol. 17 of Verdi, *The Critical Edition,* 1st ser. ed. Martin Chusid (Chicago: University of Chicago Press/Milan: G. Ricordi & Co., 1983), p. xxviii. Howard Shanet has a perceptive summary of the vices and virtues of players in small orchestras, and it no doubt would apply to the orchestras in this decade in San Francisco: "These little orchestras tended to ingrain some good habits and some very bad ones in their musicians. Since every man had to pull his full weight through the unpredictable hazards of musical theater performances, he had to be independent, resourceful, musically alert, and a good sight reader. But he also grew accustomed to playing loudly and roughly much of the time, and out

of tune some of the time; he was likely to appear in public with insufficient rehearsal, and to ignore the subtleties of blending into an artistic ensemble" (Shanet, *Philharmonic*, p. 65).

11. The two violinists—note that they are Germans—are named in advertisements in *DAC*, 12 August 1859, 2:4; and 13 August, 1:9.

12. For a brief account of Verdi's efforts, see Budden, *Operas of Verdi* 2: 121–22; also, Verdi, *Rigoletto*, p. xiii. One famous comedy that achieved contemporary dress at its premiere in 1786 was Mozart's *Le nozze di Figaro*.

13. The poster and libretto published for the opera's premiere in Venice state: "SCENA, Parigi e sue vicinanze nel 1700 circa." Announcements for performances of *Traviata* at the Tivoli, in San Francisco, for 1896 and 1898 state "period about 1700." See *Tivoli*, a looseleaf folder on the Tivoli Opera House at the San Francisco Performing Arts Library and Museum. At La Scala, Milan, the first season in which the opera was staged in the costumes of 1850 was 1906; see Martin Chusid's article "The Tempestuous Beginnings of *Traviata*" in the San Francisco Opera program for *La Traviata*, 1980. In the quarter-century before 1906, however, sopranos who fancied themselves in the style of the 1850s or of the 1890s had begun to wear nineteenth-century costumes, even as the rest of the cast remained "circa 1700." See Budden, *Operas of Verdi* 2:165. See also below, Chapter 11, n. 9.

14. *DAC*, 18 August 1859, 2:3.

15. Budden, *Operas of Verdi* 2:6.

16. *DAC*, 19 August 1859, 2:2. He seems to have miscounted the number of operas produced, for actually there were six: *Trovatore, Ernani, Lucrezia Borgia, Norma, Traviata, Attila.*

17. *DEB*, 19 August 1859, 3:2.

18. The advertisement for *Attila* in *DAC* (19 August 1859, 1:9), unlike that for *Traviata* (17 August, 1:9), does not announce, "Libretto of the opera can be obtained at Salvator Rosa's [music shop] or the Theatre." It seems, therefore, that indeed none were available, which may have inclined the non-Italian-speaking audience to stay away.

19. *SFDH*, 15 November 1854, 2:2.

20. Leach came to San Francisco with Anna Thillon (see McCabe, "Journals," 1:32) and apparently sang his tenor roles with her adequately, though without distinction. The *Wide West* (28 January 1855, 2:3) dismissed him as "an Irish ballad-singer officiating as tenor." With the Italian companies he sang baritone or bass roles, and often with so little effect that he was not mentioned in reviews. For some damning faint praise, see *DAC*, 3 November 1860, 2:3. The correspondent for *Dwight's Journal*, however, thought him better than his reviews indicated; see "Musical Correspondence, San Francisco," *DJ* 17 (28 July 1860): 141. He sang frequently, and with success, at church benefits; see, e.g., *DEB*, 1 February 1860, 3:3. Reviewing a concert, *DEB* (18 February 1860, 3:6) praises him as "very happy in the

Irish ditties of *Widow Machree, The rale ould Irish gintleman,* and *I'm not meself at all."* Whatever his failings as a singer, he was a popular artist, partly because he had made his home in San Francisco.

21. *DEB,* 19 August 1859, 3:2. Though Kaufman (*Verdi and His Major Contemporaries,* p. 335) lists Leach as Ezio in the premiere, and Roncovieri as Attila, advertisements and the review make certain that Leach sang Attila, Kammerer sang Ezio, and Alfred Pierre Roncovieri sang Leo.

22. *DAC,* 20 August 1859, 2:3.

23. *Golden Era,* 21 August 1859, 5:1.

24. *DAC,* 8 September 1859, 2:3. A news item on the benefit (*DAC,* 10 September, 2:3) states: "Some steps should certainly be taken to secure to California the services of these admirable artists, and we trust that their contemplated journey to Australia may at least be deferred."

25. On Mozart's *Requiem,* see *DAC,* 14 September 1859, 2:3; on *Lucrezia Borgia,* see the news items in *DAC,* 21 September, 2:3; 22 September, 2:3; on *Traviata,* see the news items of 27 September, 2:3; 28 September, 2:3; the "perfect jam" is mentioned in the issue of 29 September, 2:4. In Australia the Bianchis had a busy, successful two years during which they introduced the continent to *Nabucco, Attila, Macbeth, Rigoletto,* and *Traviata;* see Kaufman, *Verdi and His Major Contemporaries* pp. 267, 329, 341, 383, 416.

CHAPTER 11. THEATRICAL SCENERY AND STYLES; *TRAVIATA* AND THE NEW REALISM

1. See Kauffmann, "Two Vulgar Geniuses," pp. 496–513.

2. See Levine, *Highbrow/Lowbrow,* pp. 35–38.

3. Verdi, Letter to Camille Du Locle, 7 December 1869, in *I copialettere,* p. 221; also in Werfel and Stefan (eds.), *Verdi: The Man in His Letters,* p. 269 (Downes translation used).

4. Werfel and Stefan (eds.), *Verdi: The Man in His Letters,* p. 381.

5. Verdi, *Rigoletto,* p. xxvi.

6. Giulio Gatti-Casazza, *Memories of the Opera* (1941; rpt. London: John Calder, 1977), p. 20.

7. *SFDH,* 18 March 1855, 1:6; 1 April, 1:2; and 10, 11 July 1855, 1:3.

8. Kellogg, *Memoirs,* pp. 37–38.

9. Ibid., p. 70 (on Kellogg's costume for *La traviata*).

10. On the "glaring footlights," see ibid., p. 37; on Keene's injury, *SFDH,* 19 July 1854, 2:1; and (unless the same incident) a repetition of the accident, *DAC,* 1 August 1854, 2:3.

11. Verdi, Letter to Vincenzo Luccardi, 11 February 1846, in *I copialettere,* p. 441; also in Werfel and Stefan (eds.), *Verdi: The Man in His Letters,* pp. 115–116 (Downes translation used).

12. Luigi Agostino Garibaldi, ed., *Guiseppe Verdi nelle lettere di Emanuele Muzio ad Antonio Barezzi* (Milan: Treves, 1931), p. 303.

13. Kellogg, *Memoirs*, p. 15.

14. Soulé, Gihon, and Nisbet, *Annals*, p. 661.

15. Kauffmann, "Two Vulgar Geniuses," p. 503.

16. *DAC*, 26 May 1860, 2:3.

17. See, Hamm, *Yesterdays*, pp. 78–84; and *Complete Catalogue of Sheet Music*.

18. Hamm, *Yesterdays*, p. 87.

CHAPTER 12. A DUEL,
AND A PERIOD OF OPERATIC DOLDRUMS

1. For descriptions of Broderick, see Lotchin, *San Francisco, 1846–1856*, pp. 218–19; Rodecape, "Tom Maguire," *CHSQ* 20, no. 4, pp. 309–11; and Milton S. Gould, *A Cast of Hawks: A Rowdy Tale of Greed, Violence, Scandal, and Corruption in the Early Days of San Francisco* (La Jolla, Calif.; Copley Press, 1985), pp. 30–33. On his Friendship with Maguire, see WPA, "Tom Maguire," p. 3. For a favorable account of Terry, by E. G. Waite, see *Overland Monthly*, October 1889, pp. 434–42; for one that charges him and his seconds with arranging the duel to his advantage, see John E. B. Currey, "The Terry-Broderick Duel" (San Francisco, 1890) (typescript, with copies in the California State Library, Sacramento).

2. Field, *Personal Reminiscences*, pp. 66–71. Bancroft (*California inter pocula*, p. 764) states broadly: "No duellist has ever suffered the punishment prescribed by law in California." For Bancroft's account of the duel and trial, see ibid., pp. 763–74. California's other U.S. Senator, William M. Gwin, had fought a duel in 1853 with Joseph W. McCorkle, a Congressman from California, with rifles at thirty paces. After three shots each, with neither hit, the duel was canceled.

3. On the duelers' arrest see *DAC*, 13 September 1859, 1:1; the "immense crowd" is described in ibid., 2:2.

4. On the fighting of the duel, see *DAC*, 14 September 1859, 1:1, 2:1; also Bancroft, *California inter pocula*, pp. 763–72.

5. The editorial on Broderick's death appeared in *DAC*, 17 September 1859, 2:1; for the statement that the duel had been fought "within code," see *DAC*, 14 September, 2:1. The *Bulletin* is quoted by Bancroft, *California inter pocula*, p. 771.

6. The editorial on the legislature is in *DAC*, 14 February 1860, 2:1; for the editorial on Judge Hardy's behavior, see *DAC*, 9 May 1862, 1:1. "The court waits, and drinks, and smokes . . ." may be found in Bancroft, *California inter pocula*, pp. 772–74.

7. *DAC*, 1 October 1859, 2:2; 4 October, 2:3; 6 October, 2:3 (*"avant courier"*) and 1:9 (advertisement); 7 October, 2:3 (review). The Ferets arrived in San Francisco early in April; see *SFDH*, 8 April 1859, 3:4.

8. The opera, though composed for Paris, had an Italian text, and though its

Notes to Pages 169–172

French title commonly was used, in Paris it apparently was sung regularly in Italian. The language sung by the Feret company is nowhere specified, but most likely it was French. It also is unclear whether the work was presented in its two-act or one-act version. The opera was much admired for its unfailing melody and its attractive, clever orchestration. But for Mme Feret to sing Barnaba, a role for bass, she must have made many changes in the vocal line. See *DAC*, 6 October 1859, 1:9.

9. On the Feret school, see *DAC*, 27 June 1859, 4:1; notice of a concert with pupils is given in *DEB*, 1 November 1859, 3:1. At a concert on 21 December, in the Lyceum Theatre, Feret sang an aria from Victor Massé's *Galatée* (1852), another Opéra-comique comedy popular throughout the nineteenth century. At this concert Mrs. [Agatha] States sang "Ernani, involami"; see *DEB*, 22 December 1859, 3:3 (review). On 10 August 1871 she sang Elena in the San Francisco premiere of *I vespri siciliani*.

10. Regarding the Planel school: The advertisement in the *San Francisco Directory*, 1858, p. 221, states that the school, which "has only been established a short period," had recently been "considerably enlarged." Instruction would be given "in English, French, Spanish and Italian." The Planels also advertised their school periodically throughout 1859 and 1860 in the *Bulletin* (e.g., 8 October 1859, 1:6; 27 January 1860, 4:1) and continued to list themselves individually in the *Directory* as "teacher music" through 1864. Possibly their last public appearance as musicians occurred in October of that year; *DAC*, 28 October 1864, 1:3, reviews a concert in which they and their son participated. For 1865, Planel changed his individual listing in the *Directory* to "hotelkeeper." It seems, therefore, that, though many artists took on private pupils in the Gold Rush years (in the *Directory* for 1856, seven, including Planel, list themselves as "music teacher"), the Planel school, which lasted certainly from mid-1858 through mid-1860 and probably in some form through mid-1864, was the first institution of its kind in the city. See also Chapter 2, n. 13.

11. On the Caecilien-Verein, see *DEB*, 25 October 1859, 3:1; 29 October, 3:2. Regarding the Glee Club, an advertisement for a concert with Eliza Biscaccianti was published in *DEB*, 21 March 1860, 1:4; and an advertisement for *The Bohemian Girl* with the German Chorus appeared in *DEB*, 25 February 1860, 1:4.

12. *DEB*, 14 October 1859, 2:1; also *DAC*, 15 October, 2:2; 16 October, 2:2.

13. *DEB*, 16 November 1859, 3:3; also *DAC*, 16 November, 2:3.

14. On the "overdecorated" quality of Biscaccianti's songs in the second concert, see *DEB*, 9 November 1859, 3:1; *DAC*, 9 November, 2:3. She sang an unexciting Lucia, *DAC* (19 July 1862, 2:3) reported, because of "her recent severe illness."

15. *DEB*, 17 October 1859, 3:3; also 18 October, 3:4.

16. *DAC*, 1 November 1859, 2:4; and *DEB*, 2 November, 3:1.

17. "Positively the last" occurs in *DEB*, 20 October, 3:2; also *DAC*, 4 October 1859, 2:3.

18. *DEB*, 13 December 1859, 3:2; and *DAC*, 14 December, 2:3.

19. *DEB*, 16 December 1859, 3:3; and *DAC*, 16 December, 2:3.

20. *DEB*, 20 December 1859, 3:4. On S. W. [*sic*] Lyster as "the director," see *DAC*, 19 May 1860, 1:7.

21. *DEB*, 26 January 1860, 2:3. The report substitutes *Child* for *Daughter of the Regiment*, suggesting, probably incorrectly, a burlesque of the opera rather than merely an English version of it.

22. *DEB*, 13 January 1860, 1:3; and the reviews in *DEB*, 14 January, 3:2; and *DAC*, 14 January, 2:2.

23. On *Rob Roy*, see *DEB*, 21 January 1860, 3:2; and *DAC*, 21 January, 1:9. He had presented it in October; see *DAC*, 1 October 1859, 2:2.

24. On *The Two Figaros*, see *DEB*, 3 February 1860, 3:1; and *DAC*, 6 February, 1:9. The New Orleans English Opera Troupe had given the California premiere of Mozart's *Le nozze di Figaro*, in an English version arranged by F. Lyster, on 3 October 1859; see *DAC*, 3 October 1859, 2:3. A review (*DAC*, 4 October, 2:3) states merely that it was given "in a very acceptable manner." A news item the following year, however, states that the company's production still was in English; see *DEB*, 7 September 1860, 3:5.

25. On *Pluto and Proserpine*, see *DEB*, 6 February 1860, 3:3; and *DAC*, 8 February, 1:9, 2:2.

26. *DEB*, 6 March 1860, 3:4.

27. *DEB*, 13 March 1860, 3:5; on the chorus, see *DAC*, 13 March, 2:3: "The German Anvil Chorus was particularly well done." See also "Musical Correspondence, San Francisco," *Dwight's Journal* 17 (19 May 1860): 63. Besides those operas mentioned, others given during this season in March were Auber's *Crown Diamonds*, Rossini's *Cinderella*, Weber's *Freischütz* (in English), and Pepusch's *Beggar's Opera*. For the schedule, see McCabe, "Journals," 1:109–14.

28. *DEB*, 2 April 1860, 3:5. *DEB*, 1 November, 3:6, confirms that William Lyster had gone to London to find singers and new operas. It seems, however, that he found the singers in the United States and the new operas in London. His movements in this period are not clear. See Love, *Golden Age of Australian Opera*, pp. 16–19.

CHAPTER 13. SUCCESS OF THE MAGUIRE-LYSTER COMPANY, AND FAILURE OF *RIGOLETTO*

1. *DAC*, 19 May 1860, 1:7 (announcement). Performances with Escott are reported in Kaufman, *Verdi and His Major Contemporaries*, pp. 106, 181, 187, 391, 403–5, 420, and show her singing the operas of Mercadante, Petrella, and Verdi in Naples in 1853 and 1854, and of Verdi alone on an extensive tour of Great Britain in 1856 and 1857, during which she frequently sang *Il trovatore* in English.

2. The best accounts of Escott, of Henry Squires, and of the impresario W. S. Lyster appear in Love, *Golden Age of Australian Opera*, pp. 1–8, 46–49, 187, 275–77. In the 1860s Lyster became the "the father of Australian opera," and his chief singers then were Escott and Squires. Thompson, *American Singer*, pp. 40–41, offers a brief biography of Escott, though without mentioning her success in San Francisco or, later, in Australia. Another who similarly shortened her career is the German composer Hans Werner Henze (b. 1926), who memorialized her in his *Lucy Escott Variations*, published in 1963. These, for piano, are based on the first-act aria "Come per me sereno," from Bellini's *La sonnambula*, and are preceded by this epigraph: "Old play-bills of Italian opera performed at Drury Lane Theatre about 1820 [*sic*], show the coloratura soprano Lucy Escott as the protagonist. One of her most famous parts was Amina, in La Somnabula [*sic*]. Lucy Escott was a charming young girl with a very pleasing voice, light at the top and well balanced in all registers. Her secret love for Bellini (whom she knew only from pictures) led her existence little by little into a seclusion, which after the early death of her idol rapidly grew into an unearthly perfection that can be explained only by the pain of love; her voice became higher and higher until it could no longer be heard by human ears. By this time, grown ever smaller and more graceful, the light of the moon and the stars shone through her and she finally disappeared from this world, we imagine to live on as a nymph in the Thames. This set of variations, based on one of her favourite arias, is offered as a memory of Lucy Escott and as an obituary."

3. *DAC*, 19 May 1860, 1:7 (announcement). According to Love (*Golden Age of Australian Opera*), Squires studied music first with an organist in Troy, New York, which, being near Albany, the capital of the state, probably associated him with it. For the "American tenor," at Dodsworth's Musical Festival, Metropolitan Hall, 20 February 1852, see Shanet, *Philharmonic*, p. 120. A column, "Theatrical 'Pot Pourri,' " *DAC*, 6 August 1854, 2:3, reports Squires, "once of Albany," as singing in *La sonnambula* at the Teatro San Carlo, Naples, with great success, and ends, "Hurrah! for American Singers!" According to Kaufman (*Verdi and His Major Contemporaries*, p. 428), Squires sang *Traviata* with the Strakosch company in Louisville, Kentucky, in January 1859.

After Squires and Escott had sung opposite each other almost nightly for twelve years, the two retired from the stage, married, and on their earnings lived happily ever after in Paris. Their importance in the history of opera in Australia is great. Escott died in Paris in 1895, and Squires thereupon returned to the United States, where he died in 1907.

4. *DAC*, 19 May 1860, 1:7 (announcement).

5. *DEB*, 7 September 1860, 3:5, confirming that the Lyster production of *Figaro* was in English.

6. See "Musical Intelligence, San Francisco," *Dwight's Journal* 17 (8 September 1860): 191.

7. For a listing of performances, 19 May through 20 July, see McCabe, "Journals," 1:114–17.

8. For a review of premiere on the previous night, see *DAC*, 23 May 1860, 2:2; compared to *Lucia, DAC,* 29 May 1860, 2:3.

9. *DEB,* 26 May 1860, 3:2; *DAC,* 26 May, 2:3.

10. *DAC,* 13 June 1860, 2:2.

11. *DEB,* 13 June 1860, 3:4. Reviewing the next performance, the critic picked out as one of the opera's "gems" the "opening brindisi of the bandits" in the first act; *DEB,* 14 June, 3:4. Curiously, this chorus, which today wins little esteem, was then highly regarded.

12. The two reviews are *DAC,* 9 July 1860, 2:3; and 11 September, 2:2.

13. "Musical Intelligence, San Francisco," *Dwight's Journal* 17 (8 September 1860): 191. Love, *Golden Age of Opera in Australia,* pp. 48–51, discusses Squire's technique and quality of voice.

14. *DAC,* 9 July 1860, 2:3. The previous fall the critic for the *Bulletin* had dismissed Hodson's voice as "greatly injured by unnatural efforts to execute tenor parts"; *DEB,* 16 November 1859, 3:3.

15. Verdi, Letter to Vincenzo Luccardi, 17 February 1863, in *I copialettere,* p. 612; translated in Werfel and Stefan (eds.), *Verdi: The Man in His Letters,* pp. 230–31 (Downes translation used).

16. E.g., Henry Pleasants, *Opera in Crisis: Tradition, Present, Future* (New York: Thames & Hudson, 1989), pp. 89–90.

17. *DAC,* 9 July 1860, 2:3.

18. *DAC,* 19 June 1860, 2:2. Julius Mattfeld, *A Handbook of American Operatic Premieres, 1731–1962* (Detroit, Mich.: Information Service, 1963), p. 90, mistakenly sets the premiere in New York, 1864. On the American premiere, see *DEB,* 18 June, 3:4; the critic for *DEB,* 19 June, 3:4, blamed the poor performance in part on obvious lack of rehearsal.

19. *DAC,* 20 June 1860, 2:1. Because of the suggestion to hire another soprano to replace Durand, Love (*Golden Age of Opera in Australia,* p. 32) suggests that either Biscaccianti or Feret had bribed the critic. But I think it unlikely that Lyster, a careful, aggressive manager, would have succumbed to such pressure.

20. *DAC,* 2 July 1860, 2:3.

21. *DEB,* 2 July 1860, 3:5.

22. Kellogg, *Memoirs,* p. 36.

23. This reason is suggested by Francis Toye, *Giuseppe Verdi: His Life and Works* (1946; rpt. New York: Vintage Books, 1959), p. 271. And the French critic Bellaigue, *Verdi: Biografía critica,* p. 36, seems to agree.

24. Santley, *Student and Singer,* p. 218.

25. For a summary report on the company midway through its first season, see "Musical Correspondence, San Francisco," *Dwight's Journal* 17 (28 July 1860): 141: "De Haga has disappointed the majority. He sings terribly out of tune and his

voice is much *choked up*"; also *DAC*, 18 June 1860, 2:2: "sang as if he had a frog in his throat."

26. In *DAC*, 24 December 1860, 1:2, a summary of the company at the year's end, the critic adds an extra night to the initial season and exaggerates slightly the number of performances by Squires.

27. *DAC*, 21 July 1860, 2:2. For a summary report at the end of the company's first season, see "Musical Correspondence, San Francisco," *Dwight's Journal* 17 (8 September 1860): 191.

28. *DEB*, 19 June 1860, 3:4.

29. *DAC*, 30 August 1860, 2:2; "Musical Correspondence, San Francisco," *Dwight's Journal* 17 (8 September 1860): 191.

CHAPTER 14. THE *ANNUS MIRABILIS:* SAN FRANCISCO MAD FOR OPERA

1. McCabe, "Journals," 1:118–19. (Note: McCabe has two mistakes in his record when there were substitutions for a scheduled performance: on 30 August, *Traviata* replaced *Trovatore*, and on 10 September *Trovatore* replaced *Favorita*.)

2. *DAC*, 31 August 1860, 2:2; he had complained in an earlier review of *Traviata* of the tenor's lack of "force and energy"; see *DAC*, 26 May, 2:3.

3. *DAC*, 7 September 1860, 2:1; *DEB*, 7 September, 3:5.

4. *SFDH*, 18 September 1860, 3:2.

5. *DAC*, 18 September 1860, 2:2.

6. For the schedule, see McCabe, "Journals," 1:119. On American premieres, see Mattfeld, *Handbook of American Operatic Premieres*, p. 57, who mistakenly puts the premiere of *Lurline* in Cambridge, Mass., in 1863. The only city with two American premieres in 1860 would be New York, and then only if New York and Brooklyn were counted as one city, which they then were not—legally, socially, or culturally. Brooklyn had Mozart's *Die Entführung aus dem Serail* on 16 February 1860, and New York, Verdi's *I masnadieri* on 31 May.

7. *DEB*, 1 November 1860, 3:6 (announcement of premiere and description of scenic delights). On the U.S. premiere, see *DAC*, 1 November, 4:4. The coral is described in Santley, *Student and Singer*, p. 170.

8. *DAC*, 3 November 1860, 2:3.

9. *DAC*, 2 November 1860, 2:3; *DEB*, 2 November, 3:4; 3 November, 3:4.

10. *DAC*, 24 November 1860, 2:3.

11. *Golden Era*, 2 December 1860, 5:1.

12. On Squires as the "universal tenor," see *DAC*, 24 December 1860, 1:2. This summary report on "The Lyster Operatic Season" contains much information, a small part of which seems incorrect or, at least, ambiguously worded.

13. *DAC*, 3 December 1860, 2:3.

14. There is considerable disagreement about the city's population in 1860.

The federal census is as I have given it, but *DEB*, 22 October 1859, 2:1 (editorial), using Tax Office figures, sets the population then at 80,000. *DAC*, 16 January 1859, 1:7, estimated 80,000, and on 21 December 1862, 1:1, referring to the federal figure for 1860 as "glaringly erroneous," claimed the population then numbered "at least 70,000." *DAC*, 27 April 1865, 2:2, again referring to the federal figure as "too small," returned to its estimate of 80,000. Against the newspaper estimates, however, must be set that of Bancroft (*History of California*, vol. 6: *1848–1859*, p. 786) of about 50,000 at the close of 1859. Lotchin (*San Francisco, 1846–1856*, p. 82) adopts the federal figure for 1860. Most historians, apparently, have decided against the newspaper estimates.

15. *DAC*, 3 December 1860, 2:3.

16. Weber is quoted in White, *History of English Opera*, p. 253. White has some interesting speculations on why English opera tended to shy away from music at the important moments; see pp. 256 and 436–37.

17. *Golden Era*, 16 December 1860, 5:1.

18. A review of *Ernani* at the American Theatre, with comments on the voices of Escott and Squires, appears in *DAC*, 18 December 1860, 2:2.

19. McCabe, "Journals," 1:122. Regarding the Lyster Troupe: W. S. [William Saurin] Lyster took nine artists with him to Australia: Escott, Squires, Durand, Hodson, Ada King and Frank Trevor, who sang secondary soprano and tenor roles, Frederick Lyster, who specialized in baritone buffo parts, Anthony Reiff, the conductor, and William Lloyd, the stage manager who had designed the machinery for *Lurline* and other spectacles. This nucleus of a company dominated opera in Australia in the years 1861–67. See Love, *Golden Age of Australian Opera*, pp. 20, 87–88.

20. Degrees of madness being difficult to measure, any comparison of frenzy is treacherous. Still, among the variables entering the comparison surely must be the population of the city, the number and capacity of its theatres, the number of performances staged, and the size of the audiences.

In Venice in 1637, the first public opera house in the world, the Teatro San Cassiano, opened with a performance of Manelli's *L'Andromeda*, and the Venetians promptly fell in love with the new form of entertainment. By the end of the century there were ten public houses presenting regular opera seasons every Carnival—roughly Christmas to Lent—with frequent performances at other times. Some 350 operas had been presented and many of them more than once. The theatres were small, the audiences, by all reports, full and enthusiastic, and the city's population at the time was about 140,000, not including thousands of transients.

In New Orleans, in the years 1836–41, the chief opera house was the Orleans Theatre (cap. 1,300), the home of the French opera company specializing in French opera. The secondary theatre, where English and Italian opera as well as ballet was likely to play, was the St. Charles (cap. 4,500), at the time of its opening in 1835 the largest theatre in the United States. A third and smaller house, the Camp Street Theatre, also sometimes presented opera. According to the city's opera historian, Henry A. Kmen (see "Singing and Dancing," cited in full below), in the five-year period from the fall of 1836 through the spring of 1841 there were 602 performances of ballet and opera. Subtracting from this total some 77 performances of ballet and 46 of incomplete operas, the total becomes 479, or roughly 100 of opera each year, a figure well below San Francisco's 145 in 1860. Further, the populations in the periods compared are New Orleans, 100,000, to San Francisco, 60,000. And finally, some performances in New Orleans in these years—enough to raise cries of alarm—played to almost-empty houses. Kmen tells of audiences on occasion numbering no more than five or six. In San Francisco, apparently, the house was never less than half filled.

See Henry A. Kmen, *Music in New Orleans: The Formative Years, 1791–1841* (Baton Rouge: Louisiana State University Press, 1966) and the Ph.D thesis on which it is based, and which has lists of performances as well as more information about them, "Singing and Dancing in New Orleans: A Social History of the Birth and Growth of Balls and Opera, 1791–1841" (submitted to Tulane University, 1961 and available from University Microfilms, Inc., Ann Arbor, Michigan).

EPILOGUE

1. McCabe ("Journals," 2:221) claims that no opera was staged in 1861, and no record of any has been found. For the Civil War's effect on opera, see Kellogg, *Memoirs*, pp. 55–61, 74–75.

2. The first staged opera in 1862 was *La sonnambula* on 14 April with Biscaccianti, who, with her accompanist, George T. Evans, apparently organized a season with local artists. The company's second prima donna was Lizzie Parker; according to McCabe ("Journals," 1:131), she arrived in San Francisco from the East on 4 February, gave five concerts, and then made her operatic debut as Leonora in *La favorita*. For its third opera the troupe staged *Lucia di Lammermoor*, with Biscaccianti. In all, the season consisted of eleven performances and a benefit concert. The Bianchis, absorbing the troupe, substituted their better singers for most roles and replaced Evans as conductor with the more experienced Rudolph Herold. For some reviews of the Biscaccianti season, see *DAC*, 18 April 1862, 2:3; 19 April, 2:3; and 28 April, 2:3; and *DEB*, 15 April, 3:5; 18 April, 3:4; 19 April, 3:5; and 22 April, 3:4. For a statement implying that both the Biscaccianti orchestra and chorus were small, see *DEB*, 20 May 1862, 3:5.

3. The Bianchis, with a bass and baritone, arrived on 5 May 1862, after a voyage of 100 days from Sydney, via Honolulu; see *DAC*, 6 May 1862, 2:2; and 7 May, 2:2. The baritone was John Gregg, apparently an Australian, and the bass, Enrico Grossi, was presumably an Italian; both had been singing in Australia with the Bianchis; neither became famous. For a review of their debuts in San Francisco, in *Trovatore*, see *DEB*, 20 May, 3:5.

4. For the roster of twelve soloists, including three prima donnas, see *DAC*, 11 July 1862, 2:4. The newspaper reports do not state the orchestra size, but advertisements called the Bianchis' orchestra "efficient" and "splendid," and the critic for *DEB* (20 May 1862, 3:5) described it as "enlarged," so an estimate of twenty-five to thirty players seems reasonable. For the orchestra in New York, see Shanet, *Philharmonic*, p. 134.

5. A review of *Nabucco* (*DEB*, 26 May 1862, 3:5) states that the chorus had twenty-four male and female voices. One concert (see *DAC*, 14 April 1862, 1:7) had a mixed chorus of twenty-eight; the Garibaldi Society, for one performance, had a chorus of "over thirty voices" (*DAC*, 1 September 1862, 2:2); and the Bianchis announced a chorus of "no less than thirty-two" for a performance of *Lucia di Lammermoor* (see *DAC*, 17 April 1865, 4:2; and the Metropolitan Theatre playbill in the Bianchi folder at the San Francisco Performing Arts Library and Museum). Finally, the Caecilien-Verein, at least for its private performances, had a mixed chorus of over fifty. Hence twenty-four is probably a modest number that on occasion was increased. (But see the *DEB* review of *Macbeth*, in Appendix E.) On the chorus at the Metropolitan, New York, in 1886, see George Martin, *The Damrosch Dynasty: America's First Family of Music* (Boston: Houghton Mifflin, 1983), p. 91; for size in 1906 and 1946, see Irving Kolodin, *The Metropolitan Opera, 1883–1966: A Candid History* (New York: Alfred A. Knopf, 1966), p. 462.

6. Eleanor Scott, *The First Twenty Years of the Santa Fe Opera* (Santa Fe, N.M.: Sunstone Press, 1976), pp. 8–13.

7. For one artist against the practice, see Santley, *Student and Singer*, p. 285.

8. MacMinn, *Theater of the Golden Era*, pp. 102–5.

9. One of the last spots allowed for an insertion was the "lesson scene" in Rossini's *Barbiere di Siviglia*, and at the Metropolitan as late as the 1950s an aria frequently substituted for Rossini's "Contro un cor" was Meyerbeer's "Shadow Song" from his opera *Dinorah*.

10. The Bianchi roster in their "second season," which began on 16 July, included among the sopranos (besides Signora Bianchi) Lizzie Parker, Agatha States, and Eliza Biscaccianti. For the announced roster of twelve soloists (lacking Biscaccianti), conductor, and subscription plan, see *DAC*, 11 July 1862, 2:3, 2:4.

11. For a scuffle at the American Theatre that ended in an order for arrest, see *DAC*, 18 May 1862, 1:1; and on behavior in general, see Levine, *Highbrow/Lowbrow*, pp. 184–200.

12. Levine, *Highbrow/Lowbrow*, pp. 187–88.

13. Ibid, p. 40.

14. W. H. Auden, *The Dyer's Hand and Other Essays* (London: Faber & Faber, 1963), p. 474.

15. In addition to this review of Verdi's works, members of the company introduced the public to some selections from his *Aroldo* (1857). After a performance of *I masnadieri* one night, Signora Bianchi sang the soprano's "Grand Cavatina," probably "Ah! dagli scanni eterei" (the Cemetery scene); see *DAC*, 15

June 1863, 4:3. And after an evening of *Norma,* the company baritone, Augusto Fellini, sang an unidentified "cavatina" from *Aroldo,* probably "Mina, pensai che un angelo"; see *DAC,* 8 August 1863, 2:3.

16. On Lincoln and *Rigoletto,* see Hamm, *Yesterdays,* p. 88; and Elise K. Kirk, *Music at the White House: A History of the American Spirit* (Urbana: University of Illinois Press, 1986), pp. 78–89. Wayne D. Shirley, Music Specialist in the Music Division of the Library of Congress, reports that in the Library's collection of band music of Francis Scala, who was the leader of the Marine band in Lincoln's day, there are "band scores or parts for selections from most of the Verdi operas up through *The Sicilian Vespers* (even *Aroldo!*)" (Shirley, Letter to author, 26 March 1991.)

17. On Lincoln at *Un ballo in maschera,* see *New York Herald,* 21 February 1861, 1:6. Anna Bishop's letter to Lincoln, said by Kirk to be "the earliest letter that we know of from a performing artist to a president" (Kirk, *Music at the White House,* p. 379n.47), is dated 15 February 1861 and may be read in the Library of Congress, Lincoln Papers, Ser. 1, Reel 17, No. 7327-7328. Perhaps the most interesting aspect of the letter, which in its invitation is straightforward, is that she sent it to Lincoln via the hand of the governor of New York, Edwin D. Morgan: "... takes the liberty to request His Excellency to have the kindness to convey the enclosed to the Honorable Abraham Lincoln" (ibid., No. 7329-7330). And the governor, evidently, did as she asked.

APPENDIX C: TRANSPOSITIONS AND TUNING A IN SAN FRANCISCO

1. *DAC,* 11 July 1862, 2:4.
2. Luigi Arditi, *My Reminiscences* (New York: Dodd, Mead, 1896), pp. 53–54.
3. For more on traditional transpositions and the reasons for them, see Henry Pleasants, *Opera in Crisis,* pp. 59–66.
4. WPA, "Tom Maguire."

Works Cited

Most of the material in this book I culled from California newspapers of all types published during the Gold Rush decade. Of the dailies in San Francisco, I found most rewarding the *Alta California,* the *Herald,* and the *Evening Bulletin;* also of use were the *Evening Picayune, Pacific News,* and *Morning Call;* and out of town, the *Sacramento Union.* Of the weeklies, the most pertinent for opera were the *Golden Era* and the *Wide West.* A monthly, the *Pioneer,* also was helpful. From Boston, *Dwight's Journal of Music,* a weekly and sometimes biweekly, reported periodically on music in San Francisco.

Four works of exceptional value need a lengthier description. First there are the unpublished theatrical journals of John H. McCabe, in which he lists, day by day, the most important theatrical events, thus providing a continual, though partial, check on the city's musical activities. The "Journals" can be read at the California State Library, Sacramento, where they are catalogued under McCabe's name and the title "Theatrical Journals and Diary, 1849–1882." Because unique, they do not circulate, cannot be reproduced, and are not available on interlibrary loan.

Of equal importance is *Verdi in San Francisco, 1851–1899: A Preliminary Bibliography,* by Don L. Hixon, privately published in typescript in 1980 and available in many large or specialized California libraries. Hixon purports to list every performance in San Francisco in the nineteenth century of a Verdi opera. He gives the date, the theatre, the cast, and citations to reviews or news items in several of the city's newspapers. Needless to say, his work is fundamental to anything I have accomplished here, and though for the years 1851–63 I have been able to add twenty-three performances to those he records, while subtracting one, in time no doubt someone will improve my reckoning.

The first study of opera in San Francisco that attempted to be comprehensive was undertaken during the economic depression of the 1930s as a project of the federal government's Works Progress Administration, the WPA. A team of writers was assembled and under the title *San Francisco Theatre Research* they produced a series of monographs in typescript. Monograph 17 (in vol. 7), is *The History of Opera in San Francisco, Part I,* and Monograph 18 (in vol. 8), *Part II;* also relevant is Monograph 3 (in vol. 2, pp. 1–69) "Tom Maguire," an account of San Francisco's most famous impresario. No monograph's author is named, and many of the quotations taken from newspapers and journals lack citation. Further, as might be expected in such a pioneer work, details sometimes go awry. Yet the works' overall picture is mostly accurate, and they offer many clues to pursue. A number of California libraries have mimeographed copies, and these usually are available for copying and interlibrary loan.

Lastly, there is Thomas G. Kaufman's *Verdi and His Major Contemporaries: A Selected Chronology of Performances with Casts,* which gives the date, theatre, cast, and conductor of premieres of all Verdi's operas in most music-loving cities of the world. It is possible in Kaufman's lists to follow the careers of several singers important to this history as well to see the speed with which Verdi's operas penetrated the world.

It is mere truth to say: The lack of any one of these four books would have required mine to be far more tentative in its conclusions.

WORKS CITED

Periodicals

California Historical Society Quarterly
Daily Alta California (San Francisco)
Daily Evening Bulletin (San Francisco)
Daily Evening Picayune (San Francisco)
Daily Morning Call (San Francisco)
Dwight's Journal of Music (Boston, weekly or biweekly)
Golden Era (San Francisco, weekly)
New York Herald (daily)
New York Morning Express (daily)
Overland Monthly (San Francisco)
Pacific News (San Francisco, daily)
Pioneer Magazine (San Francisco, monthly)
Sacramento Union (daily)
San Francisco Daily Herald
San Francisco Directory of City and County Residents and Businesses
Wide West (San Francisco, weekly)

Books and Articles

Arditi, Luigi. *My Reminiscences.* New York: Dodd, Mead, 1896.

Armstrong, W. G. *A Record of the Opera in Philadelphia.* 1884; reprinted New York: AMS Press, 1976.

Auden, W. H. *The Dyer's Hand and Other Essays.* London: Faber & Faber, 1963.

Bancroft, Hubert Howe. *History of California.* Vol. 6: *1848–1859.* Santa Barbara, Calif.: Wallace Hebberd, 1970).

————. *Works.* Vol. 34: *California Pastoral, 1760–1848;* and vol. 35: *California inter pocula.* San Francisco: The History Co., 1888.

Barry, T. A., and B. A. Patten. *Men and Memories of San Francisco in the "Spring of '50."* San Francisco: A. L. Bancroft & Co., 1873.

Basevi, Abramo. *Studio sulle opere di Giuseppe Verdi.* Florence: Tipografia Tofani, 1859.

Bean, Walton. *California: An Interpretive History.* New York: McGraw Hill, 1968.

Bellaigue, Camillo. *Verdi: Biografia critica* (Milan: Treves, 1913).

Budden, Julian. *The Operas of Verdi.* 3 vols. Vols. 1–2: London: Cassell, 1973–78; vol. 3: New York: Oxford University Press, 1981.

Buffum, E. Gould. *The Gold Rush: An Account of Six Months in the California Diggings.* 1850; reprinted London: Folio Society, 1959.

Caughey, John W., with Norris Hundley, Jr. *California: History of a Remarkable State.* 4th ed. Englewood Cliffs, N.J.: Prentice-Hall, [1940] 1982.

Chorley, Henry F. *Thirty Years' Musical Recollections.* New York: Alfred A. Knopf, 1926.

Complete Catalogue of Sheet Music and Musical Works, 1870. Reprinted New York: Da Capo Press, 1973.

Crane, Clarkson. *Last Adventure: San Francisco in 1851; Translated from the Original Journal of Albert Bernard de Russailh by Clarkson Crane.* San Francisco: Westgate Press/ Grabhorn Press, 1931.

Currey, John E. B. "The Terry-Broderick Duel." Typescript. San Francisco, 1890.

Delano, Alonzo. *Pen Knife Sketches; or Chips of the Old Block.* 1853; reprinted San Francisco: Grabhorn Press, 1934.

Dempsey, David. *The Triumphs and Trials of Lotta Crabtree.* New York: William Morrow, 1968.

de Russailh, Albert Bernard. See Crane, Clarkson.

Dunn, Jacob Piatt. *Massacres of the Mountains: A History of the Indian Wars of the Far West, 1815–1875.* 1886; reprinted London: Eyre & Spottiswoode, 1963.

Field, Stephen J. *Personal Reminiscences of Early Days in California.* 1893; reprinted New York: Da Capo Press, 1968.

Garibaldi, Luigi Agostino, ed. *Giuseppe Verdi nelle lettere di Emanuele Muzio ad Antonio Barezzi.* Milan: Treves, 1931.

Gatti-Casazza, Giulio. *Memories of the Opera.* 1941; reprinted John Calder, 1977.

Gould, Milton. *A Cast of Hawks: A Rowdy Tale of Greed, Violence, Scandal, and Corruption in the Early Days of San Francisco.* La Jolla, Calif.: Copley Press, 1985.

Hamm, Charles. *Yesterdays: Popular Song in America.* New York: W. W. Norton, 1970.

Herz, Henri. *My Travels in America.* Translated by Henry Bertram Hill. Madison: University of Wisconsin Press, 1963.

Hixon, Don L. *Verdi in San Francisco, 1851–1899: A Preliminary Bibliography.* San Francisco: privately printed, 1980.

Holliday, J. S. *The World Rushed In: The California Gold Rush Experience.* New York: Simon & Schuster, 1981.

Holoman, D. Kern. *Berlioz.* Cambridge, Mass.: Harvard University Press, 1989.

Holst, Imogen. *Tune.* London: Faber & Faber, 1962.

Huntley, Henry Vere. *California: Its Gold and Its Inhabitants.* 2 vols. London: Thomas Cantley Newby, 1856.

Jensen, Luke. *Giuseppe Verdi and Giovanni Ricordi with Notes on Francesco Lucca, from "Oberto" to "La traviata."* New York: Garland, 1989.

Kauffmann, Stanley. "Two Vulgar Geniuses: Augustin Daly and David Belasco." *Yale Review* 75, no. 4 (Summer 1987): 496–513.

Kaufman, Thomas G. *Verdi and His Major Contemporaries: A Selected Chronology of Performances with Casts.* New York: Garland Publishing, 1990.

Kellogg, Clara Louise. *Memoirs of an American Prima Donna.* New York: G. P. Putnam's Sons, 1913.

Kirk, Elise K. *Music at the White House: A History of the American Spirit.* Urbana, Ill.: University of Illinois Press, 1986.

Kmen, Henry A. *Music in New Orleans: The Formative Years, 1791–1841.* Baton Rouge: Louisiana State University Press, 1966.

———. "Singing and Dancing in New Orleans: A Social History of the Birth and Growth of Balls and Opera, 1791–1841." Ph.D. diss., Tulane University, 1961.

Kolodin, Irving. *The Metropolitan Opera, 1883–1966: A Candid History.* New York: Alfred A. Knopf, 1966.

Krehbiel, Henry Edward. *Chapters of Opera, Being Historical and Critical Observations and Records Concerning the Lyric Drama in New York from Its Earliest Days Down to the Present Time.* New York: Henry Holt, 1908.

Lawrence, Vera Brodsky. *Strong on Music: The New York Scene in the Days of George Templeton Strong, 1836–1875.* Vol. 1: *Resonances, 1836–1850.* New York: Oxford University Press, 1988.

Leman, Walter M. *Memories of an Old Actor.* San Francisco: A. Roman Co., 1886.

Levine, Lawrence W. *Highbrow/Lowbrow: The Emergence of Cultural Hierarchy in America.* Cambridge, Mass.: Harvard University Press, 1988.

Lotchin, Roger W. *San Francisco, 1846–1856: From Hamlet to City.* Lincoln: University of Nebraska Press, 1974.

Love, Harold. *The Golden Age of Australian Opera: W. S. Lyster and his Companies, 1861–1880.* Sydney: Currency Press, 1981.

McCabe, John H. "Theatrical Journals and Diary, 1849–1882." 2 vols. Ms., California State Library, Sacramento.

MacMinn, George A. *The Theater of the Golden Era in California.* Caldwell, Idaho: Caxton Printers, 1941.

Maretzek, Max. *Crotchets and Quavers, or Revelations of an Opera Manager in America.* 1855; reprinted New York: Da Capo Press, 1966.

Martens, Frederick H. *A Thousand and One Nights of Opera.* New York: D. Appleton and Co., 1926.

Martin, George. *Aspects of Verdi.* New York: Dodd, Mead, 1988.

———. *The Damrosch Dynasty: America's First Family of Music.* Boston: Houghton Mifflin, 1983.

————. "La prima rappresentazione di *Un ballo in maschera* a Boston, 15 marzo 1861." *Atti del Primo Congresso Internazionale di Studi Verdiani.* Parma: Istituto di Studi Verdiani, 1969.

Mattfeld, Julius. *A Handbook of American Operatic Premieres, 1731–1962.* Detroit, Mich.: Information Services, 1963.

Monaldi, Gino. *Verdi, 1839–1898.* 2d ed. Turin: Bocca, 1926.

Neville, Amelia. *The Fantastic City: Memoirs of the Social and Romantic Life of Old San Francisco.* Edited and revised by Virginia Brastow. Boston: Houghton Mifflin, 1932.

Pleasants, Henry. *Opera in Crisis: Tradition, Present, Future.* New York: Thames & Hudson, 1989.

Rodecape, Lois Foster. "Tom Maguire, Napoleon of the Stage." *California Historical Society Quarterly* 20, no. 4 (December 1941); 21, nos. 1, 2, 3 (March, June, September 1942).

Rourke, Constance. *Troupers of the Gold Coast, or the Rise of Lotta Crabtree.* New York: Harcourt Brace, 1928.

Royce, Josiah. *California, From the Conquest in 1846 to the Second Vigilance Committee in San Francisco.* Boston: Houghton, Mifflin, 1899.

Santley, Charles. *Student and Singer: The Reminiscences of Charles Santley.* London: Edward Arnold, 1892.

Schlitzer, F. "Verdi's *Alzira* at Naples." *Music and Letters* 35 (1954).

Scott, Eleanor. *The First Twenty Years of the Santa Fe Opera.* Santa Fe, N.M.: Sunshine Press, 1976.

"Scrici." *Physiology of the Opera.* 1852; reprinted New York: Institute for Studies in American Music, Brooklyn College, 1981.

Shanet, Howard. *Philharmonic: A History of New York's Orchestra.* Garden City, N.Y.: Doubleday, 1975.

Sherman, William T. *Memoirs of General William T. Sherman, by Himself.* Bloomington: Indiana University Press, 1957.

Soulé, Frank, John H. Gihon, and James Nisbet. *The Annals of San Francisco.* New York: D. Appleton & Co., 1855.

————. *The Annals of San Francisco, Together with the Continuation, Through 1855, Compiled by Dorothy H. Huggins.* Palo Alto, Calif.: Lewis Osborne, 1966.

Starr, Kevin. *Americans and the California Dream, 1850–1915.* New York: Oxford University Press, 1973.

Strong, George Templeton. *The Diary of George Templeton Strong.* 4 vols. Edited by Allan Nevins and Milton Halsey Thomas. New York: Macmillan, 1952.

Taylor, Bayard. *Eldorado, or Adventures in the Path of Empire, Comprising a Voyage to California, via Panama, Life in San Francisco and Monterey, Pictures of the Gold Region, and Experiences of Mexican Travel.* 1850; reprinted New York: Alfred A. Knopf, 1949.

Thompson, Oscar. *The American Singer: A Hundred Years of Success in Opera.* New York: Dial Press, 1937.

Toye, Francis. *Giuseppe Verdi: His Life and Works.* 1946; reprinted New York: Vintage Books, 1959.

Upham, Samuel C. *Notes of a Voyage to California via Cape Horn, Together with Scenes in El Dorado, in the Years 1849–50.* Philadelphia, 1878.

Verdi, Giuseppe. *I copialettere di Giuseppe Verdi*. Edited by Gaetano Cesari and Alessandro Luzio. Milan, 1913.

———. *Rigoletto*. Vol. 17 of *The Critical Edition*, 1st ser. Edited by Martin Chusid. Chicago: University of Chicago Press/Milan: G. Ricordi & Co., 1983.

Ware, W. Porter, and Thaddeus C. Lockard, Jr. *P. T. Barnum Presents Jenny Lind: The American Tour of the Swedish Nightingale*. Baton Rouge: Louisiana State University Press, 1980.

Werfel, Franz, and Paul Stefan, eds. *Verdi: The Man in His Letters*. Translated by Edward O. Downes. 1942; reprinted New York: Vienna House, 1973.

White, Eric Walter. *A History of English Opera*. London: Faber & Faber, 1983.

White, Stewart Edward. *The Forty-Niners*. New Haven, Conn.: Yale University Press, 1918.

Whitman, Walt. *New York Dissected by Walt Whitman: A Sheaf of Recently Discovered Newspaper Articles by the Author of "Leaves of Grass."* Edited by Emory Holloway and Ralph Adimari. New York: Rufus Rockwell Wilson, 1936.

Works Progress Administration (WPA). *San Francisco Theatre Research*. Edited by Lawrence Estavan. Monographs 17 and 18 (in vols. 7 and 8): *The History of Opera in San Francisco, Part I* and *Part II*. San Francisco, 1938.

———. *San Francisco Theatre Research*. Edited by Lawrence Estavan. Monograph 3 (in vol. 2, pp. 1–96): "Tom Maguire." San Francisco, 1939.

Index

Entries concerning the more frequently mentioned composers and their operas are presented with general comments in a paragraph preceding the operas, which then follow alphabetically.

The abbreviation SF denotes San Francisco; prem, premiere; perf, performance; and rev, review.

Birth and death years are given for all composers and for other musicians only when certain.

An asterisk denotes an immigrant to San Francisco who settled there, at least for a great part of his or her working life, whether or not he or she became a citizen of the United States. Thus, an entry such as "Cora, Charles*, Italian professional gambler" denotes a resident, not a transient, of Italian background.

Compositor: Com-Com
Text: 11/13 Janson
Display: Janson
Printer and Binder: Haddon Craftsmen, Inc.